Islam, Women, and Violence in Kashmir

COMPARATIVE FEMINIST STUDIES SERIES
Chandra Talpade Mohanty, Series Editor

PUBLISHED BY PALGRAVE MACMILLAN:

Sexuality, Obscenity, Community: Women, Muslims, and the Hindu Public in Colonial India
    by Charu Gupta

Twenty-First-Century Feminist Classrooms: Pedagogies of Identity and Difference
    edited by Amie A. Macdonald and Susan Sánchez-Casal

Reading across Borders: Storytelling and Knowledges of Resistance
    by Shari Stone-Mediatore

Made in India: Decolonizations, Queer Sexualities, Trans/national Projects
    by Suparna Bhaskaran

Dialogue and Difference: Feminisms Challenge Globalization
    edited by Marguerite Waller and Sylvia Marcos

Engendering Human Rights: Cultural and Socio-Economic Realities in Africa
    edited by Obioma Nnaemeka and Joy Ezeilo

Women's Sexualities and Masculinities in a Globalizing Asia
    edited by Saskia E. Wieringa, Evelyn Blackwood, and Abha Bhaiya

Gender, Race, and Nationalism in Contemporary Black Politics
    by Nikol G. Alexander-Floyd

Gender, Identity, and Imperialism: Women Development Workers in Pakistan
    by Nancy Cook

Transnational Feminism in Film and Media
    edited by Katarzyna Marciniak, Anikó Imre, and Áine O'Healy

Gendered Citizenships: Transnational Perspectives on Knowledge Production, Political Activism, and Culture
    edited by Kia Lilly Caldwell, Kathleen Coll, Tracy Fisher, Renya K. Ramirez, and Lok Siu

Visions of Struggle in Women's Filmmaking in the Mediterranean
    edited by Flavia Laviosa; Foreword by Laura Mulvey

Islam, Women, and Violence in Kashmir: Between India and Pakistan
    by Nyla Ali Khan

Islam, Women, and Violence in Kashmir

Between India and Pakistan

Nyla Ali Khan

palgrave
macmillan

ISLAM, WOMEN, AND VIOLENCE IN KASHMIR
Copyright © Nyla Ali Khan, 2010.

First published in 2009 by Tulika Books, New Delhi, India.

First published in the United States in 2010 by
PALGRAVE MACMILLAN®—
a division of St. Martin's Press LLC,
175 Fifth Avenue, New York, NY 10010.

Where this book is distributed in the UK, Europe and the rest of the world,
this is by Palgrave Macmillan, a division of Macmillan Publishers Limited,
registered in England, company number 785998, of Houndmills,
Basingstoke, Hampshire RG21 6XS.

Palgrave Macmillan is the global academic imprint of the above companies
and has companies and representatives throughout the world.

Palgrave® and Macmillan® are registered trademarks in the United States,
the United Kingdom, Europe and other countries.

ISBN: 978–0–230–10764–9

Library of Congress Cataloging-in-Publication Data

Khan, Nyla Ali, 1972–
    Islam, women, and violence in Kashmir : between India and Pakistan /
Nyla Ali Khan.
        p. cm.—(Comparative feminist studies)
        ISBN 978–0–230–10764–9
        1. Sex discrimination against women—India—Jammu and Kashmir.
    2. Muslim women—India—Jammu and Kashmir. 3. Women in Islam—
    India—Jammu and Kashmir. 4. Political violence—India—Jammu and
    Kashmir. I. Title.
HQ1744.J35K43 2010
305.48'6970954609045—dc22   2010013885

A catalogue record of the book is available from the British Library.

Design by Newgen Imaging Systems (P) Ltd., Chennai, India.

First edition: October 2010

10 9 8 7 6 5 4 3 2 1

Printed in the United States of America.

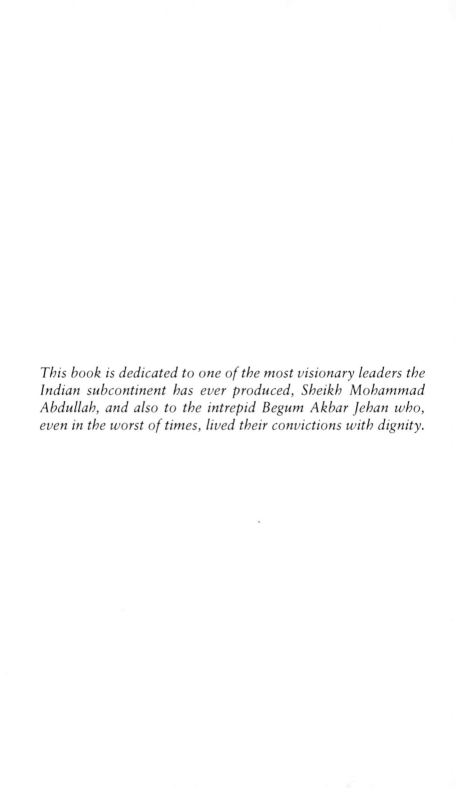

This book is dedicated to one of the most visionary leaders the Indian subcontinent has ever produced, Sheikh Mohammad Abdullah, and also to the intrepid Begum Akbar Jehan who, even in the worst of times, lived their convictions with dignity.

Contents

Illustrations

Series Editor's Foreword

Less than a year ago, *The New York Times* (23 August 2009) declared "the oppression of women worldwide" to be the "human rights cause of our time," claiming that women's liberation would "solve many of the world's problems!" Some years ago, then U.N. Secretary General Kofi Anan had announced that the status of women was the key indicator of the "development" of a nation. These pronouncements supposedly recognize the global crises in women's lives, but they also reflect a history of women's struggles and feminist movements around the globe. The Comparative Feminist Studies (CFS) series is designed to foreground writing, organizing, and reflection on feminist trajectories across the historical and cultural borders of nation-states. It takes up fundamental analytic and political issues involved in the cross cultural production of knowledge about women and feminism, examining the politics of scholarship and knowledge in relation to feminist organizing and social justice movements. Drawing on feminist thinking in a number of fields, the CFS series targets innovative, comparative feminist scholarship, pedagogical and curricular strategies, and community organizing and political education. It explores a comparative feminist praxis that addresses some of the most urgent questions facing progressive critical thinkers and activists today. Nyla Ali Khan's *Islam, Women, and the Violence in Kashmir: Between India and Pakistan* takes on some of these very questions, crafting a history of gendered violence and women's agency in a region of the world that like Palestine, embodies one of the most poignant and violent postcolonial conflicts of the twentieth, and twenty-first centuries.

Over the past many decades, feminists across the globe have been variously successful at addressing fundamental issues of oppression and liberation. In our search for gender justice in the early twenty first century however, we inherit a number of the challenges our mothers and grandmothers faced. But there are also new challenges to face as we attempt to make sense of a world indelibly marked by the failure of postcolonial (and advanced) capitalist and communist nation-states to provide for the social, economic, spiritual, and psychic needs of the majority of the world's population. In the year 2010, globalization has come to represent the interests of corporations and the free market rather than self-determination and freedom from political, cultural, and economic domination for all the world's peoples. The project of U.S. Empire building, alongside the dominance of corporate capitalism kills, disenfranchises, and impoverishes women everywhere. Militarization, environmental degradation, heterosexist State practices, religious fundamentalisms, sustained migrations of peoples across the borders of nations and geo-political regions, environmental crises, and the exploitation of women's labor by capital all pose profound challenges for feminists at this time. Recovering and remembering insurgent histories, and seeking new understandings of political subjectivities and citizenship has never been so important, at a time marked by social amnesia, global consumer culture, and the worldwide mobilization of fascist notions of "national security."

These are some of the very challenges the CFS series is designed to address. The series takes as its fundamental premise the need for feminist engagement with global as well as local ideological, historical, economic, and political processes, and the urgency of transnational dialogue in building an ethical culture capable of withstanding and transforming the commodified and exploitative practices of global governance structures, culture and economics. Individual volumes in the CFS series provide systemic and challenging interventions into the (still) largely Euro-Western feminist studies knowledge base, while simultaneously highlighting the work that can and needs to be done to envision and enact cross-cultural, multiracial feminist solidarity.

Nyla Ali Khan's eloquent, passionate history of the 60 plus year struggle for independence in Kashmir draws on her own genealogy and political legacy as part of one of the "first families" in Kashmir, textual and empirical analysis of the military and political conflicts over Kashmir between India and Pakistan, oral histories of key women nationalist leaders, feminist scholarship on women's agency in war-torn, militarized conflict zones, and a deep and unwavering commitment to a land, history, and culture that inspired visionary and progressive syncretic cultures, and poetic and spiritual texts of exceptional beauty and humanity. Khan engages with the deep trauma and reality of gendered violence in occupied, militarized territories where women constitute the ground for masculinist, patriarchal nation-projects.

Drawing on oral histories of feminist militants in nationalist struggles and against religious fundamentalisms, Khan crafts a provisional notion of women's agency that runs counter to narratives of sexualized violence and victimhood that populate scholarly and popular histories of the Kashmir conflict. Caught between the economic, political, and psychological effects of "dislocation, dispossession, and disenfranchisement," Khan argues, Kashmiri women "are positioned in relation to their own class and cultural realities; their own histories; their sensitivity to the diversity of cultural traditions and to the questions and conflicts within them; the legacies of Sufi Islam; their own struggles not just with the devastating effects of Indian occupation and Pakistani infiltration, but also with the discourses of cultural nationalism and religious fundamentalism; their own relations to the West; their interpretations of religious law; their beliefs in different schools of Islamic and Hindu thought; (and) their concepts of the role of women in contemporary societies." (p. 179)

Islam, Women and the Violence in Kashmir showcases the kind of scholarship that can create the ground for cross-racial /cross-national dialogue among and between scholars and activists in regional as well as global contexts, especially, for instance, in the current context of feminist struggles in Palestine. As Ashis Nandy states in his *Afterword*, "Nyla Ali Khan's passionate, affectionate portrait of Kashmir looks to the future with hope because her reading of Lalla-Ded and the Kashmiri women's struggle for survival is the story of the possibilities that may not have been crushed by the combined efforts of fanatic militants and the Indian army. Kashmir can still be, under an imaginative visionary arrangement, a culture mediating between South Asia and Central Asia, between India and Pakistan, and perhaps even between Islam, Hinduism, and Buddhism." (p. 200) The book will be of interest to a wide range of feminist scholars, activists, and cultural critics. It embodies the comparative praxis and vision of transnational knowledge production that is a hallmark of the CFS series.

CHANDRA TALPADE MOHANTY
Series Editor, Ithaca, New York

Preface

I belong to Indian-administered Jammu and Kashmir (J & K), a highly volatile South Asian region that is endowed with reservoirs of cultural, social, and human wealth. I was raised in the radiant Kashmir Valley located in the foothills of the Himalayas. The charm, splendor, and heterogeneity of the Kashmir Valley have enticed many a writer, historian, anthropologist, sociologist, benevolent ruler, and malevolent politician. J & K of the 1970s basked in the glory of a hard-won democratic setup, in which consideration of the well-being of the populace was supreme, marred by some political faux pas. The inhabitants of the state were neither intimidated nor hindered by the aggressively centrist policies of the government of India or the fanatical belligerence of the government of Pakistan.

Caught between rival siblings India and Pakistan, the people of the state, particularly of the Kashmir Valley, had constructed a composite national identity. Kashmiris were heavily invested in the notion of territorial integrity and cultural pride, which, through the perseverance of the populist leadership and the unflinching loyalty of the people, had sprouted on a barren landscape of abusive political and military authority. I recall that period with nostalgia and mourn the loss of a deep-rooted and heartfelt nationalism. My maternal grandfather, Sheikh Mohammad Abdullah, popularly known as the Lion of Kashmir, reigned as prime minister of J & K from 1948 to 1953. When the pledge to hold a referendum was not kept by the Indian government, Abdullah's advocacy of Kashmir independence led to his imprisonment. He was shuttled from one jail to another until 1972 and remained out of power until 1975. During the period of Abdullah's incarceration, Congress Party-led governments in New Delhi made covert arrangements with puppet regimes they had installed. Prior to the 1975 accord between the Sheikh Mohammad Abdullah-led National Conference and the Indira Gandhi-led Congress, Abdullah demanded the revocation of all central laws extended to the state that delegitimized the popular demand for plebiscite. The then prime minister, Indira Gandhi, forged an accord with Abdullah in 1975 by promising to partially restore the autonomy of the state by revoking certain central laws that had arbitrarily been imposed on J & K. The same year, Abdullah returned as chief minister of the state.

Sheikh Mohammad Abdullah and his National Conference won an overwhelming victory in the election of 1977, and he remained in office until his death in 1982.

Although my maternal grandfather has always been a large presence in my life, perhaps more in death than in life, I have been careful about not sanctifying the past. Memory is always filtered and provides an interpretive version of the past, but the conceptual framework that I have deployed in my book has been useful in enabling me to begin the process of relieving myself from the burden of history.

The refusal to wallow in grief and a desire to deconstruct the Camelot-like atmosphere of that period impelled me to undertake this colossal cross-disciplinary project regarding the political history, composite culture, and literature of the state; and the attempted relegation of Kashmiri women to the archives of memory and their persistent endeavors to rise from the ashes of immolated identities. I was further motivated to complete this project within the period stipulated by my publisher because of the plethora of mauled versions of history cunningly making their way into mainstream Indian, Pakistani, and international political discourses. This book has no pretensions about being an exhaustive discussion of the intricate politics of J & K. It is my humble attempt at speaking truth to power by employing not just traditional scholarship but oral historiography as well. Despite my emotional investment in the issue, I have tried to veer away from the seductive trap of either romanticizing or demonizing certain political actors and initiatives.

All going well, this is just the first in a series of books challenging dominant, and not necessarily accurate, discourses on J & K. Finally, *Islam, Women, and Violence in Kashmir: Between India and Pakistan* is a tribute to the resilient spirit of the inhabitants of J & K, which has made them persevere through catastrophes, upheavals, unfulfilled pledges, treacherous politics, and vile manipulations. They have emerged scathed but with an irrepressible desire to live and define their own reality. I hope to some day live that reality.

Several institutions and individuals have supported my project. I would like to express heartfelt gratitude to the College of Fine Arts and Humanities at the University of Nebraska–Kearney for its inveterate support, as well as to the office of Graduate Studies and Research for awarding me two Research Services Council Grants, enabling me to conduct archival and field research. I am especially appreciative of Don Ray's technical expertise. Michael Springer, my graduate assistant, worked diligently. Jenara Turman, my proofreader, was an absolute asset. I am greatly appreciative of the visiting professorship offered to me at the University of Oklahoma, Norman, which gave me the flexibility I required to revise my manuscript. I also learned a lot from conversations and e-mail exchanges with Krishna Misri, Neeja Mattoo, Hameeda Naeem, Parveena Ahangar, Shamim Firdous, Pathani Begum, Begum Sajjida Zameer, P.N. Duda, A. Wahid, Amar Nath Dhar, Mohammad Ishaq Khan, and R.L. Hangloo, and Mohammad Yousuf Taing. The Gujjar women I met with in the villages of Mahiyan and Ferozpora were such a delight. I appreciate the critical care with which Professor Ashis Nandy at the Centre for the Study of Developing Societies, New Delhi, read my manuscript and wrote the Afterword to this book.

I am thankful to all my interviewees in Kashmir for their time and willingness to talk with me about their years in the strife-torn state. My thanks to Ved Bhasin, editor of *Kashmir Times*, Fayaz Kaloo and Aijaz ul Haq, editors of *Greater Kashmir*, and Syed Ali Safvi, former associate editor of *Daily Etalaat*, for having provided me with public forums. Shuaib Masoodi of *Rising Kashmir* provided me with some extraordinary illustrations. My debt to my parents, Suraiya and Mohammad Ali Matto, is enormous. They have always believed in me and my dreams with unwavering faith. My daughter, Iman, has enlivened my days with her unquenchable vitality and irrepressible energy. My maternal uncle, Sheikh Nazir Ahmad, uncharacteristically gave me access to his archived collection of photographs and books. My husband, Mohammad Faisal Khan, gave encouraging comments on my work. Last but not least, I owe my inspiration to the undying loveliness and mystical beauty of Kashmir, which enlivens the soul and calls the wanderer to return.

NYLA ALI KHAN

Permissions

Translations of Lalla-Ded's *vaakh* (poem) by Sir Richard Carmac Temple in *The Word of Lalla the Prophetess*, reprinted by permission of Gulshan Books.

Translations of Lalla-Ded's *vaakhs* (poems and aphorisms) by Neerja Mattoo in a scholarly paper she presented at a conference, reproduced by kind permission of the author.

Translation of Mahjoor's poem in *An Anthology of Modern Kashmiri Verse*, translated and edited by Trilokinath Raina, reprinted by kind permission of Raina.

Excerpts from Neerja Mattoo's e-mail to author, quoted by kind permission of Mattoo.

Excerpts from Mohammad Yousuf Taing's e-mail to author, quoted by kind permission of Taing.

Excerpts from Krishna Misri's e-mail to author, quoted by kind permission of Misri.

Excerpts from P.N. Duda's correspondence with the author, quoted by kind permission of Duda.

Excerpts from Sajjida Zameer's e-mail to author, quoted by kind permission of Zameer.

Excerpts from the document on human rights violations in Indian-administered J & K formulated by G.M. Shah's Awami National Conference, reproduced by kind permission of Shah.

Excerpts from Amar Nath Dhar's e-mail to author, quoted by kind permission of Dhar.

Excerpts from A. Wahid's e-mail to author, quoted by kind permission of Wahid.

Excerpts from Mohammad Ishaq Khan's e-mail to author, quoted by kind permission of Khan.

Excerpts from R.L. Hangloo's e-mail to author, quoted by kind permission of Hangloo.

Excerpts from Suraiya Ali Matto's correspondence with author, quoted by kind permission of Matto.

Abbreviations

AISPC	All India States People's Conference
APDP	Association of Parents of Disappeared Persons
APHC	All Parties Hurriyat Conference
BJP	Bharatiya Janata Party
BSF	Border Security Force
CDR	Centre for Dialogue and Reconciliation
CRPF	Central Reserve Police Force
DM	Dukhtara-e-Milat ("Daughters of the Nation")
HM	Hizb-ul-Mujahideen
ISI	Inter-Services Intelligence
J & K	Jammu and Kashmir
JKLF	Jammu and Kashmir Liberation Front
KANA	Kashmir Affairs and Northern Areas
LOC	Line of Control
MC	Muslim Conference
MUF	Muslim United Front
NA	Northern Areas
NC	National Conference
NSG	National Security Guard
PDP	People's Democratic Party
PF	Plebiscite Front
RR	Rashtriya Rifles
SOG	Special Operations Group
STF	Special Task Force
UN	United Nations
UNCIP	United Nations Commission for India and Pakistan
UNO	United Nations Organization
WSDC	Women's Self Defense Corps

Introduction

As I sit under the bespeckled sky gazing on the enthralling beauty of Gulmarg in the Indian-administered Kashmir Valley, lush with lupines, daisies, narcissus, and red roses, nurtured by snow-covered peaks and glaciers, I watch the mutable aspects of Kashmir, sometimes joyous and sometimes despondent. I am enveloped by nostalgia for the era of lost innocence and misplaced hope that at one point in time had ensconced the Kashmiris in the heart of paradise. Smoke from the chimneys of chalets with shingled roofs creates a languid atmosphere, making the observer oblivious to the anguishes of life. The mist rises stealthily from the mountains and gives tantalizing glimpses of the ethereal vision behind the veil. The tranquil Dal lake, in which gentle ripples are created by the oar of a homebound boatman rowing his gondola on a moonlit night, calms the angst of existence. From a distance I hear sonorous voices singing folksongs lamenting the loss of a beloved or remembering the imminence of death. These songs are sung by tribal people with weather-beaten faces and jaded souls. The pain in their voices and the emotion in the lyrics echo the centuries of political, cultural, and religious persecution that these proud people have borne but have not resigned themselves to. Their isolation, caused by the rugged terrain they inhabit, has not extinguished the spark of hopeful romance and faith in the resilience of humanity. The beauty of quiet meditation and faith in providence is evoked by the rushing pristine streams in Dachigam, a wildlife sanctuary, redolent of trout. The enchanting wilderness, the mystique of which is enhanced by the soporific sound of crickets and the coverlet of purple hibiscus, provides a haven for the seeker of spiritual comfort. How can a prodigal daughter or son not return to this land of enchantment?

Indian- and Pakistani-administered Jammu and Kashmir (J & K) is a space in which conflicting discourses have been written and read. Prior to 1947 the history of Kashmir comprised four phases: Hindu and Buddhist rule, Muslim rule, Sikh conquest, and Dogra rule. In about AD 1200 the poet–historian Kalhana wrote a voluminous account of Kashmir's historical trajectory from 1182 BC, *Rajatarangini* (*River of Kings*). In this epic Kalhana writes about the tribal inhabitants of Kashmir, the Nagas, who created an agrarian society and were an idolatrous people. The history of the Kashmir

Valley through AD 1486 was recounted by Pandit Jonaraja. This task was later taken on by Srivara and Prajyabhatta, who recorded the history of Kashmir through the conquest of the Valley by the Mughal emperor Akbar in 1586 (Sufi 1979: 1).

In the earliest phase, Hinduism pervaded the fabric of Kashmiri culture and society. But the Mauryan emperor Ashoka embraced Buddhism, and during his rule, Hinduism, with its trappings of a rigid caste hierarchy, ornate rituals, and pantheon of deities, was replaced by the austerity of Buddhism in the Valley. The monasteries constructed in Kashmir during Ashoka's reign became centers of scholarly learning, and the Valley became a religious and cultural hub. The hegemonic influence of Buddhism in Kashmir declined in AD 711 with the foray of Islamic military rule, political dominance, and religious teachings.

Hindu and Buddhist rule in Kashmir was obliterated by the Muslim conquest in 1339. Prior to that, Kashmir had feared conquest by a Tartar chief. In order to nullify that threat made to the stability of the Valley during the feckless rule of Raja Sahadev, the commander-in-chief of Kashmir requested assistance from Shah Mir of Swat (now a part of Pakistan) and Rainchau Shah of Tibet. Rainchau Shah was quick to offer aid that alleviated the danger posed by the Tartar ruler. Subsequently, he employed Machiavellian strategies to assassinate the commander-in-chief, married his daughter Kuta Rani, and ascended the throne of Kashmir. Shah converted to Islam and took on the name Sadruddin (Lawrence 2005: 179–200). The dominance of Islam in the Valley was consolidated in the fourteenth century by the Sufi Naqashbandi order of Mir Sayyid Ali Hamadani, popularly known as Shah Hamadan. Hamadani first visited Kashmir during the reign of the first sultan of Kashmir, Shah Mir, who assumed the reins of power after the demise of Sadruddin.

The first sultan to implement Muslim law in the Valley was Sikander. He inherited the throne in 1394. The architectural wonders built during his reign have retained their unique ethos and are still venerated as landmarks. He founded the town of Sikandarpur (now called Nowhatta, in Srinagar), built the splendid Jama Masjid (central mosque) in Srinagar, and constructed the architecturally elegant Khanqah-i-mualla (monastery) on the banks of the river Jhelum. Mir Sayyid Ali Hamadani propagated the Islamic faith within the ornate portals of the Khanqah-i-mualla. Sikander was succeeded by Zainul Abedin (1420–1470), who was a patron of the arts. Zainul Abedin, popularly known as Budshah, proclaimed religious tolerance and invalidated discriminatory laws; today, his reign is still acclaimed for the peace, amity, and intellectual growth that it personified. Despite his remarkable contribution to the cultural, religious, and intellectual ethos of Kashmir, Budshah was unable to groom his son and successor, Haider Shah, to intrepidly position himself at the helm of affairs. With the defeat of Haider Shah by the Chak tribals in 1561, the first Muslim dynasty of Kashmir was terminated (see Lawrence 2005: 179–200; Rahman 1996; Rai 2004: 27).

Subsequently, in 1589, Mughal emperor Akbar's formidable army laid siege to and conquered Kashmir. Akbar's grandson, Shah Jahan, conquered Ladakh, Baltistan, and Kishtawar, and validated the annexation of those territories in 1634. The rule of the Afghan military commander Ahmad Shah Durrani, with its brutality and heinous militarism, replaced Mughal rule in Kashmir in 1753. This period is remembered in the annals of notoriety for its relentless oppression, cultural erosion, religious intemperance, metaphoric and literal burial of the arts, and dehumanization.

> The brutal intemperance of Afghan rule, which lasted until 1819, drove Kashmiris to urgently implore outside help. The Kashmiri Pandit community led by Birbal Dhar encouraged the Sikhs to invade Kashmir, and Birbal Dhar offered to bear the expenses of the invasion. Ranjit Singh invaded Kashmir with an army of 30,000 Sikh soldiers and captured the Valley on 15 June 1819. After five centuries of Muslim rule, during which nine-tenths of the population embraced Islam, Kashmir was once again in the hands of non-Muslims. (Rahman 1996: 12)

The demolition of Afghan rule proved to be a pyrrhic victory for the people of Kashmir. However, Sikh rule in the Valley, which lasted twenty-seven years, surpassed that of the unruly Afghans in its barbarism and cruelty. Discriminatory policies ruled the roost and the Sikh rulers made short shrift of the Kashmiri Muslim majority (see Malik 2002; Younghusband 1970). In the 1820s, the neighboring plains of the Kashmir Valley, Jammu, were ruled by Raja Gulab Singh, feudatory of the Sikh ruler Maharaja Ranjit Singh. Gulab Singh was crowned monarch of Jammu by Ranjit Singh in 1822. Under the potent overlordship of Ranjit Singh, Gulab Singh efficaciously extended his territory in the name of the Sikh kingdom, and went so far as to capture Ladakh, a region bordering China, in 1834 and Baltistan in 1840. After Ranjit Singh's demise, the hitherto genial relationship between the Sikhs and the British declined. The British had been gradually spreading their territorial control in India through the East India Company, a commercial trading company that acquired auxiliary military and governmental functions in India and other British colonies, since the middle of the eighteenth century. The subsequent upheaval at the Sikh court caused anxiety within the East India Company, which feared a Russian invasion in the face of the tottering frontier of northwestern India. The resulting interference of the British in the Sikh kingdom led to the first Anglo–Sikh war in 1845. Gulab Singh's neutrality during this war tipped the scales in favor of the British. His military strength, political acumen, and entrepreneurship did not go unnoticed (Lawrence 2005: 200–03; Rai 2004: 20–27; Khan 1978). The territories of Kashmir, Ladakh, Gilgit, and Chenab were bestowed upon the Dogra ruler Gulab Singh for the paltry sum of seventy-five lakhs, in acknowledgment of his services to the British crown. Gulab Singh was required to reimburse the British for the costs incurred by them while taking possession of Kashmir. It was stipulated that one crore of rupees would go toward indemnity. Later the British were allowed to retain the area of Kulu and Mandi, territories across the river Beas, bringing about the waiver of twenty-five lakhs from the sum that Gulab Singh owed as indemnity (Schofield 2002: 56). Prior to the sudden occurrence of war in 1845, political relations between the British and the Sikhs had deteriorated. During this systemic erosion of Anglo–Sikh relations, Gulab Singh played a significant role, which has generated tremendous controversy. Did he indulge in surreptitious dealings with the British while claiming to owe allegiance to the Sikhs? Did he enable negotiations between the British and the Sikhs, which averted an otherwise ugly situation? Why did the British sell Kashmir for a measly amount to Gulab Singh after having acquired it from the Sikhs?

The Dogras are a predominantly Hindu people who were installed as rulers of Kashmir under the Treaty of Amritsar signed in 1846. This treaty declared that "the British Government transfers and makes over, for ever, in independent possession, to Maharajah Gulab Singh and the heirs male of his body, the Kashmir Valley as well as the area of Gilgit to the north" (in Aitchison 1931: 21–22). The princely state of J & K comprised territories that at one point in time had been independent principalities: Jammu, Kashmir, Ladakh, Mirpur, Poonch, Baltistan, Gilgit, Hunza, Muzaffarabad, Nagar, and some other nondescript kingdoms. Article IX of the treaty further emphasized that the British government would provide aid and succor to the monarch of Kashmir in protecting his territories from disruptive forces. Article X underscored the monarch's allegiance to the British government. As a manifestation of his acknowledgment of the primacy of the British government, the monarch was required to present annually one horse, twelve shawl goats, and three pairs of impeccably woven Kashmiri shawls (ibid.). Thus British suzerainty indubitably asserted itself through the obeisance paid to it by the Dogra monarchy. Gulab Singh was succeeded by his son Ranbir Singh in 1847, who in turn was succeeded by his son Pratap Singh in 1885. Pratap Singh had no male heirs and tried to orchestrate the accession of a distant male relative. His maneuver, however, was quashed by the British, who facilitated the accession of Pratap Singh's nephew, Hari Singh, to the throne. The last Dogra monarch, Hari Singh, succeeded to the throne in 1925. He exercised power just as arbitrarily and unjustly as his predecessors had. A decade before the expulsion of British rule from India, Hari Singh ratified a legal settlement in British Indian courts that added Poonch, which hitherto had been bestowed by the Sikh ruler Ranjit Singh upon Gulab Singh's brother Dhyan Singh, to his territorial possessions. This significant acquisition completed the pre-partition J & K conglomeration. The Muslims in Poonch, however, have always remained ambivalent about their merger with the princely state. The reinforcing of Dogra rule by the British was "in light of [the East India Company's] concerns for stability on its northwestern frontier. Towards this end, the British sought to vacate power held in pockets in Kashmir and transfer it to the new maharajah, in whom alone a personalized sovereignty was now to vest" (Rai 2004: 27). The unquestionable and eternal authority promised to the Dogra elite in the Treaty of Amritsar was cut short exactly a century later, at the time of India's independence and partition in 1947. J & K remained an independent principality until 1947.

Although the princely state of J & K was predominantly Muslim, members of that community were prevented from becoming officers in the state's military and did not find adequate representation in the civil services. Kashmiri Muslims were disallowed from expressing their political opinions and did not have access to a free press or any other such forum. The lack of protest against autocratic and brutal rule until the end of the 1920s was attributed to the passive character of the peasantry in the Kashmir Valley (Lamb 1991: 28). The authority of the maharaja in the internal affairs of the state was paramount. Although his oppressive and exploitative methods were not thwarted, they were carefully watched by the British representative at his court. His stature was further exalted by the pompous title of His Highness. The maharaja was given the privileged position of major-general in the British Indian army and was entitled to a twenty-one gun salute— one among five "twenty-one gun" princes. The maharaja's decadence was proverbial and he indulged himself by participating in expensive sports, luxurious parties, and other extravagant hobbies. He unapologetically persecuted and exploited Kashmiri Muslims (Korbel 2002: 14).

During the autocratic rule of the Dogra maharajas there was an unrelenting regional and religious bias against Kashmiri Muslims. Kashmiri Muslims were politically, economically, and socially suppressed. Navnita Chadha Behera points to the plight of Kashmiri Muslims during Dogra rule in her complex study of Kashmir: "The lot of Muslims was even worse: they were excluded from state services, the Muslim peasantry and industrial workers were heavily taxed, and trade, business, and banking were monopolized by Punjabis and Dogras. Without access to modern education, Muslims sank into a deep distrust of rule under the Dogra Hindus" (Behera 2006: 14). The miserable plight of Kashmiri Muslims was reported by Prem Nath Bazaz, a prominent Kashmiri Pandit political and social activist, in 1941. According to him, the Muslim peasants lived and worked in despicable conditions; the Muslim masses were traumatized and victimized by official corruption (Bazaz 2002: 252–53). The subsequent awakening of a national consciousness in the state, which I delineate in chapters one and three, challenged the despotic abuse of authority.

The role played by the nation-states of India and Pakistan in the former princely state of J & K echoes the animosity created during the partition. The political and social upheaval that followed upon the creation of the two nation-states in 1947 has left legacies that continue to haunt the two countries. The partition enabled forces of violence and displacement to tear asunder the preexisting cultural and social fabric so systematically that the process of repair has not even begun. I would argue that although the "third world" intelligentsia unceasingly complains about the manipulations and shortsightedness of British imperial cartographers and administrators, the onus of the calamity engendered on 14 and 15 August 1947 does not lie entirely on the colonial power. The failed negotiations between Indian and Pakistani nationalists who belonged to the Congress and the Muslim League, the blustering of those nationalists and the national jingoism it stimulated, and the unquenchable hatred on both sides contributed to the brutal events of 1947. In the words of historian Uma Kaura (1977: 170), "the mistakes made by the Congress leadership, the frustration and bitterness of the League leadership, and the defensive diplomacy of a British Viceroy cumulatively resulted in the demand for Partition." Ever since the inception, in 1885, of proindependence political activity in pre-partition India, the Muslim leadership insisted on the necessity for a distinct Muslim identity (ibid.: 164). Kaura also underlines the inability of the nationalist leadership to accommodate Muslim aspirations because its primary concern was to ingratiate itself with the militant Hindu faction, which would have created ruptures within the Congress. Gutted homes, rivulets of blood, ravaged lands, and meaningless loss of lives were the costs of this nation building. The upsurge of ethnic and religious fundamentalism that led to the creation of Pakistan has been characterized by political psychologist Ashis Nandy as a nationalism that takes an enormous toll on a polyglot society such as India's:

> First it comes bundled with official concepts of state, ethnicity, territoriality, security and citizenship. Once such a package captures public imagination, it is bound to trigger in the long run, in a society as diverse as ours, various forms of "subnationalism"…the idea of the nation in the "official" theory of nationhood can be made available in a purer form to culturally more homogeneous communities such as the Sikhs, the Kashmiri Muslims, the Gorkhas and the Tamils. As a result, once the ideology of nationalism is internalized, no psychological barrier is left standing against the concepts of new nation-states, that would be theoretically even purer, homogeneous national units—in terms of religion, language, and culture. (Nandy 1983: 5)

The borders that were brutally carved by the authorities at the time of partition have led to further brutality in the form of those riots, organized historical distortions, and cultural depletions with which the histories of independent India and Pakistan are replete.

For India, Kashmir lends credibility to its secular nationalist image. For Pakistan, Kashmir represents the infeasibility of secular nationalism and underscores the need for an Islamic theocracy on the subcontinent. Once the Kashmir issue took an ideological turn, Mahatma Gandhi remarked, "Muslims all over the world are watching the experiment in Kashmir.…Kashmir is the real test of secularism in India." In January 1948, India referred the Kashmir dispute to the United Nations (Hagerty 2005: 19). Subsequent to the declaration of the cease-fire between India and Pakistan on 1 January 1949, the state of J & K was divided into two portions. The part of the state comprising the Punjabi-speaking areas of Poonch, Mirpur, and Muzaffarabad, along with Gilgit and Baltistan, was incorporated into Pakistan, whereas the portion of the state comprising the Kashmir Valley, Ladakh, and the large Jammu region was politically assimilated into India. Currently, a large part of J & K is administered by India and a portion by Pakistan. China annexed a section of the land in 1962, through which it has built a road that links Tibet to Xiajiang (see Rahman 1996: 5–6; Schofield 2002: 25). The strategic location of Indian-administered J & K underscores its importance for both India and Pakistan. The state of J & K borders on China and Afghanistan. Out of a total land area of 222,236 square kilometers, 78,114 are under Pakistani administration, 5,180 square kilometers were handed over to China by Pakistan, 37,555 square kilometers are under Chinese administration in the Leh district, and the remaining area is under Indian administration (*Census of India,* 1981: 156).

In order to make their borders impregnable, it was essential for both India and Pakistan to control the state politically and militarily. Even as separatist movements have surfaced and resurfaced in J & K and parts of Pakistani-administered Kashmir since the accession of the state to India in 1947, the attempt to create a unitary cultural identity bolstered by nationalist politics has been subverted by regional political forces and the comprador class, backed by the governments of India and Pakistan. The culturally, linguistically, and religiously diverse population of Indian- and Pakistani-administered J & K has been unable to reach a consensus on the future of the land and the heterogeneous peoples of the state. The revolutionary act of demanding the right of self-determination and autonomy for J & K has not been able to nurture unity amongst all socioeconomic classes (Rahman 1996: 148–49; Ganguly 1997: 78–79). Cultural notions of the people of Indian- and Pakistani-administered Kashmir in image and word have been reconstructed to emphasize the bias that reinforces the propagandist agenda of the hegemonic powers involved in the Kashmir dispute: India and Pakistan. In establishment Indian and Pakistani thought, Kashmiris are defined as different from the nationals of the two countries. The various communities in J & K—Kashmiri Muslims, Kashmiri Pandits, Dogras, and Ladakhis—have tried time and again to form a collective consciousness in order to name their cultural alterity through the nation. But due to the regional sentiments that are so entrenched in the psyche of the people, this attempt is still in a volatile stage. The symbols of nationhood in J & K—flag, anthem, and constitution—have thus far been unable to forge the process of nationalist self-imagining.

Although Pakistan distinctly expresses its recognition of the status of J & K as disputed territory, it dithers from doing so in areas of the state under Pakistani control. Pakistan arbitrarily maintains its de facto government in "Azad" (Purportedly Free) Kashmir. Old fiefdoms in the kingdoms of Hunza and Nagar were abolished and the entire area was reconstituted into five administrative districts in 1975 by the government of Pakistani Prime Minister Zulfikar Ali Bhutto. To date, the Northern Areas (NA), comprising Gilgit, Baltistan, Hunza-Nagar, Koh-e-Ghizer, Ghanche, Diamir, and Skardu, remain the disenfranchised fifth zone; administered by executive edict from Islamabad through the federal ministry for Kashmir Affairs and Northern Areas (KANA), a politically constituted, non-elected ministry, they do not have a place in Pakistan's constitution. The Northern Areas legislative council, the region's elected legislature, is a disempowered body lacking the authority to represent its constituents. South Asia affairs analyst Victoria Schofield (2001) astutely observes: "There is no question…of Pakistan ever agreeing to relinquish control of the area, either to form part of an independent state of Jammu and Kashmir or as an independent state in its own right." The germination of disgruntlement in the NA caused by the political, economic, and social impoverishment of the region has now burst into a blazing rebellion mirroring the separatist movement in J & K. There is a segment of the population that advocates the independence of the former princely state of J & K in its entirety, whereas another segment of the population is a fierce proponent of deploying politically militant and constitutional means to carve out Gilgit, Hunza-Nagar, Koh-e-Ghizer, Ghanche, Diamir, Baltistan, and Skardu, collectively known as Balawaristan, as an independent state with constitutional legitimacy. The formation of indigenous political organizations in the area, like the Balawaristan National Front, Muttehada Quami Party, and the Gilgit–Baltistan United Action Forum, is indicative of the rising demand for selfhood, liberties, enfranchisement, and constitutional status. The government of Pakistan has not engineered the de jure integration of the NA with Pakistan because it prognosticates that such an action would insidiously impair the credibility of Pakistan's demand for the Kashmir issue to be adjudged under the terms of the UN resolutions. Gilgit and Hunza are strategically important to Pakistan because of the access they provide to China through the Khunjerab pass. Therefore, advocating self-determination for the entire former princely state of J & K would irreparably damage Pakistan's political and military interests (Johnson 2003: 697–743; Rushbrook-Williams 1957: 26–35). Although now integrated into Pakistan under the rechristened name of Gilgit-Baltistan after the general elections held there in 2009, the former NA continues to remain a peripheralized (now) fifth province of Pakistan.

The once paradisiacal region coveted by kings and mystics alike, albeit for different reasons, where snow-covered peaks majestically tower over flowing rivers and streams are bordered by lilies gently swaying to the cadences of the gentle breeze, by a quirk of fate, has become a valley of guns and unmarked graves. The paean of the Mughal emperor Jahangir in 1620 to the enthralling and spiritually healing beauty of Kashmir bespeaks the passionate longing it engendered:

> If one were to praise Kashmir, whole books would have to be written. Kashmir is a garden of eternal spring, or an iron fort to a palace of kings—a delightful flower-bed, and a heart-expanding heritage for dervishes. Its pleasant meads and enchanting cascades are beyond all description. There are running streams and fountains beyond count. Wherever the eye reaches, there is verdure and running water. The red rose, the violet and the narcissus grow of themselves; in the fields, there are all kinds of flowers and all sorts of sweet-scented herbs, more than can be calculated. In the soul-enchanting spring the hills and plains are filled with blossoms; the gates, the walls, the courts, the roofs, are lighted up by the torches of the banquet-adoring tulips. What shall we say of these things or the wide meadows and the fragrant trefoil? (Rogers 1914: 114)

The breezes of Kashmir, which once had the power to heal every trauma, now cause searing wounds. The throes of pain, palpable in every withering flower and trembling leaf, can lacerate the most hardened person. The ripe pomegranate trees that once bespoke a cornucopia now seem laden with an unbearable burden. The liturgies in mosques, temples, and churches that once provided spiritual ecstasy are now jarring cacophonies. The comforting solitude that one could thrive on in various spots of the Valley now seems like a psychosis-inducing solitariness. What happened to the Valley that provided inspiration to poets, saints, and writers? Where is the beauteous land in which even a dull-witted writer could find her or his muse? Where are the majestic chinars, the fragrant pine trees, and the luxuriant weeping willows that provided harbor to those buffeted by the fates? The mesmerizing Mughal gardens in the Valley with their refreshing springs and breathtaking waterfalls bemoan the state of the riven land, the polluted streams, and the devastated people.

The seductive beauty of the Valley of Kashmir that evoked a desire to live to the hilt, untarnished by sordid passions and murky politics, is now blemished with army camps and militant hideouts. The plight of the repressed Kashmiri is similar to that of Adam and Eve in the Garden of Eden after their willful defiance of Jehovah. The palpable contrast between the enchanting beauty of Kashmir and the glazed eyes of its people is cruel. The redness of roses that once awakened sensuality now evokes the violent bloodshed and loss of innocent lives that mangle the landscape. The land in which dervishes meditated to willingly renounce the self is now a chessboard for wily politicians. The strains of mystical music are now drowned out by the cacophonous sounds of hate and virulence. The lush meadows carpeted with daisies and lupines now reek of death and destruction. The soothing fragrance of pine-covered hills has now been overwhelmed by the odor of false promises and false hope.

The tranquility of the region has been shattered by the heavy hand of political and military totalitarianism. The region resembles a vast concentration camp, swarming with soldiers. Police or military barriers abound in both urban and rural areas, and intimidation is a rather common occurrence at these checkpoints. The Valley seethes with a repressed anger generated by the humiliating brutality inflicted by Indian troops. The history of Kashmir is replete with egregious errors. As one scholar, Vincent H. Smith (1928: 176), wrote, "Few regions in the world can have had worse luck than Kashmir in the matter of government." The saga of Kashmir has been one of oppression, political persecution, and undemocratic policies. Since the pervasion of an exclusive cultural nationalism, religious fundamentalism, and rampant political corruption, it has become a challenge to lead a dignified existence in J & K.

The armed conflict has changed political combinations and permutations without either disrupting political, social, and gender hierarchies or benefiting marginalized groups. The social, economic, political, and psychological brunt of the armed conflict has been borne by the populace of Kashmir. The uncertainty created by fifteen years of armed insurgency and counterinsurgency has pervaded the social fabric in insidious ways, creating a whole generation of disaffected and disillusioned youth. Lack of faith in the Indian polity has caused Kashmiris to cultivate an apathy to the electoral process because it is a given that persons best suited to carry out New Delhi's agenda will be installed in positions of political import, regardless of public opinion. The earlier enthusiasm that accompanied democratization seems totally futile in the current leadership vacuum in the state. Lack of accountability among the J & K polity and bureaucracy has caused a large number of people to toe the line by living with the fundamental structural inequities and violence, instead of risking the ire of groups and individuals in positions of authority.

Political organizations in the Valley have eroded mass bases and are in a moribund state. There seems to be an unbridgeable gulf between figures of authority and the electorate, who have been deployed as pawns in the devious political game being played by Indian and Pakistani state-sponsored agencies. The glaring lack of a well-equipped infrastructure in the Valley makes unemployment rife and underscores the redundancy of the educated segment of the population. The counterinsurgency operations undertaken in J & K by the Indian military and paramilitary forces were ferocious and cruel, and have alienated the disillusioned populace.

I start from the premise that the syncretic ethos of Kashmir has been violated by the outburst of religious nationalism, secular nationalism, and ethnonationalism that have facilitated political and social structural violence. The well-crafted theoretical fiction of a syncretic culture by the advocates of a Kashmiri polity empowered them in a circumscribed fashion to choose an idiom within which they could arbitrarily remove the distinction between religion and politics. I consider the shape of women's empowerment or lack thereof in the syncretic ethos of Kashmir, and the new languages of resistance, negotiation, and empowerment it adopts in the cacophonous social and political situation created by various nationalist discourses. I draw from the cultural and ideological spaces I was raised in; the cherished verses of the Sufi poetess Lalla-Ded, in whose immortal poetry the legendary beauty of Kashmir endures pain and strife but lives on; conversations with my maternal grandmother that are etched in my memory; informative and enlightening discussions with my parents, who have continued to live in the strife-torn Valley through years of unbearable hostility and the psychological trauma of armed conflict with an unparalleled stoicism; informal conversations with friends and acquaintances who are victims of the politics of dispossession; and the extensive reading that I have done over the years on the conflictual history and politics of J & K. I also draw from field work conducted during my annual trips to Kashmir in July 2005, 2006, and 2007 among predominantly agricultural communities in areas bordering the Line of Control between India and Pakistan. Against the backdrop of the politically tumultuous situation in J & K, which has led to an increase in gender-based violence, I attempt to show that the muted voices of marginalized laypeople, particularly women, have not been raised loud enough against the atrocities to which they are subjected by Indian paramilitary forces, Pakistan-sponsored insurgents, counterinsurgency forces, and religious fundamentalists. I also emphasize the necessity of foregrounding women's perspectives in issues of nationalist ideologies, religious freedom, democratic participation, militarization, intellectual freedom, and judicial and legal structures in a milieu that does not co-opt them into mainstream political and cultural discourses or first-world feminist agendas.

Using self-reflexive and historicized forms, drawing on my heritage and kinship in Kashmir, I explore the construction and employment of the Kashmiri political and cultural landscape, and gender, in secular nationalist, religious nationalist, and ethnonationalist discourses in J & K. I question the exclusivity of cultural nationalism, the erosion of cultural syncretism, the ever-increasing dominance of religious fundamentalism, and the irrational resistance to cultural and linguistic differences. I also question the victimization and subjugation of women selectively enshrined in the prevalent regressive social discourse and the uncritically rendered folklore of traditional Kashmiri Islamic and Hindu cultures, such as limited educational and professional opportunities; the right of a husband to prevent his wife from making strides in the material world; the kudos given to a hapless wife who agrees to live in a polygamous relationship; the bounden duty of the woman to bear heirs; the unquestioned right of a husband to divorce his barren wife; confinement of the woman to her home where she is subjected to material and emotional brutality; the hallowed status of a woman who conforms to such cultural dogmas; the social ostracization of a woman who defies them; and the status of woman as a fiefdom facilitating political and feudal alliances.

The upsurge of gender-based violence has circumscribed the mobility of women who are caught between the devil and the deep blue sea. I, for one, would not have been able to conduct my field research without the armed bodyguard my parents provided. As a woman, it would have been difficult and dangerous for me to venture into secluded rural areas that are cordoned by paramilitary troops. The ethnographic field research that I undertook was a method of seeking reconnection sans condescension by simultaneously belonging to, and resisting, the discursive community of traditional Muslim Kashmiri and Gujjar rural women. I was further motivated by the desire to critically observe the sociopolitical discourse in Kashmir through an oblique focus from the margins instead of from an elitist center. My goal was to engage in reflective action as an educator working with diverse cultural and social groups. I was challenged to examine my own locations of privilege and seek emotional empowerment in order to understand the systems that have generated the culture of silence. This culture generates problematic stereotypes, alliances, and biases within and outside the community. I seek in the collision of modernity and communal memory a horizontal relationship producing intersectionalities between different cultural spaces, times, and ways of knowing the self in relation to the family, society, and the larger cultural landscape. Acknowledging our complicity in oppression, reconceptualizing paradigmatic structures, and mobilizing cultural and political coalitions is riddled with conflict, but it is the need of the day for us to engage in these processes.

In chapter one, "Conflicting Political Discourses," I delineate the origins of the Kashmir conflict and the perspectives on it. I look at the discourse of "Kashmiriyat" as a significant attempt to form a national consciousness in order to name its cultural alterity through the nation. In chapter two, "Cultural Syncretism in Kashmir," I analyze the recorded poems and paradigmatic sayings of Lalla-Ded, a Sufi mystic. I retrieve the rich details of her life that have been relegated to the background in the documented version of history. I incorporate hitherto unpublished opinions of scholars of Kashmiri and Urdu literature, as well as of scholars of mysticism in the Kashmir Valley, on the impact of Lalla-Ded on the Kashmiri Muslim and Kashmiri Pandit communities. I also foreground the revival of indigenous cultural institutions in J & K. In chapter three, "Political Debacles," I underline the repercussions of India's antidemocratic strategies in the state, which instigated oppositional and dissident responses. In chapter four, "Militarization of J & K," I delineate the fundamental structural inequities in the J & K polity, exacerbated by political and military intrusions of the Pakistani administration and the engendering of political resistance. In chapter five, "Negotiating the Boundaries of Gender, Community, and Nationhood," I analyze the effects of nationalist, militant, and religious discourses and praxes on a gender-based hierarchy. I write about the radical political and socioeconomic changes in the role of Kashmiri women between 1947 and 1989. I report the reminiscences of two of the three surviving members of the women's militia that was formed at the height of the struggle against political and military tyranny. I address the traditional freedoms and prerogatives of Kashmiri women in the land of a spiritual luminary like Lalla-Ded.

Entrenched gender inequities are intensified in situations of armed conflict, in which the agency assumed by women in the public sphere is given legitimacy by male authoritative figures and is subsumed within masculinist discourse. In my book, I explore the concept of agency in the context of revival of nationalism, fight for self-determination, armed insurgency, counterinsurgency, imposition of quasi-democratic processes, and experiences of women within these discourses. The concept of agency is a problematic one that has been defined as "a temporally embedded process of social engagement, informed by the past (in its habitual aspect), but also oriented toward the future (as a capacity to imagine alternative possibilities) and toward the present (as a capacity to contextualize past habits and future projects within the contingencies of the moment)" (Emirbayer and Mische 1998: 964); or another definition (Professor of Sociology in the Department of Sociology and Philosophy at the University of Exeter, England, Pickering): "The dance of agency, seen asymmetrically from the human end, thus takes the form of a dialectic of resistance and accommodation, where resistance denotes the failure to achieve an intended capture of agency and practice, and accommodation an active human strategy of response to resistance, which can include revisions to goals and intentions as well as to the material form of the machine in question and to the human frame of gestures and social relations that surround it" (Fuchs 2001: 30). How did Kashmiri women express their political agency during the resuscitation of cultural pride and nationalist awakening in the 1930s; during the "Quit Kashmir" movement in the 1940s; at the onset of the militant movement in the late 1980s; and during the era of gross human rights violations by the Indian army, paramilitary forces, Pakistani-trained militants, mercenaries, and state-sponsored organizations in the 1990s and 2000s? How did these women navigate the undulating, often impenetrable terrain of formal spaces of political power?

I have chosen to deploy oral evidence in my book, which has allowed me to approach events, notions, and literatures about which there was meager evidence from other sources. The use of oral history has empowered my interviewees and correspondents, people of J & K, in significant ways, bringing acknowledgment of hitherto disregarded opinions and experiences. In some instances, I have taken the liberty of reproducing e-mail responses, which I received from my interviewees, verbatim. I was keen on providing personal reminiscences from participants about landmark events without mediating between oral evidence or historiography and more elitist versions of history. My primary goal is to ensure that future generations of the former princely state of Jammu and Kashmir do not forget, because if we stop remembering, we stop being.

Chapter One

Conflicting Political Discourses, Partition, Plebiscite, Autonomy, Integration

Despotism during the Dogra Regime and the Awakening of Nationalism

Maharaja Hari Singh ruled the princely state of Jammu and Kashmir (J & K) with an iron fist and employed forceful means to extinguish the flames of an antifeudal nationalism. Dogra rule in the Kashmir Valley was particularly tyrannical and created stifling socioeconomic conditions for the populace. Although Muslims constituted a large percentage of the population of the state, out of thirteen battalions in Kashmir, just one was Muslim. Muslims were disallowed from owning and carrying firearms and sharp instruments. Kashmiri Muslims lived in such circumscribed conditions and under such strict surveillance that they were required to seek a license to slaughter a chicken for an ordinary meal. There was a strict ban on cow slaughter in the state. The sheep or goats that Muslims sacrificed on religious occasions were heavily taxed, transforming the existence of these people into the proverbial albatross. Most edible items, salable artifacts, and ceremonial services were taxed. Kashmiri farmers worked as mere serfs on the lands that were bestowed by the Dogra monarch on his clansmen (Khan 1958: 5–7). Because of their military and political supremacy, Dogras were endowed with high-ranking and lucrative positions in the military as well as in the civil services, in addition to their enormous landholdings. Muslims were denied the right to acquire an education; excluded from the civil services; and disenfranchised and prevented from participating in political activities without governmental permission. Such unapologetically discriminatory practices created an endemic ignorance and conscripted existence for the Muslim inhabitants of the princely state.

In an endeavor to enable the formation of representative governments in Indian states, the All India States People's Conference (AISPC) adopted a constitution in 1939 that underlined deploying legitimate means to help the people of the state form a responsible and representative government under the aegis of the monarch. Once the AISPC drafted and proclaimed its objectives, a number of organizations were formed in order to achieve concretization of these objectives. Intellectually and politically drawn to the nationalist reform movements of the late nineteenth and early twentieth centuries, the Kashmiri Pandits, for example, formed a Hindu revivalist party; in Jammu, political organizations, whose hallmark was their exclusionary regionalism, were formed solely for Dogras, of which the Dogra Sabha, established in 1903, and the Yawak Sabha, established in 1915, were the primary ones. These organizations did not seek involvement just with political issues but focused on social reform as well, particularly on improving the conditions of Hindu women. Following the institutionalization of Hindu organizations, Kashmiri Muslims, led by their religious leader, the *mirwaiz*, formed the Anjuman-i-Nusrat-ul-Islam. Besides the dissemination of Islamic teachings, the Anjuman aimed at social reform and educational improvement for the Muslims of the Valley.

While the political mobilization of Kashmiri Muslims was still in an embryonic stage, it was pulverized by a governmental edict banning all Muslim organizations. The grievances of the Muslims were exacerbated by the labor crisis in the silk mill in Srinagar, Kashmir, which was owned by the monarch. Most of the underpaid, overworked, and shabbily treated laborers in the mill were Muslim (for details, see Ganju 1945). These widespread exploitative practices and the resentment engendered by them impelled eminent members of the Muslim community to voice their protest in a memorandum. The memorandum was presented to the governor-general of India, Lord Reading: "In addition to specifying grievances, the memorandum called for an increase in Muslim employment, improved education, land reforms, protection of Muslim religious establishments from encroachment, the abolition of forced labor, equitable distribution of resources, a state constitution, and a legislative assembly that would give Muslims proper representation" (for an informative discussion, see Rahman 1996). The increasing atrocities inflicted on Kashmiri Muslims by Maharaja Hari Singh's regime in terms of religious irreverence, violating their right to worship, desecrating their places of worship, and razing entire villages to the ground instigated a volcanic antimonarchical eruption (Sibtain 1992: 117–50).

When the first few Kashmiri Muslims to have obtained degrees at institutions of higher education, such as the Aligarh Muslim University in British India, returned to the state in the 1920s, they were imbued with "newfangled" ideas of nationalism, liberty, and democracy.

> Things were now moving very fast in the Indian subcontinent. In December 1929, the Indian National Congress adopted, in Lahore, the resolution of complete independence as its goal; a mass civil disobedience movement followed which electrified the subcontinent from Gilgit to Cape Comorin. Kashmir too felt its repercussions; people began to be deeply excited with what was taking place in the rest of the country. It seems astounding today, but is, nevertheless, a fact that the Dogras, ostrich-like, refused to see the writing on the wall or to be moved by these soul stirring developments. And when a number of Muslim young men—among them Sheikh Mohammad Abdullah—educated at different universities in India and deeply moved by the Congress struggle for freedom returned home, a spark was applied to the explosive matter which had accumulated in the Valley. (Bazaz [1967] 2005: 29)

A group of these young graduates, who were well educated but denied opportunities that would have enabled them to climb the socioeconomic ladder, started convening regular meetings at a house in Fateh Kadal, Srinagar, and from these seemingly innocuous gatherings evolved the "Fateh Kadal Reading Room Party." Members of the Reading Room Party wrote articles for various publications in which their subversive voices expressed resentment against the arbitrary and discriminatory practices of the Dogra regime.

The torch of cultural pride and political awakening in the princely state of J & K was lit by Sheikh Mohammad Abdullah, a prominent member of the Fateh Kadal Reading Room Party, in 1931: "Sheikh Abdullah was an imposing figure. His six feet four inches of height towered over his countrymen, and his intellect attracted the attention and respect of those who were associated with him in his revolutionary efforts" (Korbel 2002: 17). For the first time in decades, the Kashmiri people, particularly the Muslim population, acknowledged the leadership of a man who overtly challenged the hitherto impregnable authority of the maharaja. They responded to his revolutionary politics with a zeal that was previously unknown. Abdullah's inspirational speeches, concern for the well-being of the masses, commitment to the cause of freedom, as well as his charisma, motivated the Kashmiri people to throw off the yoke of oppression and docility. Despite persecution, he continued to vociferously fight for the political, economic, and religious rights of the Kashmiri people.

Ahmad Ullah Shah, the senior mirwaiz, had been unequivocally accepted by the Srinagar Muslims as their religious leader, and his authority had been ratified by the Dogra regime. When his son

Muhammad Yusuf Shah assumed the leadership of the Jama Masjid worshippers in 1931, he had expected to don his father's mantle and exercise the same unquestioned authority. But, to his surprise, his stature was undermined by a young politician of obscure origins and revolutionary political opinions, Sheikh Muhammad Abdullah. Abdullah, a political greenhorn at that point, challenged the hegemony of the mirwaiz. As a strategy to eliminate the threat posed to his hegemonic position by Abdullah's rising popularity and clout, Yusuf Shah contemptuously labeled him a heretic. Abdullah vociferously retaliated by aligning himself with Mirwaiz Hamadani. That political move widened the gap between the two mirwaizeen (religious leaders). A couple of months after Abdullah and Hamadani formed the Muslim Conference (MC), Yusuf Shah founded the Azad Conference, and in April 1933 Abdullah's *Sher* (lion) followers and Yusuf Shah's goatee-wearing *Bakra* (goat) followers fought a violent battle during the *Id-uz-Zuha* (religious festival) prayers. But Shah's servile attitude toward the Dogra monarchy and his inclination to toe the official line made him an unappealing figure to the repressed Muslim masses. He sank further into the morass of servility and unpopularity by accepting a fiefdom worth Rs. 600 from the Dogra regime. In the twilight of his political life, Shah reverted to the security of his priestly edifice (Copeland 1991: 248).

Formation of the All Jammu and Kashmir Muslim Conference and Its Subsequent Secularization into the National Conference

Regardless of the ongoing political maneuverings, Sheikh Mohammad Abdullah created a legitimate forum for himself and the state's Muslim population by founding the All Jammu and Kashmir Muslim Conference (MC) in 1932. In order to redress the grievances aired by Kashmiri Muslims, the British government sent the Glancy Commission to Srinagar, the summer capital of J & K. The investigations made by the commission led it to ask the maharaja to give the populace the right to elect a legislative assembly in order to redress the alienation of the Muslim population. The maharaja's devious policies and unwillingness to deploy quasi-democratic measures caused the uprising of 1933, which was put down with unwarranted violence. Subsequently, a civil disobedience movement was organized by Abdullah and his ally, Chaudhri Ghulam Abbas, but the maharaja was adamant in his refusal to relent. The flames of revolution, however, could not be doused, and the first democratic election in the state was held in 1934.

The era of political and social upheaval in the state between 1930 and 1960 invoked an assertion of a revolutionary self invigorated with unfaltering cultural pride, rejecting the bondage that was deterring it from soaring high.

> Come, gardener! Create the glory of spring!
> Make Guls [flowers] bloom and bulbuls [a type of bird] sing—
> create such haunts!
>
> The dew weeps and your garden lies desolate;
> Tearing their robes, your flowers are distracted;
> Breathe life once again into the lifeless gul and the bulbul!
>
> Rank nettles hamper the growth of your roses;
> Weed them out, for look thousands
> Of laughing hyacinths are crowding at the gate!
>
> Who will set you free, captive bird, Crying in your cage?
> Forge with your own hands
> The instruments of your deliverance!
>
> Wealth and pride and comfort, luxury and authority,
> Kingship and governance—all these are yours;
> Wake up, sleeper, and know these as yours,
>
> Bid good-bye to your dulcet strains; to rouse
> This habitat of flowers, create a storm,
> Let thunder rumble—let there be an earthquake!
>
> (Mahjoor 1972: 68–69)

The articulation of the religious and economic rights of Muslim subjects by Abdullah in the 1930s revived regional sentiment with an unparalleled ferocity (Rai 2004: 278). As Sumantra Bose succinctly points out, in the years prior to 1947, the rallying banner and political ideology of the MC mobilized a collective sense of pride in regional identity. The charismatic leader of the party, Sheikh Mohammad Abdullah, had the political will and astuteness to create an efficiently organized network of young men who were committed to the party's ideology. Abdullah's emphasis on a shared Muslim identity, which brought Kashmiri nationalism out of the dark chambers of tyranny and promised social and political enfranchisement, was a light at the end of the tunnel for an abject, debased, and politically disenfranchised people (Bose 2003: 25).

The formation of secular local political organizations that espoused a nationalist and socialist ideology in the 1930s and 1940s, such as the Kashmiri Youth League, Peasants Association, Students Federation, Silk Labour Union, Telegraph Employees Union, and so on, enabled popular political leaders, especially Sheikh Mohammad Abdullah, to focus on the structural inequities legitimized by the state rather than on just religious and sectarian conflict. Although the MC won fourteen out of twenty-one seats allotted to Muslim voters in the State Assembly, the assembly had only consultative powers. Two years later, however, fresh elections were held, because the elected members of the legislature fiercely protested their restricted powers. Abdullah's disillusionment with the insularity of the Muslim population and the supersession of nationalist aspirations by sectarian ones inspired him to forge a secular movement in the state. In order to disseminate his progressive ideas, Abdullah and a Kashmiri Hindu secularist and democratic socialist, Prem Nath Bazaz, founded an Urdu

LEST WE FORGET   KASHMIRI TRADERS WITH JENAB SHER-I-KASHMIR, SHEIKH MOHAMMAD   IN BOMBAY IN THE YEAR 1936
ABDULLAH,
WITH BEST COMPLIMENTS
QAZI MOHD SIDIQ

Kashmiri traders with Sheikh Mohammad Abdullah, Bombay, 1936. (*Courtesty*: The Archives of the National Conference, with the permission of the general secretary of the National Conference, Sheikh Nazir Ahmad)

weekly, *Hamdard*, in 1935. Consequently, the MC was replaced by the secular All Jammu and Kashmir National Congress (NC), presided over by Abdullah, in June 1939.

In order to align itself with the purportedly secular and nationalist Indian National Congress, the younger generation of MC leaders, including Sheikh Mohammad Abdullah, Bakshi Ghulam Mohammad, and Maulana Sayeed Masoodi, strove to transform a communally oriented political movement into a secular movement for political, economic, and social reforms. The nature of this transformation was articulated by Sheikh Mohammad Abdullah in his address to the MC's annual session in March 1938:

> We desire that we should be free to set our house in order and no foreign or internal autocratic power should interfere in our national and human birthrights. This very demand is known as Responsible Government....The first condition to achieve Responsible Government is the participation of all those people...they are not the Muslims alone nor the Hindus and the Sikhs alone, nor the untouchables or Buddhists alone, but all those who live in this state....We do not demand Responsible Government for 80 lakh Muslims but all the 100% state subjects....Secondly, we must build a common national front by universal suffrage on the basis of joint electorate. (Quoted in Hassnain 1988: 88)

A unitary national identity was forged by the young leadership of the MC in order to expound the political expediency of a constituent assembly, adult suffrage, and protective measures for minorities. As I mentioned earlier, the MC was converted into the All India Jammu and Kashmir NC in 1939. In 1944, the NC sought reconstitution of the political, economic, and social systems of J & K. The NC came to be identified with socially leftist republicanism and the personality of Abdullah (Bose 2003: 21).

Veteran journalist and Abdullah's contemporary and cofreedom fighter Prem Nath Bazaz observed about the formation of the NC that the communal politics in the state were fraying the traditional religious tolerance. Sheikh Mohammad Abdullah and some of his colleagues had the political foresight to recognize the malignant effects of communalism and lent vigorous support to the secularization of politics. This timely political move won the approbation and full-fledged support of emancipated Hindus and Muslims (Bazaz [1967] 2005: 34). Josef Korbel, the Czech chairman of the United Nations Commission for India and Pakistan, noted the prestige accorded to Sheikh Abdullah's NC in terms of the support it enjoyed at the organizational and grassroots level (Korbel 2002: 246). At the national level, the NC made a concerted effort to reach out to various socioeconomic classes and to align itself with other political movements that had socialist leanings.

Sheikh Abdullah and his political organization fought tooth and nail against Dogra autocracy and demanded that the Treaty of Amritsar be revoked and monarchical rule ousted. He described the Dogra monarchy as a microcosm of colonial brutality and the NC's "Quit Kashmir" movement as a ramification of the larger Indian struggle for independence. At the annual session of the NC in 1945, the unity and integrity of India were recognized and the demand for India's independence and the right of self-determination for the various ethnic/cultural groups in the country was put forth. Abdullah's political ideology was well delineated in the London *Times*:

> The Sheikh has made it clear that he is as much opposed to the domination of India as to subjugation by Pakistan. He claims sovereign authority for the Kashmir Constituent Assembly, without limitation by the Constitution of India, and this stand has a strong appeal to Kashmiris on both sides of the Ceasefire line and if this movement of purely Kashmiri nationalism was to gain ground, it might well oblige India, Pakistan, and the United Nations to modify their view about what ought to be done next. (*The Times*, 8 May 1952, quoted in Taseer 1986: 148; see Appendix A, 175–178)

Abdullah's patriotic fervor and his unquenchable zeal to improve the socioeconomic position of Kashmiris, debilitated by feudalism, remained an integral part of his political persona till the day he died (see Appendix C, 180).

The first president of the NC was Abdullah's Communist ally, G.M. Sadiq. Despite the establishment of an executive council, council of ministers, and a juridical and legislative branch of public administration, the maharaja retained his supreme authority. Abdullah explicitly declared the antimonarchical stance of his organization to the British Cabinet Mission, which was to chart the course of India's destiny, including that of the princely states:

> The fate of the Kashmiri nation is in the balance and in that hour of decision we demand our basic democratic right to send our elected representatives to the constitution-making bodies that will construct the framework of Free India. We emphatically repudiate the right of the Princely Order to represent the people of the Indian States or their right to nominate personal representatives as our spokesmen.

(Opening Address by Honorable Sheikh Mohammad Abdullah, Jammu and Kashmir Constituent Assembly, Srinagar, 1951; see Appendix C, 180)

This well-articulated demand for the introduction of democratic measures was brazenly ignored by the administration as well as by the British Cabinet Mission.

The "Quit Kashmir" Movement

Abdullah launched the "Quit Kashmir" movement to oust the Dogra monarchy. But the movement did not garner the support he had hoped for. On the contrary, he was accused of having vested interests and of having started the agitation for the purpose of regaining the immense popularity he had enjoyed, which had diminished due to his political and personal alliance with the first prime minister of independent India, Jawaharlal Nehru (Korbel 2002: 22). The "Quit Kashmir" movement did not bolster Abdullah's position among the Muslims of Kashmir, and it antagonized the Hindus and Sikhs of the state who venerated the maharaja because they owed him their political, economic, and religious privileges in the predominantly Muslim Kashmir Valley (Bazaz 1950: 4–5).

In May 1946 Abdullah was sentenced to nine years in prison for having led the seditious "Quit Kashmir" movement against the maharaja's regime. Abdullah's defense against the charges leveled at him during the infamous "Quit Kashmir" trial reinvigorated the national identity of the people of J & K, an attempt to underline a strategic syncretism enabling legitimate opposition to despotic rule:

Where law is not based on the will of the people, it can lead to the suppression of their aspirations. Such law has no moral validity even though it may be enforced for a while. There is law higher than that, the law that represents the people's will and secures their well being; and there is the tribute of the human conscience, which judges the ruler and the ruled alike by standards that do not change by the arbitrary will of the most powerful. To this law I gladly submit and that tribunal I shall face with confidence and without fear, leaving it to history and posterity to pronounce their verdict on the claims that I and my colleagues have made not merely on behalf of the four million people of Jammu and Kashmir but also of the ninety-three million people of all the States of India [under princely rule]. This claim has not been confined to a particular race or religion or color. It applies to all, for I hold that humanity as a whole is indivisible by such barriers and human rights must always prevail. The fundamental rights of all men and women to live and act as free beings, to make laws and fashion their political, economic and social fabric, so that they may advance the cause of human freedom and progress, are inherent and cannot be denied though they may be suppressed for a while. I hold that sovereignty resides in the people, all relationships political, social and economic, derive authority from the collective will of the people. (Quoted in Bhattacharjea 2008: 237–38)

On 29 September 1947, the maharaja ordered Abdullah's release while the state was going through a period of chaos. Soon after his release, Abdullah categorically stated his position at a public rally in Hazuribagh, Kashmir:

Our first demand is complete transfer of power to the people in Kashmir. Representatives of the people in a democratic Kashmir will then decide whether the State should join India or Pakistan. If the forty lakhs of people living in Jammu and Kashmir are by-passed and the State declares its accession to India or Pakistan, I shall raise the banner of revolt and we face a struggle. Of course, we will naturally opt to go to the Dominion where our own demand for freedom receives recognition and support. We cannot desire to join those who say that the people must have no voice in the matter. We shall be cut to pieces before we allow alliance between this State and people of this type. In this time of national crisis Kashmir must hold the beacon light. All around us we see the tragedy of brother killing brother. At this time Kashmir must come forward and raise the banner of Hindu–Muslim unity. In Kashmir we want a people's government. We want a government which will give equal rights and equal opportunities to all men—irrespective of caste and creed. The Kashmir Government will not be the government of any one community. It will be a joint government of the Hindus, the Sikhs, and the Muslims. That is what I am fighting for. (*People's Age*, quoted in Krishen 1951: 38)

Abdullah's first public speech after being released from jail was attended by a mammoth crowd, an estimated 30,000 people (figure averaged from the Resident's reports, which were submitted fortnightly). All through his political life, Abdullah remained consistent in his antipathy toward the autocratic Dogra monarchy, feudalism, Punjabi hegemony, and communalism. The populist measures employed by Abdullah's NC enabled it to win the support of the majority of the Muslim populace in the Valley (sourced from interviews with political activists and academics in Kashmir, in 2006).

Despite the support that the "Quit Kashmir" movement launched by Abdullah's cadre received from various regional councils and state Congress committees, the movement was crushed tactically and militarily. On 20 May 1946, speaking at a public rally at the Shahi Masjid (mosque), Srinagar, Abdullah thunderously condemned the 1846 Treaty of Amritsar, which had legitimized the Dogra possession of Kashmir (Copeland 1991: 251). In addition to the brutal opposition that the NC encountered from the Dogra regime, it faced vociferous resistance from a section of the MC leadership who vehemently opposed any attempt to create a syncretism that would bridge the divide between Hindus and Muslims.

As the NC made its support of secular principles and its affiliation with the All India National Congress more forceful, the gulf between the upholders of secularism and the guardians of an essential Muslim identity became wider. The communally oriented group characterized itself as the Muslim segment of society attempting to undermine the political dominance of the Dogra maharaja and create an Islamic theocracy governed according to Islamic laws and scriptures. Despite its tenacious hold on secular principles, the NC found itself gasping for breath in the quagmire created by the maharaja's duplicitous policies. For example, the maharaja's government had passed a special ordinance introducing two scripts, Devanagari and Persian, in Kashmir's government schools, and, under the Jammu and Kashmir Arms Act of 1940, had prohibited all communities except Dogra Rajputs from owning arms and ammunition. Such communally oriented policies created a rift between the Muslim leadership of the NC and their Hindu colleagues.

The rift within the organization was further widened by Mohammad Ali Jinnah's insistence that Abdullah extend his support to the Muslim League and thereby disavow every principle he had fought for. Abdullah's refusal to do so sharpened the awareness of the Muslim League that it would be unable to consolidate its political position without his support. Initially, the Congress supported the "Quit Kashmir" movement and reinforced the position of the NC on plebiscite. The Congress advised the maharaja, right up to 1947, to gauge the public mood and accordingly accede to either India or Pakistan. Nehru's argument that Kashmir was required to validate the secular credentials of India was a later development. Jinnah refuted the notion that Pakistan required Kashmir to vindicate its theocratic status and did not make an argument for the inclusion of Kashmir in the new nation-state of Pakistan right up to the eve of partition. As Behera (2006) writes, "If Kashmir was integral to the very idea of

Pakistan, it is difficult to see why the Muslim League and the Muslim Conference did not ask the Maharaja to accede to Pakistan until as late as 25 July 1947." The Congress's support to and furtherance of partition, however, eroded the notion of a united India.

Sheikh Mohammad Abdullah, on the contrary, was ambivalent about the partition because he did not agree with the rationale of the two-nation theory. He was equally ambivalent about acceding to India, because he felt that if that choice was made, Pakistan would always create juggernauts in the political and economic progress of Kashmir. As for the idea of declaring Kashmir an independent state, he recognized that "to keep a small state independent while it was surrounded by big powers was impossible" (Abdullah 1993: 60). Was Abdullah willing to concede the necessity of political compromise and accommodation? Did Abdullah draw attention to the political, cultural, and territorial compromises that the autonomy model might entail? He did categorically declare that "Neither the friendship of Pandit Nehru or of Congress nor their support of our freedom movement would have any influence upon our decision if we felt that the interests of four million Kashmiris lay in our accession to Pakistan" (quoted in Brecher 1953: 35). The decision to accede to either India or Pakistan placed Maharaja Hari Singh in a dilemma. On the one hand, if the state acceded to India, the maharaja would be forced to hand over the reins of political power to an organization that had vociferously opposed his regime, the Congress, and the NC. On the other hand, if the state acceded to Pakistan, the maharaja's Dogra Hindu community would find itself in a position of subservience. Consequently, the maharaja disregarded the advice of the Congress and the British about the infeasibility of independence and opted for that choice because it would allow him to maintain his political paramountcy. He was unable to recognize how independence would enhance the political and military vulnerability of the state. Hari Singh's decision to maintain his political paramountcy was supported by Pakistan, but not by India.

Standstill Agreement

On 15 August 1947, Maharaja Hari Singh's regime ratified a standstill agreement with the government of Pakistan (see Appendix A, 175–178). This agreement stipulated that the Pakistan government assume charge of the state's post and telegraph system and supply the state with essential commodities. Given the political and personal affiliations of the Congress with the NC and its antipathy toward monarchical rule, the maharaja and his cohort considered it worthwhile to negotiate with Pakistan's Muslim League in order to maintain his princely status. But this already tenuous relationship was further weakened after the infiltration of armed groups from Pakistan into J & K. After Pakistani armed raiders and militia attempted to forcefully annex Kashmir on 22 October 1947, the maharaja did a political volte-face by releasing NC leaders from prison, seeking Indian military help to keep the Pakistani forces at bay, and acceding to India in order to protect his own security and interests. Subsequent to his release after sixteen months of incarceration, Sheikh Abdullah delivered a speech at a public rally at the Hazratbal shrine where he declared the establishment of a popular government to be the priority and primary concern of the people of Kashmir, and relegated the accession issue to the background.

Invasion by Pakistani Tribal Militia and Military Leaders

The validity of the division of India into the nation-states of India and Pakistan along religious lines was unequivocally challenged by Sheikh Abdullah: "My organization and I never believed in the formula that Muslims and Hindus form separate nations. We did not believe in the two-nation theory, or in communalism....We believed that religion had no place in politics" (Abdullah 1993: 86; see Appendix B, 179). Abdullah's noncommunal politics were vindicated by the ruthlessness of the Pakistani tribal raiders' miscalculated attack, which drove various political forces in the state to willy-nilly align themselves with India. Although the raiders, or *Qabailis*, were unruly mercenaries, they were led by well-trained and well-equipped military leaders who were familiar with the arduous terrain, and the raiders launched what would have been a dexterous attack if they had not been tempted to pillage and plunder on the way to the capital city, Srinagar (Dasgupta 1968: 95). En route to Srinagar, the tribal raiders committed heinous atrocities: they raped and killed several Catholic nuns at a missionary school, and tortured and impaled an NC worker, Maqbool Sherwani (Copeland 1991: 245). The brutal methods of the raiders received strong disapprobation from the people of the Valley who had disavowed a quintessentially Muslim identity and replaced it with the notion of a Kashmiri identity. This political and cultural ideology underscored the lack of religious homogeneity in the population of Kashmir. The raiders antagonized their coreligionists by perpetrating atrocities against the local populace, including women and children. The undiplomatic strategies of the tribal raiders and Pakistani militia expedited the attempts of the All India National Congress to incorporate Kashmir into the Indian Union (for a clearer picture of the ramifications of the tribal invasion, see Appendix B, 179).

Validity of the Provisional Accession to India and Role of the United Nations

On 26 October 1947, Maharaja Hari Singh signed the "Instrument of Accession" to India, officially ceding to the government of India jurisdiction over defense, foreign affairs, and communications (see Lamb 1991 for discussions on the legitimacy of the "Instrument of Accession"; see Appendix A for a delineation of the circumstances in which Hari Singh signed the "Instrument of Accession," 175–178). The accession of J & K to India was accepted by Lord Mountbatten with the proviso that once political stability was established in the region, a referendum would be held in which the people of the state would either validate or veto the accession. After signing the Instrument of Accession, the maharaja appointed his political adversary, Sheikh Mohammad Abdullah, as the head of an interim government. The political monopoly of the NC was bolstered by the organization of a "National Militia," which was established by Abdullah's trusted lieutenants, Bakshi Ghulam Mohammad and G.M. Sadiq. In keeping with Abdullah's socialist politics, this organization had a women's wing as well, which I discuss at length in chapter five. I provide oral testimonies from two of three surviving members of the women's militia, in chapter five, about the political and cultural initiatives taken by them during the Pakistani tribal invasion.

Bose (2003: 36) observes that on 27 October, Abdullah told a correspondent of *The Times of India* that the tribal invasion was a pressurizing attempt to terrorize the people of the state and, therefore, needed to be strongly rebuffed (see Appendix B, 179 for Abdullah's excoriation of the belligerence and treachery of the tribal invaders). Pakistan's first prime minister, Liaquat Ali Khan, termed the accession of J & K to India "fraudulent" and declared that the very existence of Pakistan was a sore spot for India (quoted in Dasgupta 1968: 36). On 2 November 1947, Pandit Jawaharlal

Nehru, the first prime minister of independent India, reiterated his government's pledge to not only the people of Kashmir, but also to the international community, to hold a referendum in Indian- and Pakistani-administered J & K under the auspices of a world body like the United Nations, in order to determine whether the populace preferred to be affiliated with India or Pakistan. Nehru emphasized this commitment several times at public forums over the next few years.

In January 1948 India referred the Kashmir dispute to the United Nations (Rahman 1996: 15–19). Prime Minister Nehru took the dispute with Pakistan over Kashmir beyond local and national boundaries by bringing it before the UN Security Council and seeking a ratification of India's "legal" claims over Kashmir. The UN reinforced Nehru's pledge of holding a plebiscite in Kashmir, and in 1948 the Security Council established the United Nations Commission for India and Pakistan (UNCIP) to play the role of mediator in the Kashmir issue. The UNCIP adopted a resolution urging the government of Pakistan to cease the infiltration of tribal mercenaries and raiders into J & K. It also urged the government of India to demilitarize the state by "withdrawing their own forces from J & K and reducing them progressively to the minimum strength required for the support of civil power in the maintenance of law and order." The resolution proclaimed that once these conditions were fulfilled, the government of India would be obligated to hold a plebiscite in the state in order to either ratify or veto the accession of J & K to India (Hagerty 2005: 19). Sir Zafarulla Khan, Pakistan's minister of foreign affairs, while discussing the volatile Kashmir issue at the UN on 16 January 1948, said that the maharaja's government had attempted to brutally quell the spirit of revolution in Kashmir: "They were mowed down by the bullets of the State Dogra troops in their uprising but refused to turn back and received those bullets on their bared breasts" (United Nations Security Council: 65).

This political stalemate led to the resumption of bitter acrimony in 1948. Sheikh Mohammad Abdullah's NC voiced its disillusionment with the wishy-washy role of the UN Security Council. It expressly declared on 22 April 1948 that the Security Council resolution was "yet another feature of power politics on which the Security Council has embarked ever since its inception." Abdullah condemned the machinations of imperialist powers like the United States and the United Kingdom, which "saw Kashmir only as the neighbour of Russia and therefore an essential base in the encirclement of Russia for future aggression" (Krishen 1951: 19–20). A provisional cessation of hostilities, however, occurred in January 1949, with the establishment of a political and military truce.

> The ceasefire line left the Indians with the bulk of Jammu and Kashmir's territory (139,000 of 223,000 square kilometres, approximately 63 per cent) and population. The Indians had gained the prize piece of real estate, the Kashmir Valley, and they also controlled most of the Jammu and Ladakh regions. These areas became Indian Jammu and Kashmir (IJK). The Pakistanis were left with a long strip of land running on a north–south axis in western J & K, mostly Jammu districts bordering Pakistani Punjab and the NWFP...a slice of Ladakh (Skardu), and the remote mountain zones of Gilgit and Baltistan (the Northern Areas or NA). (Bose 2003: 41)

The de facto border carved in 1949 worked to India's territorial and political advantage.

The president of the UN Security Council, General A.G.L. McNaughton of Canada, endeavored to outline proposals to resolve the dispute. He proposed a program of gradual demilitarization and withdrawal of regular Indian and Pakistani forces, which were not required for the purposes of maintaining law and order from the Indian side of the cease-fire line. He also proposed disbandment of the militia of J & K, as well as of forces in Pakistani-administered "Azad" Kashmir. McNaughton recommended continuing the administration of the Northern Areas (NA) by the local authorities, subject to UN supervision. He recommended the appointment of a UN representative by the secretary general of the UN, who would supervise the process of demilitarization and procure conditions necessary to holding a fair and free plebiscite (Das 1950). Although McNaughton's proposals were lauded by most members of the Security Council, India stipulated that Pakistani forces must unconditionally withdraw from the state, and that disbandment of Pakistani-administered Kashmir troops must be accomplished before an impartial plebiscite could be held (Rahman 1996: 90–91). In the interests of expediency, the UNCIP appointed a single mediator, Sir Owen Dixon, the United Nations representative for India and Pakistan, Australian jurist and wartime ambassador to the United States, to efficiently resolve the conflict.

A meeting of Sheikh Mohammad Abdullah's National Conference was convened on 18 April 1950, in order to pass a resolution expressly warning the United Nations to take cognizance of Pakistan's role as the aggressor (Korbel 2002: 170). The Communist writer Rajbans Krishen wrote an entire book to establish that the UN, its Commission, and its representative, Sir Owen Dixon, were instruments of the

United States and the United Kingdom to annihilate the progressive movement pioneered by Sheikh Mohammad Abdullah in order to create in Kashmir, with the aid of Indian and Pakistani capitalists, a military base for an attack on the Soviet Union (ibid.: 257). The Communist leader in Kashmir, G.M. Sadiq, underscored the skepticism prevalent in Kashmir at the time:

> ...the time has come for India to withdraw the Kashmir question from the Security Council...[as] the Kashmiris realized that the talk of fair plebiscite was a mere smokescreen behind which the Anglo-American powers were planning to enslave the Kashmiris. Nothing will suit them better than the façade of trusteeship in Kashmir behind which they can build war bases against our neighbours [*sic*]. (*Delhi Express*, 1 January 1952)

Even as Abdullah was aware of the infeasibility of withdrawing the Kashmir issue from the UN, the NC reiterated its commitment to securing the right of self-determination for the people of Kashmir. It was suspicious of the UN, which was subservient to the hegemony of the United States and the United Kingdom and flinched when it came to holding a plebiscite in Kashmir (Korbel 2002: 259). Abdullah declared that if a plebiscite was held in Kashmir and the people of Kashmir did not validate the accession to India that would not imply that, "as a matter of course Kashmir becomes part of Pakistan....It would regain the status which it enjoyed immediately preceding the accession [i.e., independence]" (*The Hindu*, 26 March 1952). In 1949 Abdullah candidly told Michael Davidson, correspondent of the London *Observer*, that, "Accession to either side cannot bring peace. We want to live in friendship with both the Dominions" (quoted in Saxena 1975: 33).

The insistence on rejecting the trajectory charted out for them by the power structures of India, Pakistan, and the West, and the urge to proclaim themselves a nation that is capable of exercising the right of self-determination has haunted the psyche of the Kashmiri people for decades. The distrust that pervaded the Kashmir political scene was outlined by the Communist paper *People's Age*, which assessed the report of the United Nations Commission to the Security Council as an instrument of the political intrigues and machinations of imperialist powers against the engendering of democracy in J & K. It was critical of the complicity of Pakistan with these powers to destroy the beginnings of a democratic mass movement. It evaluated the attempt of the United States and the United Kingdom to preside over a purportedly "free and fair" plebiscite that would be held "under the direction of the military and political agents of American imperialism, masked as the UNO Commission officers," as a strategy on their part to create and secure war bases on the subcontinent against the Soviet Union and China (Krishen 1951: 38).

As a placatory measure, in 1949 the UNCIP declared that "the Secretary-General of the United Nations will, in agreement with the Commission, nominate a Plebiscite Administrator who shall be a person of high international standing" (Dasgupta 1968: 402–03). Needless to say, the plebiscite was never held. The inability of the Indian government to hold a plebiscite is regarded by the Pakistani government and by proindependence elements in Kashmir as an act of political sabotage. The Indian government has been rationalizing its decision by placing the blame squarely on Pakistan for not demilitarizing the areas of J & K under its control, which was the primary condition specified by the United Nations for holding the plebiscite. Josef Korbel, the Czech UN representative in Kashmir, observes that ten weeks after the Security Council had passed an injunction calling on both India and Pakistan to demilitarize the Kashmir region within five months, Sir Owen Dixon found that not an iota of work had been done in that regard. Although both parties had agreed to hold a plebiscite in the state, they had failed to take any of the preliminary measures required for a free and fair referendum. Sir Owen Dixon, therefore, decided to take matters into his own hands and asked for the unconditional withdrawal of Pakistani troops. This was followed by a request to both countries to enable the demilitarization of Kashmir. The then prime minister of Pakistan, Liaquat Ali Khan, agreed to initiate the process by calling for the withdrawal of his troops. But this request, which would have enabled the maintenance of law and order, was denied by India (Korbel 2002: 171). The rationale that India provided for its denial was the necessity to defend Kashmir and maintain a semblance of order. India vehemently opposed any proposal that would place Pakistan on the same platform as India, and that would not take into account the incursion of Kashmir territory by Pakistani militia and tribesmen. In order to neutralize the situation, Sir Owen Dixon suggested that while the plebiscite was being organized and held, the entire state should be governed by a coalition government, or by a neutral administration comprising nonpartisan groups, or by an executive formed of United Nations representatives. But his proposal did not meet with the approval he expected. He noted, in 1950, that the Kashmir issue was so tumultuous because Kashmir was not a holistic geographic, economic, or demographic entity, but, on the contrary, an aggregate of diverse territories brought under the rule of one maharaja (Schofield 2002: 4–10). In a further attempt to resolve the conflict, Sir Owen Dixon propounded the trifurcation of the state along communal or regional lines, or facilitating the secession of parts of the Jhelum Valley to Pakistan (Ganguly 1997: 3–4, 43–57; Rahman 1996: 4).

Despite the bombastic statements and blustering of the governments of both India and Pakistan, however, the Indian government has all along perceived the inclusion of Pakistani-administered J & K and the NA into India as unfeasible. Likewise, the government of Pakistan has all along either implicitly or explicitly acknowledged the impracticality of including the predominantly Buddhist Ladakh and predominantly Hindu Jammu as part of Pakistan. The coveted area that continues to generate irreconcilable differences between the two governments is the Valley of Kashmir. Dixon lamented:

> None of these suggestions commended themselves to the Prime Minister of India. In the end, I became convinced that India's agreement would never be obtained to demilitarization in any such form, or to provisions governing the period of the plebiscite of any such character, as would in my opinion permit the plebiscite being conducted in conditions sufficiently guarding against intimidation and other forms of influence and abuse by which the freedom and fairness of the plebiscite might be imperiled. (*The Statesman*, 15 September 1950)

Sir Owen Dixon nonetheless remained determined to formulate a viable solution to the Kashmir issue and suggested that a plebiscite be held only in the Kashmir Valley subsequent to its demilitarization, which would be conducted by an administrative body of UN officials. This proposal was rejected by Pakistan, which, however, reluctantly agreed to Sir Dixon's further suggestion that the prime ministers of the two countries meet with him to discuss the viability of various solutions to the Kashmir dispute. But India decried this suggestion. A defeated man, Sir Dixon finally left the Indian subcontinent on 23 August 1950 (Korbel 2002: 174). There seemed to be an inexplicable reluctance on both sides, India and Pakistan, to solve the Kashmir dispute diplomatically and amicably. Sir Dixon's concluding recommendation was a bilateral resolution of the dispute with India and Pakistan as the responsible parties, without taking into account the ability of the Kashmiri people to determine their own political future.

After Dixon's inability to implement conflict mitigation proposals, Frank Graham was appointed as mediator in 1951. Graham proposed the following: a reaffirmation of the cease-fire line; a mutual agreement that India and Pakistan would avoid making incendiary statements and that would reassert that Kashmir's future would be decided by a plebiscite; and steady attempts at demilitarization. But he was unable to dispel the doubts raised by the governments of India and Pakistan on securing the approval of both governments on a strategy for withdrawal of forces from the state, and agreement of both governments on a plebiscite administrator (ibid.: 239–40). Given the unviability of its proposals, the UN soon bowed out of the political quagmire, leaving an unhealed wound on the body politic of the Indian subcontinent: the Security Council resolutions affirming that the future of the state should be decided by its denizens (for the reasoning behind the notion that the UN could have played a constructive role in the resolution of the Kashmir conflict, see Appendix A, 175–178).

Jawaharlal Nehru's Stance vis-à-vis Plebiscite in Jammu and Kashmir

In August 1952, Nehru declared in the Indian parliament: "We do not wish to win people against their will with the help of armed force; and if the people of Kashmir wish to part company with us, they may go their way and we shall go ours. We want no forced marriages, no forced unions" (Bhattacharjea 2008: xiv; Lamb 1991: 46–47; Noorani 1964: 61). But, once again, he equivocated and sought to capitalize on the formation of the de facto border by declaring in 1955 that he had asked his Pakistani counterparts to consider resolving the Kashmir issue by converting the de facto border into a permanent international one between the two nation-states. Nehru's endeavor to renege on his oft-repeated promise of holding a plebiscite created a hostile obstinacy in Pakistan. After the troubling failure of Sir Dixon's various proposals, the London *Times* (6 September 1950) observed:

> Like most great men, Nehru has his blind spot. In his case it is Kashmir, the land of his forebears which he loves "like a woman." Because he is not amenable to reason on this subject, but allows emotion to get the better of common sense, Kashmir remains a stumbling block in the path of Indo–Pakistan friendship. So long as it is so India's moral

standing is impaired, her will to peace is in doubt, and her right to speak for Asia is questioned by her next-door neighbor [*sic*]. Critics may well ask, if self-determination under United Nations auspices is valid for Korea [as India advocates], why is it not valid for Kashmir?

Nehru's sentimentalism and vacillation regarding Kashmir, perhaps, played a large role in keeping this issue of international dimensions in limbo. The Kashmir dispute has thus remained troublingly infantile in its irresolvability. The remushrooming of the separatist movement in Kashmir in 1989 and the subsequent creation of a political vacuum has allowed the insidious infiltration of distrust and suspicion into the relationship between Kashmir and the two nuclear powers in the Indian subcontinent, India and Pakistan.

Naya (New) Kashmir Manifesto

The NC's collaboration with the Congress was a cause of celebration for the Indians but was absolute anathema for the Pakistanis. New Delhi looked upon the affirmation of Kashmir as a legitimate part of the Indian Union as a validation of India's secular status. Nevertheless, in the years leading up to 1947 the NC established itself as an agent of political mobilization. In September 1944, representatives of the organization formulated and adopted a manifesto entitled "Naya Kashmir" (for details, see Mir 2003). This manifesto propounded a program of democratization and progressive social change under the new regime. The Naya Kashmir manifesto explicitly delineated the conception of a representative government that would enable the devolution of administrative responsibilities to districts and villages. The monarch would be a mere titular head. It declared Urdu the lingua franca that would bridge the gulf between Kashmiri- and Dogri-speaking parts of the state. It advocated a socialist system in which the state would control the means of production so as to ensure the fairest distribution of goods, power, and services to its members. The good of society would be considered a responsibility of the state, but the state would serve as an administrator and a distributor, not as a disseminator of ideology or doctrine. The manifesto underlined the necessity of abolishing exploitative landlordism without compensation, enfranchising tillers by granting them the lands they worked on, and establishing cooperatives. It also addressed issues of gender, and instituting educational and social schemes for marginalized sections of society.

The new government headed by Sheikh Mohammad Abdullah and Mirza Afzal Beg passes the landmark "land to the tiller" legislation, 1950. (*Courtesy*: The Archives of the National Conference, with the permission of the general secretary of the National Conference, Sheikh Nazir Ahmad)

The Naya Kashmir manifesto sought to create a more democratic and responsible form of government. On 13 July 1950, the new government headed by Sheikh Mohammad Abdullah made a landmark decision.

> Between 1950 and 1952, 700,000 landless peasants, mostly Muslims in the Valley but including 250,000 lower-caste Hindus in the Jammu region, became peasant-proprietors as over a million acres were directly transferred to them, while another sizeable chunk of land passed to government-run collective farms. By the early 1960s, 2.8 million acres of farmland (rice being the principal crop in the Valley) and fruit orchards were under cultivation, worked by 2.8 million smallholding peasant-proprietor households. (Bose 2003: 27–28)

This metamorphosis of the agrarian economy had groundbreaking political consequences. The NC, which had orchestrated this transformation, won the unstinting support of thousands of erst-while disenfranchised peasants. But displaced landlords and officials in the erstwhile Dogra regime made no bones about their hatred of the political supremacy of the new class of Kashmiri Muslims. This hatred unleashed a reign of terror and brutality against the Valley's new political class. The atrocities inflicted by the Indian state led to mass arrests and political repression, culminating into a midnight coup against Abdullah and his regime.

In August 1952, Abdullah reiterated the commitment of his orga-nization to the principles of secularism and democracy that would enable the forging of ties with the Indian nation-state: "The supreme guarantee of our relationship with India is the identity of secular and democratic aspirations, which have guided the people of India as well as those of Jammu and Kashmir in their struggle for emancipation, and before which all constitutional safeguards will take a secondary posi-tion" (quoted in Soz 1995: 121–39). For the layperson, Sheikh Abdullah embodied the "new Kashmir" in which the hitherto peripheralized Muslim population of the Valley and marginalized women would rein-sert themselves into the language of belonging. "The National Conference initially envisaged a limited role for women but later had a radical pack-age for women in the historical document 'Naya Kashmir.'...This was when no other political formation in the subcontinent had projected women's issues in this perspective" (Misri 2002: 4). After having read the provision for women's rights in the document, I would underscore Misri's opinion about the radical nature of the package for women:

> Women citizens shall be accorded equal rights with men in all fields of national life: economic, cultural, political and in the state services. These rights shall be realized by affording women the right to work in every employment upon equal terms and for equal wages with men. Women shall be ensured rest, social insurance and education equally with men. The law shall give special protection to the interests of mother and child. (Quoted in Bhattacharjea 2008: 74.)

Abdullah, with his socialist politics, sought to challenge the safely guarded domain of privilege and power that had disenfranchised the Muslim majority, reinforced the seclusion of Kashmiri women, and made their support irrelevant for the Dogra sovereigns and later for the regimes installed by New Delhi. Interestingly, it was the Kashmiri Muslims led by Sheikh Mohammad Abdullah who rallied around the notion of regional nationalism (for Abdullah's vociferous espousal of the need to redress the grievances of impoverished and down-trodden Kashmiri masses, see Appendix C, 180).

"Kashmiriyat"

As I mentioned in the introduction, the various communities in the state of J & K—Kashmiri Muslims, Kashmiri Pandits, Dogras, and Ladakhis—have tried time and again to form a national consciousness in order to name a cultural alterity through the nation. The construction of "Kashmiriyat," or a syncretic cultural ethos, by Sheikh Abdullah's NC involved culling selected cultural fragments from an imagined past that would enfold both the Pandits and the Muslims. As Mridu Rai (2004: 284–85) points out, "This espousal of a 'secular' ideology, read through a secularly written history, was intended also as a way to keep at bay a centre in Delhi that had begun to encroach upon Kashmiri 'autonomy' increasingly in the early 1950s." But due to the regional sentiments that are so well entrenched in the psyche of the people, this attempt is still in a volatile stage.

The notion of "Kashmiriyat," forged by my maternal grandfather Sheikh Mohammad Abdullah, was not handed down to me as an unachievable and abstract construct; on the contrary, it was crystallized for me as the eradication of a feudal structure and its insidious ramifications; the right of the tiller to the land he worked on; the unacceptability of any political solution that did not take the aspirations and demands of the Kashmiri people into consideration; the right of Kashmiris to high offices in education, the bureaucracy, and government; the availability of medical and educational facilities in Jammu, Kashmir, and Ladakh; the preservation of literatures, shrines, and historical artifacts that defined an important aspect of "Kashmiriyat"; formation of the Constituent Assembly of J & K to institutionalize the constitution of the state in 1951, which was an enormous leap toward the process of democratization; the fundamental right of both women and men to free education up to the university level; equal opportunities afforded to both sexes in the workplace; the nurturing of a contact zone in social, political, and intellectual ideologies and institutions; and pride in a cultural identity that was generated in a space created by multiple perspectives.

"Kashmiriyat" was the secular credo of Sheikh Mohammad Abdullah's All Jammu and Kashmir NC, popularized in the 1940s and 1950s to defeat the centralizing strategies of the successive regimes of independent India (see Rai 2004 for a theorization of "Kashmiriyat" that is similar to mine). This significant concept does not attempt to simplify the ambiguity and complexity of religious, social, and cultural identities. It neither attempts to assert a fixed identity nor reinforce the idea of purity of culture. I would veer away from adopting an image of this secular credo that is created by the unitary discourses it deplores. On the contrary, "Kashmiriyat" brings about a metamorphosis in the determinate concept of the Indian state and creates a situation in which the nation-states of India and Pakistan are forced to confront an alternative epistemology. At a time of political and social upheaval in the state, this notion engendered a consciousness of place that offered a critical perspective from which to formulate alternatives. Without negating the historicity of the notion, this theoretical fiction was deployed by Sheikh Abdullah's NC in order to forge a strategic essentialism that would enable the creation of a sovereign Kashmiri identity. It certainly was not a lawless notion, as Mridu Rai (ibid.: 296) is quick to point out: "...this notion of cultural harmony was predicated on the requisite condition of protecting Kashmiri Pandit privileges and a consequent subsumption of the majority of Muslims." Professor R.L. Hangloo, eminent historian of Kashmiri Pandit descent at the University of Hyderabad, provided a complex and concise definition of "Kashmiriyat":

Kashmiriyat is a far wider concept than the harmonious relationship cutting across religious and sectarian divisions. *Kashmiriyat* is the externally endowed and internally evolved phenomenon of co-existence at the social, religious, political, spatial, cultural and other institutional levels among Kashmiris of all shades that inhabited Kashmir. *Kashmiriyat* has evolved as a result of special circumstances that are rooted in Kashmir's topographical centrality that entitled Kashmir to imbibing, interacting and assimilating a variety of world cultures in consonance with Kashmiri sensibilities that reflect a nuanced and sophisticated approach that did not disturb the patterns of production and cultural manners reflecting the Kashmiri genius. This specificity has stemmed from the historical processes that the region of Kashmir has embraced both in peace and turmoil for centuries. Kashmir has always been surrounded by some of the world's greatest civilizations such as China, Persia/Iran, Central Asia and India. Kashmir and Kashmiris were always at the center of this world and not on the periphery which is reflected in the assimilation of their residual practices of religions. Note that while Kashmir may be on a fairly marginal point on the map of the state of India, Kashmir as a region was historically at the epicenter of a much larger world space and world civilization. This centrality endowed the region with a superiority and self identity that has assimilated the social and religious-cultural traditions of this greater region and traits of greater cultures throughout history to evolve and strengthen what came to constitute *Kashmiriyat*. This sense of superior self identity has grown over centuries as *Kashmiriyat* among Kashmiris both within and out side Kashmir.

Living together, untroubled by diversities of religion, racial, cultural, material, and political and other identities, the notion of *Kashmiriyat* became the bedrock of identity which consolidated itself increasingly when Islam entered into the Valley. Before the thirteenth century, even though there were plural religious sects, they neither saw eye to eye with each other nor were they external to Kashmir in tality. Shaivites facilitated the decline of Buddhists in Kashmir; the Vaishnavas had to keep their identity concealed to escape the wrath of the Shaivites. The pre-Islamic history is replete with religious, ethnic, racial and other conflicts. The battles of Dammaras, Ekangas, Tantrins, Khasas and others were perpetual features of pre-Islamic Kashmiri society. There was a long drawn conflict and contestation within Islamic society before rapprochement took place between the orthodox Muslims and heterodox sects. The entrance of Islam in Kashmir coincided with the end of this struggle. It was this rapprochement that disallowed Kashmiris from seeing any contradiction between the preaching of Islam and the practice of upholding the Heretical tradition (that is, acknowledging the divine power of the local, the Rishi) in Kashmir. Therefore the kind of Islam that entered Kashmir was devoid of any orthodoxy. It was only after the arrival of Islam that Lalleshwari and Sheikh Noor-ud-din (Nund Reshi) interacted to produce the atmosphere and philosophy of co-existence and tolerance at popular level. This interaction entailed massive changes in the world view of Kashmiris that reflected a truly remarkable and world encompassing shift in every aspect of their sensibility as well.

Is J & K a Postcolonial State?

Uncertainty about the status of the former princely state has loomed large since 1947. In an atmosphere of unpredictability, in the frightening darkness of political intrigue, in the paranoia of political deception, the fungi of undemocratic policies and methods continue to grow unabated. The unresolved Kashmir dispute poses a danger of monstrous proportions to the stability of the Indian subcontinent. Is the former princely state of J & K a postcolonial state? Postcolonialism refers to a phase undergone after the decline and dismantling of the European empires by the mid-twentieth century, when the peoples of many Asian, African, and Caribbean countries were left to create new governments and forge national identities. The ideology that has been propounded by the governments of India and Pakistan reflects and produces the interests of state-sponsored agencies and institutions on both sides of the Line of Control (LOC). These institutions have couched the debased discourse of exploitation in the language of culture and religion, a strategy that has led to the relegation of the subjectivity, historical understanding, and traditions of the Kashmiri populace. As the eminent Palestinian–American scholar Edward Said (1991: 29) noted, "All human activity depends on controlling a radically unstable reality to which words approximate only by will or convention." Representatives of the privileged center of power silence the voices that are on the margins of mainstream society and politics. These privileged centers have always constrained reality by imposing their ideological schema, which underpins their powerful positionality, on it. Their ability to conjure images and restretch boundaries that serve their set of beliefs has rendered them a force to reckon with. These ideas expounded by the powers-that-be portray Kashmiris as a stereotypical and predictable entity.

This delineation of the Kashmiri subject was foregrounded by an imperial agent of the British Raj, Sir Walter Lawrence, Settlement Commissioner of J & K, in his *The Valley of Kashmir* ([1895] 2005). This politically and culturally misleading portrayal of the Kashmiri subject has been underscored by the policies of the governments of India and Pakistan vis-à-vis Jammu and Kashmir, which is why the authority of democratically elected representatives in that region has always been curbed. The policies of the two governments follow the much-trodden path of totalitarianism and spell a pattern of doom for Kashmir. The unnecessary and unjustified postponement of the resolution of the Kashmir conflict has insidiously gnawed at the tenuous relations between India and Pakistan. The issue has also, for better or worse, been thrust onto the stage of global politics, and its volatility has contributed to the destabilization of the Indian subcontinent. Josef Korbel (2002: 304) wrote with foresight that "whatever the future may have in store, the free world shares with India and Pakistan common responsibility for the fate of democracy and it awaits with trepidation the solution of the Kashmir problem. Its own security may depend on such a settlement."

Chapter Two

Cultural Syncretism in Kashmir

Shiv chuy thali thali rozaan
Mav Zaan Hyound ta Mussalman
Trukhay chukh ta panunuy paan parzaan
Ada Chay Saahibas Zaani Zaan
                        (Lalla-Ded, quoted in Mattoo 2007)

Shiva abides in all that is everywhere
Then do not discriminate between a Hindu and a Muslim
If you are wise seek the Absolute within yourself
That is true knowledge of the Lord
                        (from "Lalla-Ded's Vaakhs")

Kashmiris have taken pride in inhabiting a cultural space between Vedic Hinduism and Sufi Islam. The traditional communal harmony in Kashmir enabled the peaceful coexistence of Muslims and Hindus, highlighted by mutual respect for their places of worship and an ability to synthesize not just cultural but religious practices as well (for conceptualizations of "Kashmiriyat," see Kaw 2004; Razdan 1999; Rushdie 2005; Whitehead 2004: 335–40). Deep reverence for each other's shrines and the relics housed in those shrines is a well-entrenched aspect of the culture. Salman Rushdie (2005: 57) describes this sentiment of "Kashmiriyat" succinctly in his fictionalized account of the history of J & K, *Shalimar the Clown*: "The words Hindu and Muslim had no place in their story. . . . In the Valley these words were merely descriptions, not divisions. The frontiers between the words, their hard edges, had grown smudged and blurred."

A fitting symbol of this syncretic ethos of Kashmir is Lalla-Ded, a figure revered by both the Pandits and Muslims of Kashmir. Lalla-Ded was born in 1334 into a Kashmiri Brahman home in Simpur village, about four miles from Srinagar, the summer capital of Kashmir. She was brutalized in a marriage that was arranged for her by the elders once she reached puberty. Unwilling to acquiesce to the constraints placed on the "traditional" woman and questioning the self-abnegation of women that disallowed them from reconciling their private selves with their roles as public contributors to the community, Lalla-Ded disavowed the psychosocial narratives inscribed on the female body in defiance of the continued conscription of women (Bhatnagar, Dube, and Dube 2004: 30).

Challenging a Patriarchal and Hierarchical Society

I would argue that by committing the sacrilegious act of crossing the threshold of her husband's house in order to choose a life of asceticism, Lalla-Ded subverted the traditional reliance on male authority. She was a *yogini*, a professed woman ascetic, who disseminated the yogic doctrines with an unquenchable zeal. Her passionate pursuit of self-knowledge led her down the tortuous path of a yogic life, but the flame of her devotion blazed bright. Lalla-Ded is a watershed in the cultural and spiritual development of Kashmir. Her role counters Prem Nath Bazaz's assessment of the "splendid" role that Kashmiri women of ancient times played in the social and cultural life of Kashmir. Bazaz's assessment is glorious but romanticized, and discounts the disparagements that intellectually inclined women had to combat in order to emerge as public figures.

> Broadly speaking, from early times to the thirteenth century they enjoyed remarkable freedom, wielded ample power and exercised responsibility, which gave them a high position in society....At times Kashmiri women have risen to pinnacles of glory and distinguished themselves as rulers (Yashomati, Sughandha, Didda and Kota) in their own right, as regents of minor princes, as powerful queens-consort (Ishandevi, Vakpushta, Ananglekha, Srilekha, Suryamati and Jayamati), as diplomats in peace and war (Radda Devi, Kalhanika), as commanders of armies (Silla, Chudda), as thrifty landladies, as builders and reformers and as preceptors of religious lore. (Bazaz [1967] 2005: 12)

But unconditional freedom from sexualized hierarchies does not exist in any social matrix. Bazaz's assessment of Kashmiri women in ancient times is sanguine but mythical in that it ignores the "internal dynamics of patriarchal and hierarchical societies, essentially biased against women. Rigid, reprehensive customs and conventions placed women inferior to men in status, rights, power and freedom in these

The Shah Hamadan mosque (Khanqah-i-mualla) on the banks of the Jhelum, Srinagar. (*Courtesy*: Amin Studio, Srinagar)

societies. Discrimination and inequality were accepted as a natural scheme of things" (Misri 2002: 7). The women whose positions on the political and artistic zenith Bazaz chooses to foreground were affiliated with the royalty in a monarchical regime basking in the freedom from economic constraints and societal limitations that women of other classes were tormented by. But Lalla-Ded sought, in the social arrangement to which she had access, concepts and tools for a new society that would be liberated from gendered forms of oppression. She intervened in patriarchal national history by speaking from her location about the political realities that had woven the web of prevalent social relations. Lalla-Ded's cognizance of how a woman's aspirations for personal emancipation are mediated by her responsibility toward her community, and the ways in which this sense of responsibility inflects her own emancipatory thought, underscores her importance for me. She rejected a sexualized persona in order to break the power nexus that underlined the objectification of "the damsel in distress."

Religious Humanism in the Teachings of Lalla-Ded

Although a Sufi mystic, childless Lalla-Ded eroded the construct of woman as goddess or mother that binds her to a form of subordination that is the ultimate paradigm of social relationships in traditional societies. Most historians are of the opinion that Sheikh Noor-ud-Din Wali, the founding father of the predominant Sufi sect in the Kashmir Valley, Rishiism, acknowledged Lalla-Ded as his spiritual mentor. There is a legend that the infant Noor-ud-Din adamantly refused to be suckled by his mother, Sudra. When the infant was brought to Lalla-Ded, she reprimanded him for his rejection of nourishment. Subsequently, the boy allowed his mother to nurse him. Later, Lalla-Ded facilitated Sheikh Noor-ud-Din Wali's immersion into the intellectual radicalism generated by her philosophy of religious humanism (Bazaz [1959] 2005: 138). The recorded poems and paradigmatic sayings of Lalla-Ded and of Sheikh Noor-ud-Din Wali enrich Kashmiri literature and add layer upon layer to the culture. (For renditions of syncretic Kashmiri literature with a rich spiritual content, see Kaul 1999; Murphy 1999; Parimoo 1978; Sufi 1979.)

After extensive research on poetry and literature in the Kashmiri language, Sir George Grierson (1911) drew the inference that

Lalla-Ded is the oldest Kashmiri author. Her verses continue to retain their relevance in various parts of the Valley even centuries after the decline of mysticism: "Lal Vakyas [wise sayings], rich in philosophical theme and content, rolled down to generations through word of mouth in Kashmiri, language of the masses" (Misri 2002: 9). A prolific scholar of Lalla-Ded's religious philosophy, Professor Amar Nath Dhar, sent me an eloquent e-mail (18 April 2008) about Lalla-Ded's composite spiritualism and its cohesive impact on Kashmiri society, which dissipated because of the relegation of the syncretism that was lived by Lalla-Ded and Noor-ud-Din Wali to circumscribing political, literary, and cultural realms:

> Nund Rishi alias Sheikh Noor-ud-Din Wali was greatly influenced by Lalla-Ded. Holding her in very special regard, he was not averse to the Hindu belief in the avtarhood of Lalla-Ded. The Rishi order founded by him evolved in the Valley itself after the advent of Islam. It was Sheikh Noor-ud-Din Wali's unqualified veneration for the saint-poetess Lalla that had a great impact on devout Kashmiri Muslims, his followers. That explains why for centuries the Muslims in the Valley have continued to own her, delighting in memorizing her sayings and quoting them on festive occasions such as marriage ceremonies and cultural functions, as the Kashmiri Pandits do as well. The Sufis in Kashmir, especially those who were not alien to the Valley but rooted in the humanistic Rishi tradition nurtured by Noor-ud-Din Wali (Nund Rishi) and his followers, contributed a lot to the preservation of the composite Kashmiri ethos.

Although she was born into a Hindu family, Lalla-Ded "was greatly influenced by Islamic Sufiistic thought and may, in truth, be said to be above all religious conventionalities" (Sufi 1979: 167). The most significant contribution of Lalla-Ded to the Kashmiri language and literature is that she translated the sophisticated, esoteric concepts of Saiva philosophy and her mystic experiences into the vernacular and made them accessible to the masses. She employed metaphors, idioms, and images from experiences with which ordinary people could relate in her translations of abstruse concepts. Her deployment of the easily recitable verse form of the *vaakh* in Kashmiri, the language of the masses, has enabled the incorporation of her utterances into the common mode of speech. She sought to forge a relationship with her Creator that did not require the intercession of a religious male figure, a Brahman priest or a mullah. The significance of Lalla's vaakhs was made much clearer for me by the candid and forthright e-mail exchange that I had with a knowledgeable historian of Kashmiri Pandit descent at the University of Hyderabad, Professor R.L. Hangloo, about the immediate application in and beyond our everyday lives of Lalla's teachings:

> Lalleshwari, popularly known as Lalla Arifa and Lalla-Ded was born in A. D. 1335. Like Indian Bhakti and Sufi saints she mediated her understanding of religion to the popular masses in the local language, i.e. Kashmiri. She was revered by all Kashmiris equally. Her sayings remained popular in Kashmir in every age because of the overtones of humanism, Bhakti, and *Tassawuf* in them. Her poetry traveled from one generation to the next orally. It was Sir George Grierson and Dr. L. Barnett who first edited these *vaakh* verses under the title *Lalla Vaakini* for the Royal Asiatic Society in the early part of the twentieth century. It was around the same time that a Kashmiri writer, Muhammad-ud-Din Fauq, brought to the notice of the reading public the personality of Laleshwari when he wrote a book entitled *Khawatin-i-Kashmir* in Urdu, published from Lahore around 1902. After him G. M. D. Sofi made references to Lalla's poetry in one of the two volumes of his book *Kashir*, published in 1949, very briefly. After Sofi, it was Gopinath Raina who published some of her work in 1956. The other works are by Jialal Kaul and the most recent one is by Nil Kanth Kotru, published in 1989. After the advent of the armed insurgency in J & K and the exodus of Kashmiri Pandits in 1989, it was B. N. Sopori who brought out an English rendering of Lalla's *vaakhs* in 1999.
>
> The impact of Lalla's *vaakhs* has to be studied in the changing historical scenario of Kashmir. Although her *vaakhs* represent the credo of secularism and spirituality, they have been misinterpreted for sectarian interests. Her profound saying that, "*Sare Samhan Akse Raze Lamhan Ada Kyazi Ravehe Khan Gav*" (all Kashmiris should be united in their attitude), was used by some groups that demanded a separate homeland in Kashmir without understanding her spirit, attitude, and nuances of her age. Lalla-Ded is the common heritage of all Kashmiris, Hindus and Muslims alike, like other Sufi and Bhakti saints. My understanding is that whenever Kashmir has faced a crisis of communal, sectarian, or of any other nefarious nature, Lalla has been visited and revisited by Kashmiris of all shades. (E-mail to author 4 January 2010)

While further researching Lalla-Ded as a mystic and a poet, I found Sir Richard Carnac Temple's heartwarming translations of her verses. I was particularly inspired by the one in which the self is foregrounded as the cure of all spiritual, physical, mental, and material afflictions:

> Lady, rise and offer to the Name,
> Bearing in thy hand the flesh and wine.
> Such shall never bring thee loss and shame,
> Be it of no custom that is thine.
>
> This they know for Knowledge that have found—
> Be the loud Cry from His Place but heard—
> Unity Betwixt the Lord and Sound,
> Just as Sound hath unison with Word.
>
> Feed thy fatted rams, thou worldly one,
> Take them grain and dainties, and then slay.
> Give thy thoughts that reek with "said and done"
> Last-fruits of Knowledge, and cast away.
>
> Then shalt see with Spirit-eyes the Place
> Where the dwelling of the Lord shall be:
> Then shall pass thy terrors of disgrace:
> Then shall Custom lose her hold on thee.
>
> "Think not on the things that are without,
> Fix upon thy inner self thy Thought:
> So shalt thou be freed from let or doubt":—
> Precepts these that my Preceptor taught.
>
> Dance then, Lalla, clothed but by air:
> Sing, then, Lalla, clad but in the sky.
> Air and sky: what garment is more fair?
> "Cloth," saith Custom—Doth that Sanctify?
>> (" 'Cloth,' saith Custom—Doth that Sanctify?"
>> in Temple [1924] 2005: 172–73)

Lalla-Ded was a visionary whose promethean verses broke the intractable frameworks of conventional thought and behavior, which pinioned the self.

Self-Awareness Erodes Constrictive Conventions

Lalla-Ded preempted the modern-day psychoanalytic promulgation of the concept of self-awareness:

Lalla has yet another hard saying. The sense of it adopted in the English wording is that she utters a cry of despair. Like Christian in *The*

Pilgrim's Progress, she has been bearing on her back a burden of worldly illusions and pleasures, compared to a load of sugar-candy, and the knot of the porter's string that supports it has become loose and galls her. She has found that such a burden produces toil and pain. Her wasted life in this workaday world has become a weariness, and she is in despair. She has recourse to her Guru, her spiritual Teacher. His words cause her intolerable pain, such as that experienced by the loss of a beloved object—the worldly illusion that she must abandon. She learns that the whole of the flock of factors that make up her sentient existence have lost their proper ruler, the mind; for it is steeped in ignorance of Self. (Ibid.: 227)

Recognizing one's strengths and weaknesses enables one to pave the tortuous path toward self-advancement—a much sought after goal that would allow people of different intellectual dispositions to relegate life's peripherals to the background and face the vicissitudes of fate with courage and faith in themselves.

It is a Herculean task not just to recognize the self, but to channelize the confidence that the said recognition fosters. Self-awareness enabled Lalla-Ded, unobstructed by a false consciousness, to practice religious, cultural, and social iconoclasm in an idolatrous and cult-worshipping society. Again anticipating the psychoanalytic emphasis on maintaining serenity and verbalizing destructive emotions in order to defang them, Lalla-Ded exhorts the believer to

> Keep thy mind calm as the Peaceful Sea,
> Slaking and quenching the fires of Wrath,
> Lest from thy bondage thou set them free
> And the words of rage, as flames, break forth:
>
> Words that shall sear, as with fire, thy mind
> Burnt in anger to be healed in truth.
> What are they? Nothing. Nothing but wind,
> When thou hast weighed them in scales of Truth.
>   (Ibid.: 181)

In an age in which the culture was pervaded by conservative sensibilities, well-defined gender roles, and the confinement of women to home and hearth, Lalla-Ded's blatant mockery of confining conventions was condemned by the upholders of the hegemonic order.

Her honed self-knowledge and sublimation of needs highlighted by society taught Lalla to maintain an unscarred mind in the face of thoughtless condemnation and adversity. Critical intelligence, particularly when expressed by a woman to break down societal, religious, and cultural edifices, has always been intimidating and has invited virulent criticism, as it did in Lalla's case. The ravages of time and the putative liberation of women in the twenty-first century have not diminished the potency of Lalla-Ded's radicalism or the tangible beauty of her poetry and its pertinence in this day and age. Professor Neerja Mattoo (2007), emeritus professor of English at Maulana Azad Women's College, Srinagar, Kashmir, and author of several publications on Kashmiri literature, astutely draws a comparison between Lalla-Ded and medieval Christian women mystics:

> For them [medieval Christian women mystics], too, the only way to validate their words and to get out of the all-pervasive, constricting presence of male authority was this claim of a personal relationship with God. After all, it was from God Himself that all the authority of the Church, all of whose top functionaries were male, was drawn. These women were thus able to establish some authority of their own. We can say that in this "confession" they did not require a "Confessor," but they could be alone.

I had an enlightening conversation with Mohammad Yousuf Taing (e-mail to author July 2007), former secretary of the Cultural Academy and director general of culture, J & K government, in which he pointed out that it is also believed that Lalla-Ded was greatly influenced by discourses on mysticism and on the different schools of Sufi thought given by Mir Syed Ali Hamadani, Shah Hamadan, a regal Central Asian Islamic scholar and mystic who disseminated and perpetuated Islamic teachings in predominantly Brahmanical fourteenth- and fifteenth-century Kashmir. In fact, educated Kashmiri Muslims are of the firm opinion that the verses that Lalla-Ded composed after having forged a spiritual alliance with Shah Hamadan and other Muslim scholars reverberate with Islamic thought.

> Lalla fills her teaching with many things that are common to all religious philosophy. There are in it many touches of Vaishnavism, the great rival of Shaivism, much that is reminiscent of the doctrines and methods of the Muhammadan Sufis, who were in India and Kashmir well before her day, and teaching that might be Christian with Biblical analogies, though the Indians' knowledge of Christianity, if any, must have been very remote and indirect at her date. (Temple [1924] 2005: 165)

The Ziarat Sheikh-ul Alam, Chirar-i-Sharif, Srinagar, tomb of Noor-ud-Din Wali, was burned down during militancy in 1995. (*Courtesy:* Amin Studio, Srinagar)

Lalla-Ded's secular and anachronistic teachings were a death knell for orthodox religion. Sheikh Noor-ud-din Wali placed Lalla-Ded in the role of the mother who honed his knowledge of the ethos of Kashmir (for a delineation of Lalla-Ded's religious philosophy, see Bamzai 1994; Murphy 1999).

Impact of Lalla-Ded's Teachings on Pandit and Muslim Communities

Lalla-Ded's poignant verses, pulsating with the pain and damnation of peripheralized social and economic groups, were not written down but were ensconced in the language and cultural discourse of the hoi polloi, and continue to reverberate in the day and age of political paranoia and religious fundamentalisms. She chose to break the mold of patriarchy in a stiflingly traditional society by not allowing her intellectual and spiritual freedoms to be curbed.

In an illuminating e-mail (dated 4 April 2008) about the impact of Lalla-Ded's teachings on Kashmiri Pandit women, Professor Neerja Mattoo wrote:

> Although Kashmiri Pandit women in the past have revered Lalla-Ded, taken pride in acknowledging her as their great ancestress, quoted her *vaakhs* as proverbs to suit all occasions when a stoical response is required, the deeper Saivite philosophy and the questions she raises regarding Reality and Self-Realization and to which she supplies answers seem to have stayed out of their domain. These demand an intellectual rigour and a highly evolved sensibility, which most women, kept in subjugation in a patriarchal system, did not possess. Brahmanism, which Lalla had defied all through by preferring to use the language of commoners, Kashmiri, to communicate with them, however, appropriated the significant and esoteric part of her work. The only legacy left for women was her proverbial patience in suffering the cruelty of the mother-in-law, who acted as the tool of an oppressive system by even denying her enough food. It is ironic that while her real message was for everyone, irrespective of class, caste, gender, or religion, radical for those times, the only lesson women generally learned from it was that of submission. But, of course, women who had broken free from social confines on a spiritual quest after renouncing the material world were certainly influenced by her. Among these is the seventeenth-century mystic poet Roph Bhavani, the content of whose *vaakhs* is also the theory and practice of Saivism. Although there is a brooding intellectuality in Roph Bhavani's *vaakhs*, written in a highly Sanskritized form of Kashmiri and, therefore, quite different from the common idiom that Lalla-Ded used, her message is the same: free yourself from prejudice, cleanse yourself from the sense of Duality, meditate on the Absolute, and realize your own spiritual potential. The following *vaakh* from Roph Bhavani's work, *Rahasyopadeasha*, shows her acknowledging Lalla-Ded as her guru:

> *Om gwar antar that nirmalan*
> *Shuddham atyant vidyadharan*

Lal naam Lal parmagwaram
Shiv Madhav naham parman Brahma Soham

(With Om I begin, and instal in a cleansed mind my Guru,
Who is most pure and greatly learned
Lal is your name, my ultimate Guru!
Neither Siva nor Madhav am I, but Brahma Himself,
   the Supreme Self)

Unfortunately, the present generation of Kashmiri women seems to have lost touch with this great mystical tradition. Since it no longer forms part of their daily discourse—most of them are aware of Lalla-Ded, at best, as a name alone. The meaning and import of her *vaakhs* remains an unfamiliar territory. A pity, indeed!

Through her poetry, Lalla-Ded questioned restrictive cultural mores, religious, social, economic, and gender hierarchies, and the relevance of esoteric knowledge. She deconstructed traditional dichotomous categories and anticipated the postmodern notion of the implosion of the Supreme and Nature, the individual Self with the Universal Self. The true devotee, from the nondualist point of view, "is one who recognizes that He is all in all and that all creation and all experiences are but modes of Him" (Temple [1924] 2005: 169). Lalla renders her teachings with sensuous imagery, making them easier to visualize. For instance, she illustrates her teaching of the unity of the Self with the Supreme using the analogy of the melding of ice, snow, and water. She explains that the three are different, but the sun enables the blending of all three. Similarly, true knowledge enables the soul to recognize not only its oneness with the Supreme, but also with the entire universe (ibid.: 179).

Erosion of Monolithic Religious and Political Structures

Lalla-Ded's oracular sayings, replete with double entendres, have made her verses an intricate part of Kashmiri culture. The analogies that she employed in order to make her philosophy and religious teachings comprehensible render her verses eclectic and esoteric. By challenging oppressive attitudes, which had been internalized by the masses, Lalla-Ded interrogated official historiography and exhumed the corpses of subaltern historiography. Her ability to challenge the oppressiveness created by the nexus between the institutions of patriarchy and feudalism enabled her to acknowledge the marginalized classes of society. For instance, Lalla-Ded foregrounds the work of artisans and peasants, which hitherto had been relegated to the background, in the following verse:

> *Lal ba drayas kapas poshi satsuy*
> *Katsi tu dooni karnam yatsay lath*
> *Tuy yeli khaernas zaeviji tuye*
> *Vovuri vaana gayam alaeney lath,*
> *Dwobi yeli chhaevnas dwobi Kani pethay*
> *Saz ta saaban mathsnam yatsuy*
> *Sutsi yeli phirnam hani hani kaetsuy*
> *Ada Lali me praevum paran gath*

> I, Lal, set out, hoping to bloom like a cotton flower,
> But was beaten and trampled by ginner and carder,
> Shredded and spun into so fine a yarn,
> And hung and hit by a weaver on his loom,

> Thrashed and kneaded on the washerman's stone,
> Pasted and plastered with soap and clayey earth,
> Till the tailor's skilful scissors worked on my limbs,
> And I found my place in the highest Abode! (In Mattoo 2007)

Lalla-Ded does not allow her vision of reality to be clouded by idyllic mysticism. On the contrary, her visceral poetry and the fluidity of her language create ripples in the stagnant pools of tradition and fumigate the sewers of power.

Here is another example of Lalla-Ded's erosion of monolithic religious and political structures:

> *Deev vatta divar vatta*
> *Petha bon chhuy ikavaath*
> *Pooz Kas karakh hutta Batta*
> *Kar manas tu pavans sangaath*

> Your idol is stone, the temple a stone too—
> All a stone bound together from top to toe!
> What is it you worship, you dense Brahmin?
> True worship must bind the vital air of the heart to the mind. (Ibid.)

In this vaakh, Lalla-Ded shatters the complacency of the priest who exploits the ignorant, poor, and superstitious masses. She mocks religiosity and conformity to insipid traditions that diminish the spiritual aspect of faith in the Unseen. Her unequivocal condemnation of the self-righteousness and hypocrisy of the Hindu priest surpasses the language and leitmotifs in the world of conventional women. Her syncretic faith transcended barriers of religion, caste hierarchies, and race. Although Lalla-Ded's gender and social position did not endow her with authority, she did not hesitate to challenge social, gender, and religious constructs that underscored the privilege of the few and reinforced the subservience of the many.

Lalla-Ded's complete disapproval of kitsch magical practices, designed to be formidable and give uncritical believers a false sense of security, is further underlined in the following vaakh:

> *Zal thamavun hutavan turnaavun,*
> *Urdagaman parivarzith chareth*
> *Kaathdeni dwad shramanaavun,*
> *Antih sakalay kapat chareth*

> Stilling the waters or quenching a fire,
> The cursed practice of seeming to fly,
> Or to make a wooden cow yield milk,
> In the end it is deceit and fraud (Ibid.)

Lalla-Ded categorically declared that the renunciation of such practices and aspiration to unify one's being with the Supreme consciousness should be the ultimate goal of the true believer. Her articulation of her mystic experiences and her pooh-poohing of the shallowness of men falsely claiming to have knowledge of the supernatural facilitated her repudiation of gender and social constructs in an age in which female submissiveness was deeply embedded in the culture.

In an e-mail to me (dated 25 December 2009), renowned Kashmiri historian and author of *Biographical Dictionary of Sufism in South Asia* (2009), Mohammad Ishaq Khan, wrote

> Lalla-Ded's seminal impact on the evolution of Kashmiri Muslim society is traceable to her eulogisation as an *avatara* of underprivileged Kashmiris by her junior contemporary, Shaikh Nuruddin Rishi. Consequently, legendised both as a rebel against the caste-ridden Brahmanic society and a Muslim woman mystic in the folk consciousness, even the *Shari'ah*-conscious Sufis and scholars at a later stage—particularly close disciples of the revered Shaikh Hamza Makhdum—extolled her to the skies in their hagiographies. Significant as this development was in spiritual as well as social terms, it did affect the way women began to be viewed during Kashmir's transition to Islam over centuries of acculturation. Women Sufis now began to

wield immense spiritual and social influence along with men. That Lalla-Ded accorded a place of equal social worth to women can be gauged from the fact that not long ago there was no dearth of Kashmiri mothers who by virtue of their knowledge of *Lal Vaak* played the role of educators; this despite the fact that they were seemingly denied influence or empowerment in our traditional and patriarchical society.

Through her poetry, Lalla-Ded played a significant role in raising consciousness and in foregrounding the dispensability of cultural and social practices that benighted the masses. Her voice created perceptible cracks in the edifice of iconicized womanhood and the figure of the "native woman," which was similar to that of the Victorian woman as upholder of the culture of silence.

In her path-breaking poetry, Lalla-Ded intelligently voiced the agonizing plight of the marginalized that lacerated the heart and seared the mind, brought about by a debilitating culture. She extricated herself from the midst of monstrous structures and the agony that they caused in order to achieve the ideal of self-realization, which did not require self-mortification but the proverbial endurance of Sufi saints and prophets. Even to aspire to self-actualization was a radical notion, particularly for a woman, in an age of stifling conventions and traditionalism.

Portrayal of Women in Nationalist Literatures

Most nationalist movements and literatures of independence have portrayed women as icons of cultural preservation. In the nationalist and postcolonial phase of nations, gender divisions have been reinforced by the hallowed figure of the "native woman" (Gandhi 1998: 83). The complexity in the varying positions of women has been ignored to preserve nationalist portraits of the "native woman" that do not concede to the female subject the right to foreground her own "distinct actualities" (Minh-ha 1989: 5). For instance, the iconicization of Lalla-Ded as goddess–mother in nationalist literatures limits her sphere of influence within Kashmiri folklore and social practices. I oppose this decapacitating iconicity of "woman" that traditional Islamic, Hindu, and Victorian concepts of femininity endorse. Lalla-Ded deemphasized the roles imposed by conjugality and motherhood in order to widen her identity without totally dismissing the cultural definition of womanhood. "Her indomitable spirit and profound creativity were too expansive to be encased in outmoded familial and societal structures" (Misri 2002: 9). The Sufi mystic located agency in possibilities created in the variability of spaces in which identity is formed. Lalla-Ded's unsurpassed Sufi mysticism and the eloquent verse that ensued from it led to her being owned as much by the Pandits of the Valley, as Lalla Ishwari, as by the Muslims of the Valley, as Lalla Arifa (Bamzai 1994; Jha 1996; Khan 1994; Ray 1970).

Mohammad Yousuf Taing, a noted scholar and historian in addition to his work for the Cultural Academy and J & K government, elaborated on Lalla's deconstruction of traditional societal mores through her verse:

Lalla's impact on Kashmiri mind and literature would not have been as pervasive if she had only assumed the role of a preacher of traditional thought. She is primarily a poet and then a preacher. The ecstasy of her poetic expression and its inherent *Rasa* is of such quality that the preacher assumes the role of a bard. It surmounts the barrier of religion and has a universal appeal. That is the reason that she has dominated the poetic space in Kashmir for 700 odd years. Even in the twentieth century a modern poet like Mirza Arif (1910–2004) could proclaim;

  "*Nangay naychenav Lalla aik Gura Shahdoni.*"
  (Lalla was made to dance in nude by just a word from her teacher.)

Lalla's image as a nude ascetic roaming and dancing around takes her beyond the realm of the ordinary. She emerges as an eternal bold rebel who transcends the mores and rules of tradition, and is still accepted as a person of unblemished spiritual grandeur. It is significant that she gives up this nude dance when she recognizes a true man of God. It is a beautiful metaphor that when she saw Mir Syed Ali Hamdani, the great Muslim saint (717–786 Hijira) she hastened to jump into a baker's oven. When she came out, she was in beautiful bridal apparel and exclaimed,

  "I have seen a true man after all, hence this dress."

Lalla is the forerunner of the Bhagti stalwarts of pre-partition India. It is yet to be established that her *vaakhs* had not reached them, but poets like Bhagat Kabir, Tulsi Das, and Ravi Das came on the scene after the advent of great Lalla. In an ancient and rich language like Kashmiri she is still the most unexplored and mysterious mount of poetic excellence. Even in the 20th century such tall poets as Dina Nath Nadim (1915–1988) and Rehman Rahi (1925–) are emulating the glory of her poetic style. She continues to be the inspiration for many generations of Kashmiri elite and, of course, its common folk especially women who still take pride in reciting the tribute which the spiritual progenitor of

Kashmiri ethos, Sheikh Noor-ud-Din Wali, had paid her some six hundred years ago,

> "*Ami Padma\n Purchi Lalley, yemi ais Amrit galley chaive*"
> (Remember the Lalla from Padman Pur who made us drink nectar by gulps)

Lalla started a procession of female poets in Kashmir, e.g., Haba Khatoon, Arni Mal, and now living poets like Mahfooza Jan and Naseem Shafi. (E-mail to author 12 December 2009)

Resurgence of the Literature of Jammu and Kashmir

Subsequent to 1947, when India gained independence from British dominion, there was a regeneration of interest in folk literatures, mythologies, poetry, and so on. Cultural organizations that had been in dire straits because of the lack of intellectual and financial support were rejuvenated and reclaimed in the nationalist climate. Some of these organizations were Prem Sangeet Niketan Bazam-i-Adab, Himalaya Bhand Theatre, Kala Kendra Club, Kashmir Art Society, Rashtrabhasha Prachar Samiti, Kashmir Cultural Society, and Progressive Artists Association (Bazaz [1967] 2005: 10–12). The Academy of Arts, Culture and Languages, which was established in Srinagar on 24 October 1958, provided creative artists with a much needed forum. This institution enjoyed the patronage of Sadar-i-Riyasat Karan Singh and Prime Minister Bakshi Ghulam Mohammad. The Academy gained the status of an autonomous corporate organization in 1963, and it disseminated the reservoirs of creativity and artistic talent throughout the state.

In order to encourage local artists, the Academy provided subsidies for productions and awarded actors, musicians, writers, playwrights, and poets for their work. Kashmiri, spoken in the Kashmir Valley, and Dogri, spoken in the Jammu region, were no longer confined to the domestic realm but were deployed in literary and public discourse. The Academy unearthed Kashmiri and Dogri manuscripts from the crumbling archives of history and collective memory, edited and published them; among these were Abdul Ahad Azad's voluminous book on Kashmiri language and poetry, *Kashmiri Zaban aur Shayiri*; and selected Kashmiri poetry by Nadim, Haba Khatoon, Haqqani, Maqbool Kralwari, Parmanand, Rasul Mir, Wahab Parey, and Lakshman Koul. The Academy also published two spectacular volumes of the poetry of mystic masters, under the title *Sufi Shaeyir*.

Cultural Academy, Srinagar. (*Courtesy*: Amin Studio, Srinagar)

Some of the other notable Kashmiri works of literature and poetry are Master Zind Koul's *Sumaran* (Remembrance), Dina Nath Nadim's *Kwang Posh* (Saffron Flower), Nadim's opera *Heemat Nagirai*, and Rahman Rahi's *Naoroz Saba* (New Year's Breeze). Ghulam Nabi Khayal translated Omar Khayyam's poetry and Aristotle's *Poetica* into Kashmiri. Amin Kamil undertook the Herculean task of compiling three volumes on Kashmiri mystic masters. The ancient Hindu text *Bhagwad Gita* was translated into Kashmiri by Sarwanand Koul Premi.

In 1964 the Academy further supported the revival and enhancement of cultural activities by opening two schools of music and fine arts in Srinagar and Jammu, where classes were held in painting, classical music, and drama. Exquisite arts such as papier-mâché, carpet weaving, crewel work, shawl weaving, and walnut wood carving were also revived in the 1950s and 1960s (ibid.). This revival of cultural activities in J & K echoed the ramification of nationalist pride that was making inroads all over the Indian subcontinent.

Chapter Three

Political Debacles*

Democratic Processes and Radical Socioeconomic Measures

Subsequent to the awakening of Kashmiri nationalism; pride in the unique cultural ethos; institution of a populist government headed by Sheikh Mohammad Abdullah in Indian-administered J & K; bolstering of an alternative epistemology in the form of "Kashmiriyat"; and legitimization of progressive socialist measures in Indian-administered J & K; India agreed to hold a free and impartial plebiscite in the state. (After tremendous reluctance to accede to either the dominion of India or Pakistan, it became a hobson's choice for the maharajah to sign the "Instrument of Accession" enabling the provisional accession of J & K to India. See Appendix A, 175–178). Initially, the prime minister of India, Jawaharlal Nehru, in tandem with the prime minister of Kashmir, Sheikh Mohammad Abdullah, conceded the inviolable right of the people of J & K to chart their own political course At a mass public rally in Srinagar in 1948, Nehru, with the towering Abdullah by his side, solemnly promised to hold a plebiscite under United Nations auspices.

But Abdullah's ascendancy received vituperative opposition not just from royalist elements, but also from Ladakh's Tibetan Buddhists who were apprehensive about the sudden rise of a new Kashmiri Muslim elite and were particularly fearful of the implications of its land reform policies for the Buddhist clergy's enormous private landholdings in Ladakh. As the elected head of government, Abdullah pushed through a set of major reforms, the most important of which was the "land to the tiller" legislation, which destroyed the power of the landlords, most of whom were non-Muslims. They were allowed to keep a maximum of 20 acres, provided they

* The works of Tariq Ali, Prem Nath Bazaz, Sumantra Bose, Jyoti Bhusan Dasgupta, Balraj Puri, and Victoria Schofield have influenced my conceptualization of the complexity of the Kashmir issue.

Jawaharlal Nehru, with Sheikh Mohammad Abdullah by his side, pledges to hold a UN-supervised plebiscite in J & K, Srinagar, 1948. (*Courtesy*: The Archives of the National Conference, with the permission of the general secretary of the National Conference, Sheikh Nazir Ahmad)

worked on the land themselves: 188,775 acres were transferred to 153,399 peasants, while the government organized collective farming on 90,000 acres. A law was passed prohibiting the sale of land to non-Kashmiris, thus preserving the basic topography of the region (Ali 2003: 237).

The new economic plan of the state, formulated and executed by Abdullah's government, underlined cooperative enterprise as opposed to malignant competition, in keeping with Abdullah's socialist politics, which implied the organization and control of marketing and trade by the state. This revolutionary economic agenda in a hitherto feudal economy enabled the abolition of landlordism; allocation of land to the tiller; cooperative guilds of peasants; people's control of forests; organized and planned cultivation of land; the development of sericulture, pisciculture, and fruit orchards; and the utilization of forest and mineral wealth for the betterment of the populace. Tillers were assured of the right to work on the land without incurring the wrath of exploitative creditors, and were guaranteed material, social, and health benefits (Korbel [1954] 2002: 204). These measures signaled the end of the chapter of peasant exploitation and subservience, and opened a new chapter of peasant emancipation.

Sheikh Abdullah's unsurpassed achievement during his years as the prime minister of J & K from 1948 to 1953 was the abolition of the exploitative feudal system in the agrarian economy. He was also responsible for the eradication of monarchical rule. A.M. Diakov, a Soviet specialist on India, wrote about the progressive and democratic policies adopted by Abdullah's National Conference (NC): "After the Second World War, a national movement in Kashmir developed the program of doing away with the Maharaja, of turning Kashmir into a democratic republic, of giving to the people of Kashmir the right of self-determination" (Diakov 1948). The Dogra monarchy was formally abolished in 1952, and the last monarch's heir apparent, Karan Singh, was declared the titular head of state. Disregarding the attempts of the Indian government to ratify its authority in J & K, the UN Security Council passed a resolution in March 1951 reminding the governments and authorities concerned of the premises of the Security Council resolutions of 21 April 1948, 3 June 1948, and 14 March 1950, and the United Nations Commission for India and Pakistan (UNCIP) resolutions of 13 August 1948 and 5 January 1949, according to which a final decision about the status of the state would be made in accordance with the wishes of its people expressed in a free and fair referendum held under the impartial auspices of the UN. This resolution also determined that the convening of a constituent assembly as recommended by the general council of the All Jammu and Kashmir National Conference, and any decision that the assembly might take and attempt to execute determining the political affiliation of the entire state or any part thereof, would be considered as not in accordance with the above principles and would therefore be disregarded (Dasgupta 1968: 406–07). When Sheikh Abdullah first voiced his unrelenting opposition to autocratic rule in the state, his political stance was applauded by some sections of the Indian press, which, by foregrounding his position, further brought it out of the catacombs of provincialism:

> It is imperialism's game to disrupt the great democratic movement led by the NC.... There is no doubt that the NC would defeat these disruptive efforts by placing in the forefront the issue of ending the present autocratic regime and establishing a fully democratic government in accordance with its program. (*Communist*, October 1947, quoted in Krishen 1951: 3–4)

Despite the injunction of the Security Council, Abdullah and his organization convened a constituent assembly in 1951. The NC regime was faced with unstinting opposition in the Hindu-dominated southern and southeastern districts of the Jammu region. Disgruntled elements comprising officials in the former maharaja's administration who had been divested of their authority by the installation of a democratic regime in the state, and Hindu landlords stripped of their despotism by the NC administration's populist land reforms, founded an organization called the Praja Parishad in late 1947, which was at loggerheads with Abdullah's regime since 1949 (see Bose 1997: 104–64).

Despite all odds, Abdullah sought to maintain Kashmir's autonomous status. Tariq Ali makes an astute observation regarding Abdullah's locus standi:

> If Abdullah had allied himself with Pakistan, the Indian government and its troops would have been unpleasantly disarmed. But he considered the political and social ideologies of the Muslim League extremely conservative and was afraid that if Kashmir acceded to Pakistan, the Punjabi feudal lords who were at the helm of the ship of policy making in the Muslim League would hamper political and social progress. In order to prevent such an occurrence, Abdullah agreed to support the Indian military presence in the State provided under United Nations auspices in J & K. (Ali 2003: 165)

The purportedly autonomous status of J & K under Abdullah's government provoked the ire of the Hindu nationalist parties, which sought the unequivocal integration of the state into the Indian Union.

The unitary concept of nationalism that these organizations subscribed to challenged the basic principle that the nation was founded on, namely, democracy. In such a nationalist project, one of the forms that the nullification of past and present histories takes is the subjection of religious minorities to a centralized and authoritarian state buttressed by nostalgia of a "glorious past." As Bose (2003: 58) is quick to point out, the unequivocal aim of the supporters of the integration of J & K into the Indian Union was to expunge the political autonomy endowed on the state by India's constitutional provisions. According to the unitary discourse of sovereignty disseminated by the Hindu nationalists, J & K was not entitled to the signifiers of statehood—a prime minister, flag, and constitution. The concept of nationalism constructed by Hindu nationalists bred relentless violence and the delusions of militant nationalisms.

Although Sheikh Mohammad Abdullah viewed the accession of J & K to India as a strategic and pragmatic necessity, and sought to justify it by deploying the rhetoric of socialism and secularism, he continued to harbor hopes for the creation of a sovereign Kashmir. In October 1949, the Constituent Assembly of India reinforced the stipulation that New Delhi's jurisdiction in the state would remain limited to the categories of defense, foreign affairs, and communications, as underlined in the Instrument of Accession. This stipulation was provisional and its final status would be decided upon the resolution of the Kashmir issue. Subsequent to India acquiring the status of a republic in 1950, this constitutional provision enabled the incorporation of Article 370 into the Indian Constitution, which ratified the autonomous status of J & K within the Indian Union. Article 370 stipulates that New Delhi can legislate on the subjects of defense, foreign affairs, and communications only in just and equitable consultation with the government of the state of J & K, and can intervene on other subjects only with the consent of the J & K State Assembly.

At this point in time, Abdullah made some controversial observations in an interview with the London *Observer*. He voiced his concern over the increased vulnerability and instability of J & K caught between two countries that were hostile toward each other. He expressed his solicitude over the political and economic hardships that the location of the state would cause its populace. The only viable option, according to him, was for J & K to have a neutral status vis-à-vis both India and Pakistan. However, because of the ruptured politics within the state given its diverse political, religious, and ethnic affiliations, the sovereign and autonomous status of J & K would need to be acknowledged and guaranteed not just

by India and Pakistan, but also by the UN and other world powers. Abdullah's candid observations created a furor in New Delhi.
His "politically incorrect" views met with particular objection
from India's right-wing deputy prime minister, Vallabhbhai Patel.
Abdullah withdrew his remarks in an interview with *The Hindu*
a couple of months later (Dasgupta 1968: 194). In 1952 Abdullah
voiced his relentless hostility toward Hindu majoritarianism in the
stronghold of the Hindu right-wing Praja Parishad. He referred to
the attempts of the Congress Party and the central government to
enforce the complete integration of J & K into the Indian Union
as juvenile, impractical, and ludicrous (ibid.: 196). In March
1952 Abdullah stated that "neither the Indian Parliament nor any
other Parliament outside the state has any jurisdiction over our
state....No country—neither India nor Pakistan—can put spokes
in the wheel of our progress" (Delhi Radio, Indian Information
Service). He further declared that "the existence of Kashmir did not
depend on Indian money, trade, or defense forces, and he did not
expect any strings to be attached to Indian aid. Threats and taunts
would not intimidate him into servile submission" (*The Times*, 26
April 1952).

Delhi Accord of 1952

The negotiations in June and July 1952 between a delegation of the
J & K government led by Abdullah and a minister of his cabinet,
Mirza Afzal Beg, and a delegation of the Indian government led by
Nehru, resulted in the Delhi Accord, which maintained the status
quo on the autonomous status of J & K. In a public speech made on
11 August, Abdullah earnestly declared:

> This briefly is the position which the Constitution of India has accorded
> to our State. I would like to make it clear that any suggestions of alter-
> ing arbitrarily this basis of our relationship with India would only con-
> stitute a breach of the spirit and letter of the Constitution, it may invite
> serious consequences for our harmonious association of our State with
> India. The formula evolved with agreement of the two Governments
> remains as valid today as it was when the Constitution was framed and
> reasons advanced to have this changed seem completely devoid of sub-
> stance. In arriving at this arrangement, the main consideration before
> our Government was to secure a position for the State which would be
> consistent with the requirements of maximum autonomy for the local
> organs of State Power which are the ultimate source of authority in the

State while discharging obligations as a unit of the Federation. (quoted
in Soz 1995: 128)

At the talks held between the representatives of the state government
and the Indian government, the Kashmiri delegation relented on just
one issue: it conceded the extension of the Indian Supreme Court's
arbitrating jurisdiction to the state in case of disputes between the
federal government and the state government, or between J & K
and another state of the Indian Union. But the delegation shrewdly
disallowed an extension of the Indian Supreme Court's purview to
the state as the ultimate arbitrator in all civil and criminal cases
before J & K courts. It was also careful to prevent the financial
and fiscal integration of the state with the Indian Union. The representatives of the J & K government ruled out any modifications
to their land reform program, which had dispossessed the feudal
class without any right to compensation. It was also agreed that
as opposed to the other units in the Union, the residual powers of
legislation would be vested in the State Assembly instead of in the
central government.

But this was an ephemeral victory. It became increasingly clear,
over the years, that the autonomy issue remained unresolved and anti-
autonomy factions in Jammu and Ladakh did not lose their political
clout. Abdullah tried to defuse the complicated situation in 1953 by
proposing a plan for devolution of authority to the provinces within
the state through the Constituent Assembly's basic principles committee. According to this plan, the Kashmir Valley and Jammu regions
would be entitled to elected assemblies and separate councils of ministers with the authority to debate and legislate on certain affairs of
local and regional importance. This multipronged devolution was
intended to maintain the autonomy of Indian-administered J & K
while mollifying regional and sectarian opposition in the Jammu and
Ladakh regions (Bose 2003: 63). But the sectarian conflict in Jammu
and Ladakh, fueled by right-wing Indian nationalist elements, could
not be appeased with anything short of the overthrow of the Abdullah
regime. From the 1960s, militant Hindu groups in the Jammu province have advocated and supported the secession of the Hindu majority province from the Muslim-dominated Kashmir Valley, which is
a politically unwise demand that negates the social, religious, and
cultural complexities of the Jammu province. If this demand is fulfilled, the three predominantly Muslim districts—Doda, Rajouri, and
Poonch—of Jammu's six districts would rather cast their lot with the
Muslims of Kashmir Valley than align themselves with the Hindus

of Jammu, in keeping with the logic of the partition of India (Bazaz [1967] 2005: 151).

Rupture within the National Conference and Installation of the Bakshi Government

In 1953 Abdullah appointed a subcommittee, comprising members from the Muslim, Pandit, Sikh, and Dogra groups, which propounded four viable options for Kashmir's future. All of them involved holding a referendum and independence for part or whole of the disputed territory. The subcommittee recommended, on the suggestion of Maulana Masoodi, general secretary of the NC, that the people of Kashmir be offered the option of independence besides the option of acceding to either India or Pakistan. Abdullah decided to publicly advocate this option as a feasible choice. But in the summer of 1953, an unbridgeable rift occurred among the top brass of the NC that pitted Abdullah and Mirza Afzal Beg (Kashmiri Muslims) against Shyamlal Saraf (a Kashmiri Pandit), Giridharilal Dogra (a Jammu Hindu), and Bakshi Ghulam Mohammad (also a Kashmiri Muslim). Abdullah's proindependence stance received a severe blow when the dissident faction of the NC was joined by the Constituent Assembly speaker, G.M. Sadiq, and D.P. Dhar, deputy minister of interior. The former Soviet Union's stance on the Kashmir issue seemed to have had an influence on this group. The fallout of the rift was the dismissal of Sheikh Mohammad Abdullah as prime minister by the titular head of state, Karan Singh, and his arrest under the Public Security Act, a coup authorized by Nehru. Abdullah would be shuttled from one jail to another for the next twenty-two years, until 1975. A few days later Abdullah loyalists, including Mirza Afzal Beg, were also arrested under the same act. Subsequent to Abdullah's arrest, Bakshi Ghulam Mohammad was installed as prime minister. Bakshi's de facto regime was given a semblance of legitimacy by being formally ratified by members of the NC general council and Constituent Assembly delegates in specially convened sessions. In September 1953, Nehru, who earlier had underscored Abdullah's importance to the resolution of the Kashmir issue, did a political volte-face: he justified Abdullah's undemocratic eviction from office before the Indian parliament by asserting that the latter's "autocratic" methods had resulted in the loss of the majority of his cabinet and had caused trauma to the electorate. The well-planned coup in Kashmir that led to Abdullah's prolonged detention, the mass arrests of his loyalists, and the fabricated shows of loyalty to the new regime unveiled the strategies deployed by New Delhi as measures that lacked political and ethical legitimacy. One of the dissenters who was given a position of political import in the new regime, Syed Mir Qasim, makes candid observations in his autobiography about the overwhelming popular protests against Abdullah's removal and the police brutality that was deployed to quell the unrest (Qasim 1992: 68–70). The blatant suppression of defiance made it amply clear that any attempt to erode New Delhi's supreme authority would be tantamount to political hara-kiri.

I met with the former Sadr-i-Riyasat (governor) and former crown prince of the princely state of J & K, Karan Singh, at his quasi-regal home in New Delhi in the summer of 2007. Fortunately, he was willing to answer the questions I had regarding the 1953 coup. Debonair and composed, Karan Singh has a keen mind and was intent on rationalizing his political decisions, including the debacles he had presided over. He was also gracious enough to give me a copy of his autobiography in which he has unapologetically written about his role in that manifestation of political wiliness and despotism. He has written about his acceptance of the office of Sadr-i-Riyasat, a constitutionally legitimate position, and of the repercussions of his momentous decision:

> I knew that I had irrevocably severed my links with the feudal system and also that, however cordial our relations would be on the surface, my father would not easily forgive me for accepting the new office. I realized that the Sheikh was an inveterate foe of our dynasty and that by accepting it I was virtually placing myself at his tender mercies. I also knew that the reaction among my own community, the Dogras of Jammu, would be hostile, at least to begin with. And yet I was convinced that the old order had passed never to return; that whatever the future might hold there was no future for me or my people unless I threw in my lot with Jawaharlal Nehru and the new India that he has done so much to create and was guiding with such courage and foresight. (Singh 1994)

When I asked Karan Singh whether his office had entailed work of political import, he averred that subsequent to the 1953 coup, his was the only office that enjoyed constitutional legitimacy. While he thought Sheikh Mohammad Abdullah was a political stalwart, he saw him as a "Kashmiri leader of the Kashmiris, not of the entire state of J & K." Karan Singh, whose nostalgia for the monarchical era and the reverence his father, Maharaja Hari Singh, enjoyed in Jammu province remains unmitigated, spoke rather derisively of his father's and Abdullah's nemesis: the chimera of the independence of the former princely state of J & K. Regarding Abdullah's dalliance with the notion of independence, as Karan Singh would have one believe, he writes in his autobiography that, "the Sheikh's speeches became more and more strident, and it became increasingly clear that he was seriously working on the idea of some sort of independent status for Kashmir which, inevitably, would imply a virtual negation of the Accession to India" (ibid.: 156). He decries Abdullah's launching of what he terms "the anti-Dogra movement" as in essence an antimonarchical socialist movement. He perceives Abdullah's unwillingness to appease the Dogra monarchy as his inability to mollify the Dogra people of Jammu. In his conversation with me in July 2007, he seemed unwilling or unable to recognize the multiple political ideologies that exist among the populace of Jammu despite the hegemony of the monarchy in that province. In an antirepublican spirit, he characterizes Abdullah's nationalism as "Kashmiri chauvinism" (ibid.: 153). (For Abdullah's vocalization of his populist and nationalist ideology, see Appendix C, 180).

Karan Singh's underlying hostility toward Sheikh Mohammad Abdullah seems to be burnished by his bitter memories of Abdullah's outrage at the autocratic nature of the Dogra monarchy and the suppression of the underprivileged Muslims of the state. He talked to me of "the song and dance" that Abdullah had made about Maharaja Hari Singh's regime by launching a republican movement, which precipitated the eradication of the monarchy and removed every possibility of Karan Singh's ascension to the throne. Singh's antipathy toward the advocates of self-determination comes through clearly in his autobiography, in his description of the amenability of Bakshi Ghulam Mohammad, whose repressive regime was the harbinger of the corrosion of the autonomy of Indian-administered J & K and the nationalism of the Kashmiri people. He writes that Bakshi and the Sheikh were poles apart. In a laudatory tone, Singh characterizes Bakshi as a pragmatic impresario who dispassionately fostered public relations, especially with the people of Jammu. Unlike the Sheikh and Mirza Afzal Beg, Bakshi did not assiduously nurture Kashmiri nationalism, a brazenly anti-Dogra sentiment, and he diminished the sticky political problem of plebiscite (Singh 1994: 153).

Contrary to what Karan Singh would have one believe, however, the dismissal of Sheikh Mohammad Abdullah's de jure regime and the installation of Bakshi Ghulam Mohammad's de facto government plunged the Valley into utter political and ethical turpitude, which reverberated in later years. According to the current general secretary of the NC and nephew of Sheikh Mohammad Abdullah, Sheikh Nazir

Ahmad, the events of 1953 drastically altered the political landscape of Indian-administered J & K. Abdullah's dismissal and subsequent incarceration, which cast Nehru in the mold of a deceiver, engendered an irreparable distrust between the populace of the state and the government of India (e-mail to author 6 April 2008). Bakshi Ghulam Mohammad and the Communists leveled a series of allegations against the UN military observers for their purported encouragement of the protestors (Korbel [1954] 2002: 264). G.M. Sadiq accused the UN observers of encouraging subversive clandestine activities between pro-Pakistan elements in Kashmir and the imperialist powers, and declared that the government of Kashmir would not approve the appointment of Fleet Admiral Chester Nimitz, whom they perceived as the "nominee of an imperialist power," as plebiscite administrator (*The Hindustan Times*, 26 October 1953). Nehru validated the opposition of the Communists to Fleet Admiral Nimitz: "It will not be fair to any of the big powers to ask them to supply a representative as a plebiscite administrator, however admirable he may be, because that would be embarrassing and needlessly creating suspicion, not in my mind necessarily, but in some other big power's mind" (speech made on 17 September 1953). As Bose (2003: 67) astutely observes, the vicissitudes of decades of political uncertainty that buffeted Abdullah were clearly intended to underscore the agonizing predicament of persons who did not endorse the Indian agenda in Kashmir. Only those willing to disaffirm their political, cultural, and social ideologies in obeisance to the Indian state could hope to play a significant role in legitimized political institutions.

Abdullah's Kashmiri nationalism and patriotism, manifested in the successfully implemented land reform policies, had endowed him with an iconic stature that bordered on the messianic, especially in the Muslim-dominated Kashmir Valley. The dictatorial regime of Abdullah's former trusted lieutenant, Bakshi Ghulam Mohammad, lasted an entire decade, until 1963. During that period Bakshi was at the helm of an unrepresentative government that enjoyed the security blanket of New Delhi's protection. New Delhi cashed in on Bakshi's dependent status by insidiously undermining democratic institutions in Indian-administered J & K and eroding the state's autonomy with the complicity of the state government. The autonomy of the state within the Indian Union, which had been proclaimed in 1950 by a constitutional order formally issued in the name of the president of India, was rescinded in 1954 by the proclamation of another dictum that legalized the right of the central government to legislate in the state on various issues. The state was financially and fiscally integrated into the Indian Union; the Indian Supreme Court was given the authority to be the undisputed arbiter in Indian-administered J & K; the fundamental rights that the Indian Constitution guaranteed to its citizens were to apply to the populace of Indian-administered J & K as well, but with a stipulation that those civil liberties were discretionary and could be revoked in the interest of national security. In effect, the authorities had *carte blanche* for the operation of unaccountable police brutality in the state.

The Bakshi government required the ratification of New Delhi for its existence. Bakshi unashamedly declared in the Constituent Assembly that Kashmir's accession to India was irrevocable and the bond that had been forged between the Indian Union and Indian-administered J & K was unbreakable (Korbel [1954] 2002: 246; Dasgupta 1968: 212–13). This declaration was backed by Nehru, who was careful to qualify his validation with the assertion that the government of India would honor its commitment to hold a plebiscite in Kashmir: "let me say clearly that we accept the basic proposition that the future of Kashmir is going to be decided finally by the good will and pleasure of the people. That is the policy that India will pursue" (speech in the Indian Parliament, 11 August 1951; see *Jawaharlal Nehru's Speeches* 1963: 184; also see "Appendix A" 175–178). This was a clever initiation of the erosion of Article 370, which, for all intents and purposes, had been relegated to the background by Nehru's central government in collusion with Bakshi's state government.

The J & K Plebiscite Front

Despite brazen and pervasive corruption within the state under Bakshi's government, the police and military apparatuses were unable to quell political opposition. In August 1955, a group comprising eight legislators from the Constituent Assembly initiated a political movement called the J & K Plebiscite Front (PF). The first president of this organization was Abdullah's trusted colleague, Mirza Afzal Beg. Beg spearheaded this movement during his probationary period. The credo of the PF was "self-determination through a plebiscite under UN auspices, withdrawal of the armed forces of both nations from Kashmir, and restoration of civil liberties and free elections" (Dasgupta 1968: 227–28). The "seditious" goals of this organization unleashed state-sponsored violence against its members and supporters, creating a repressive atmosphere that was meant to insidiously gnaw at any semblance of autonomy that Indian-administrative J & K retained. In 1956 the Constituent Assembly validated a draft constitution for the state, built on the premise that the state of Indian-administrated J & K was and, indubitably, would remain an integral part of the Union of India (Noorani 1964: 73). This unambiguous premise assigned the political inclinations of the people of Kashmir to an obscure position. In fact, Nehru unabashedly declared that the legality of the accession of Kashmir to India was now a moot issue. The undemocratic approach of Nehru and the Kashmiri comprador class did not go unchallenged, and Sheikh Mohammad Abdullah wrote protest letters from prison to his former ally Nehru, and to his former trusted political comrade G.M. Sadiq, the procommunist speaker of the assembly. Despite his incarceration, Abdullah's larger-than-life political status and clout, reified by his die-hard supporters, kept alive the issues of self-determination and special status (Schofield 2002: 97). When the draft constitution was placed before the house, Mirza Afzal Beg moved a motion of adjournment for exactly two weeks, in order to enable Abdullah to be present. The assembly was presided over by Sadiq, who ruled the motion out of order. Subsequently, Beg and his followers protested and boycotted the proceedings (Dasgupta 1968: 97). The large-scale repressive measures deployed by the government of India paved the way for it to firmly entrench the state's new constitution on 26 January 1957. This development was followed by a resolution of the UN Security Council, which reiterated that the final status of J & K would be settled in accordance with the wishes of the people of the state as expressed in a democratic plebiscite. In effect, the convening of a constituent assembly as recommended by the general council of the All Jammu & Kashmir NC would not determine, in any way, shape, or form, the political future of the state. The course of the political destiny of J & K would be charted by the voice of its people raised at a democratic forum under the auspices of the UN (ibid.: 408). The resolution affirmed that the Kashmir issue was still pending final settlement and, despite claims to the contrary by Nehru's Congress government, was under consideration by the Security Council. The reiteration of earlier UN resolutions regarding the Kashmir issue made explicit the disputed status of the state. However, the UN was unable to retard or prevent certain political developments in Indian and Pakistani-administered J & K.

Legitimization of Undemocratic Processes

Soon after validating the new constitution, the Constituent Assembly dissolved itself and sought the organization of midterm elections in order to constitute a new legislative assembly. At the time, the jurisdiction of the Election Commission of India did not extend to J & K. Although the election that was held in June of 1957 had a semblance of political equity, Abdullah's *bête noir* and a politician whose notoriety was by then unsurpassed, Bakshi Ghulam Mohammad, won his seat without any contest. Bose (2003: 75) makes some interesting observations about the mockery of the electoral process in the state that year, in which Bakshi Ghulam Mohammad's NC won 66 seats. Electoral contests of dubious authenticity occurred for only 28 seats. In brazen disregard of democratic processes, of 43 Kashmir Valley seats, 35 were won by official NC candidates without even the semblance of a contest; 30 NC candidates, including Bakshi, won overwhelming victories without an iota of opposition; and another 10 NC candidates were elected after the nomination papers filed by opposing candidates were invalidated. Not surprisingly, the official responsible for vetting the nomination papers was an unscrupulous Bakshi adherent, Abdul Khaleq. In the Jammu region, there was a contest of sorts for 20 of the 30 seats—the NC won 14 seats, the Praja Parishad bagged 5, and a party representing "low-caste" Hindus secured 1 seat.

The organization of a well-manipulated electoral process had enabled New Delhi to ensure the victory of the stooge faction that it patronized. Bakshi Ghulam Mohammad, who had been elected as the leader of the NC legislative party without dispute, was reinstalled as prime minister. Bakshi and his cohorts were firmly entrenched not just in the Legislative Assembly, but in the Legislative Council as well. The monopolization of both houses of the assembly by a political faction sponsored by New Delhi legitimized a full-scale intervention of the central government, allowing the incorporation of non-Kashmiri officials in important administrative positions and the subsequent marginalization of the well-educated segments of Kashmiri Muslims. The Pandit population of the Valley, which was a small minority, enjoyed privileges in the political, civil, and economic structures of which the Muslim majority was deprived.

During these fateful years in the history of Kashmir, a wide fissure was created within the ruling clique when Bakshi, in his signature style, did not incorporate any members of the Communist faction headed by G.M. Sadiq into the cabinet that he formed subsequent to the 1957 elections. Bakshi's inability or unwillingness to appease this faction motivated Sadiq to create a separate organization, the Democratic National Conference, with the rebel Communist group of fifteen legislators. New Delhi recognized the threat that the rebelliousness of this faction could cause not just to the constructed political stability within the state, but also to India's relationship with China, which was already on the decline. The Chinese government had ratified an agreement with the military regime in Pakistan that specified that after the Kashmir dispute between the governments of Pakistan and India had been settled, the preeminent authority concerned would initiate negotiations with the government of the People's Republic of China in order to implement a boundary treaty to replace the present agreement. It reinforced its alliance with Pakistan's military regime by underlining that if that supreme and indisputable authority was Pakistan, then the provisions of the present agreement would be reinforced (Dasgupta 1968: 389–91). The prospect of the Pakistan–China alliance being bolstered spurred New Delhi to bring about a rapprochement between Bakshi's and Sadiq's warring factions in 1960. Sadiq and his cohort were reincorporated into the cabinet. A couple of years after this reconciliation, in 1962, assembly elections were held in the state, and Bakshi and his cabinet colleagues Sadiq, Mir Qasim, and Khwaja Shamsuddin won their assembly seats without even a peep of opposition (Bose 2003: 78). That year elections were held to 60 seats in the entire state, out of which the Bakshi-led NC suspiciously won 55 while the Praja Parishad won 3 (telephone conversation with Sheikh Nazir Ahmad, general secretary of the NC, 8 January 2009).

Bakshi's arrogance, and rampant deployment of corrupt and illegal methods and malpractices in political processes, soon caused him to be an embarrassment for the "democratic" government of the Republic of India, and his mentors in New Delhi had to ask him to step down from the position of prime minister of the state. Bakshi resigned in November 1963. The political bigwigs in New Delhi were concerned that another unopposed election in the state would tarnish India's reputation as the largest democratic republic. So Nehru's unsolicited advice to Bakshi was that he would gain more credibility and the elections could boast of an air of fairness if he lost a few seats to "bona fide opponents." Bakshi's political indebtedness to Nehru and his clique prevented him from discounting Nehru's advice, and he was replaced as prime minister by a hitherto unknown political entity, Khwaja Shamsuddin. Although the new government was headed by Shamsuddin, Bakshi's political clout buoyed by his goondaism remained a formidable presence. Consequently, his political rival, who enjoyed the patronage of the same political forces that had enabled Bakshi's ascendancy, was not accommodated in the new government (Puri 1995: 45–49).

Theft of the Sacred Relic at Hazratbal Mosque and Abdullah's Resurgence

In December 1963, the simmering fury against New Delhi's dubious strategies in J & K finally erupted in volcanic proportions. The anger of the masses was fueled by the theft of a relic, believed to be a hair from the beard of the prophet Mohammad, from the Hazratbal shrine in Srinagar. In the wake of the unleashed chaos, a central action committee was formed to investigate the theft. The committee was headed by Maulana Masoodi, former general secretary of Abdullah's NC

Façade of the Hazratbal mosque, Srinagar (*Courtesy:* Amin Studio, Srinagar)

(who was assassinated in December 1990 by pro-Pakistan separatists), and comprised G.M. Karra, Srinagar district chief of the NC in the 1940s, and Maulvi Farooq (see Dasgupta 1968: 20), a religious leader with a small band of devotees whose political survival was contingent on the blessings of pipers who called the tune on both sides of the fence between India and Pakistan. The repercussions of the theft of the ancient relic were so widespread that they shook the foundations not just of the picturesque Valley, but of Bengal and neighboring Pakistan as well. Shamsuddin was replaced as prime minister of Indian-administered J & K by G.M. Sadiq, New Delhi's blue-eyed boy, who shrewdly constituted a cabinet that comprised his loyalists. He also astutely determined that in order to ensure the stability of his administration and prevent a large-scale revolt, it would be politically expedient to release Sheikh Mohammad Abdullah, who had been in incarceration since 1958. Abdullah and his comrade-in-arms, Mirza Afzal Beg, were released in April 1964. Abdullah returned to the Valley with a heightened, iconic status and was greeted by an ecstatic crowd of 250,000 people. The summer capital of Indian-administered J & K was festooned with NC flags and in their delirium people seemed to have stormed the citadels of state power to give Abdullah a welcome accorded, in the Homeric period, to beings of godlike prowess and beneficence. Addressing a mammoth gathering of 150,000 people on 20 April, Abdullah stridently said that in 1947 he had challenged Pakistan's ability to wield the religion card to annex Kashmir and now he was challenging India's authority to declare the Kashmir dispute moot and just hypothetical (ibid.: 323).

Despite the discrediting of Abdullah's politics by various national and regional factions along the political spectrum, and despite some of his own questionable political decisions, it is hard to deny his contributions in carving a substantial niche for the people in Indian-administered J & K, particularly the Muslims of the Valley. Nor can it be denied that Abdullah fought a courageous and titanic battle against the mammoth political forces of India and Pakistan to voice the sentiments of marginalized Kashmiris.

Irony of Fate

Perhaps it was an irony of fate that, soon after Abdullah's talks with Nehru regarding the Kashmir imbroglio, Nehru died—on 27 May 1964. Prior to the change in Nehru's stance toward Kashmir, the two stalwarts had shared a commonality of vision: they were tied by an umbilical cord of antidespotic, socialist political beliefs. Abdullah

Subsequent to his talks with Indian Prime Minister Jawaharlal Nehru in 1964, Sheikh Mohammad Abdullah traveled to Pakistan with his loyalists Maulana Masoodi and Mirza Afzal Beg to hold talks with Pakistan's General Ayub Khan. (*Courtesy*: The Archives of the National Conference, with the permission of the general secretary of the National Conference, Sheikh Nazir Ahmad)

came from an unpretentious Muslim background and was motivated to fight the structural inequities and state-sponsored injustices wrought by the peripheralization of Kashmiri Muslims who were quarantined in the alleyways of poverty, illiteracy, and despondency, and who could not touch the corridors of economic and social prestige even with a bargepole. Nehru came from an elite background, had been groomed in the privileged hallways of Harrow and Cambridge, and was a proud personage, often arrogant or condescendingly superior in manner. His intellectual grooming exacerbated his patronizing tone and manner. Despite the fact that the two figures, Abdullah and Nehru, occupied different rungs of the social and economic hierarchy, the rapport between them was of critical importance to the installation of a democratic regime in Kashmir when the tide of separatism in 1947 threatened to drown out the Indian presence in the state (Ali 2003: 229).

Following his talks with the Indian premier, Sheikh Abdullah went to Pakistan with Maulana Masoodi and Mirza Afzal Beg, in sanguineness and good cheer, to hold talks with the Pakistani president, General Ayub Khan. After a series of hopeful conversations with Ayub Khan, Abdullah felt confident that the talks were making headway. He visited Muzaffarabad, the capital of Pakistani-administered Kashmir, and was exuberantly welcomed by a sea of people (ibid.: 240). During that period, Abdullah did not once waver on his demand for self-rule, but he required the cooperation of Pakistan in looking for a viable solution to the conflict that had caused more corrosion than the two countries were willing to admit. The heartwarming response to Abdullah and his stance, particularly in the Kashmir Valley, was not well received either by New Delhi or its ward at the time, G.M. Sadiq. Interestingly, Abdullah, whose earlier bitter experience with Bakshi had not taught him the lesson that discretion was the better part of valor, forged an alliance with his erstwhile Brutus in order to orchestrate a coup d'état. Sadiq turned to New Delhi for support, but New Delhi, true to character, decided to cash in on the internecine battle that had polarized the Muslims of the Valley into pro-Bakshi, tacitly supported by the Abdullah faction, and pro-Sadiq groups, thereby disaffirming their cultural, linguistic, and social unities. Further alienation and marginalization of dissident opinions was created by New Delhi with the political externment of Sheikh Mohammad Abdullah.

The Sheikh's daughter, my mother, Suraiya Ali Matto, poignantly recalls the period of her father's political externment:

I was asked by my parents to join them in Kodaikanal, a place hitherto unknown to me, in 1965. My father had been externed to this South Indian hill station soon after his return from the Haj pilgrimage along with my mother. Kodaikanal is in Tamil Nadu, and back then it was known not just for being a tourist resort but also for its good missionary schools to which children from elite families were sent. We were lodged in an old, well-preserved mansion of an erstwhile nawab, called Koh-i-Noor. My parents and I were given the uppermost apartment; the basement and the ground floor were occupied by security officials and guards. My father was grudgingly allowed mobility within the small hill station, which had a golf course, a lake, and a shopping mall. The luxurious touristy hotels were situated around the lake, and every evening we would go out for long walks either around the lake or on the golf course. My father was a strict disciplinarian who stuck to his regimen—studying Tamil in the mornings; indulging in his favorite pastime, cooking, in which he was assisted by my mother, Begum Akbar Jehan, and at times by me. Reading newspapers regularly, listening to the radio or television news, and reading good books became his daily routine. A deeply religious man, he said his prayers five times a day and recited the Quran, which became his routine. His punctuality, discipline, and regularity saved him from either going insane or being afflicted by depression, except once. All three of us had more or less adjusted ourselves in our God forsaken prison where anyone who was cordial towards us was regarded as a suspect by the security personnel who followed us like shadows wherever we went. None of us had access to the single telephone installed for the security officials; letters addressed to us were censored. We were on the verge of giving up hope of papa ever being released from Kodaikanal. Then suddenly one morning he complained of severe thirst and weakness. Lately, he had started eating candies and mangoes. He would be depressed and fatigued especially when feelings of persecution set in and he expressed that he was being subjected to slow poisoning. His condition was reported to the Government of India by the District Collector, T. N. Seshan, who later became the 10th Chief Election Commissioner of India. Various tests were conducted on my father by the doctors. The results absolutely shocked the doctors—his blood sugar had crossed the danger mark. That is when he was shifted to the All India Institute of Medical Sciences, New Delhi, where he was kept for nearly three months. Subsequently, he was moved to 3 Kotla Lane in New Delhi. Eventually, the Government of India led by Prime Minister Indira Gandhi initiated diplomatic negotiations with him, supposedly, for a viable resolution to the Kashmir conflict. The rest is history. My father remained clear headed about his political ideology during his time in externment and even until he breathed his last. All that while my mother stood like a rock beside him. Not once did she buckle under pressure or try to weaken his resolve. (Conversation with author, 21 November 2009)

The government of India made several strategic moves to break the spirit of dissident politics and the revolutionary zeal of the people of J & K, the most systemically damaging of which was to expunge the composite culture of Kashmir in an attempt to disseminate the unitary discourse of Indian nationalism.

In December 1964, the Union government declared that two highly federalist statutes of the Indian Constitution would be enacted in J & K: Articles 356 and 357. These draconian articles enabled the central government to autocratically dismiss democratically elected state governments if it perceived a dismantling of the law and order machinery. A constitutional order implementing these statutes was decreed by New Delhi (see Bose 2003 and Puri 1995 for further details). In 1965, the Union government fortified its autocratic powers in Indian-administered J & K by getting several corrosive amendments passed in the State Assembly: the Sadr-i-Riyasat, or titular head of the state, was replaced by a governor, a political nominee appointed by the central government; the title of head of government was changed from prime minister to chief minister, which was the regular title of heads of government within the Indian Union; and state representatives to the lower house (Lok Sabha) of India's Parliament would no longer be nominated by the state legislature but would be elected. These amendments were highly centrist and were designed to corrode the autonomy of J & K provided by Article 370.

Legitimacy of Article 370

All doubts about the attenuation of Article 370 were removed when the ruling faction of the NC, led by Sadiq, heralded the dissolution of the party and its subsequent integration into the Indian nationalist Congress Party. This attempt at discounting a historic political movement that foregrounded a separate Kashmiri identity was an exclusionary tactic deployed by the Union government. The Congress Party's working committee unhesitatingly accepted the integration of the NC (Sadiq faction or Democratic National Conference) into it. This substantive development proclaimed the victory of the Hindu nationalist project in Indian-administered J & K, which had sought the subsumption of religious minorities into a centralized and authoritarian state since the 1940s. The furtherance of the Hindu nationalist agenda in the state was enabled by the complicity of one of the architects of democracy and secularism, Jawaharlal Nehru. His adherence to the unitary discourse of nationalism galvanized the suppression of demands for the autonomy of the Indian-administered J & K state (Puri 1995: 89). These integrative and centralist measures were met with massive opposition, which the Indian government suppressed with bloody maneuvers. The volcanic nature of the protests in the Valley gave a veneer of legitimacy to its action of large-scale repression of leaders of the Plebiscite Front. Abdullah was also arrested, for the umpteenth time, under the Defense of India Rules, to further hush the voices of dissent. The uproar in Kashmir was an opportune moment for Pakistan to jump in the fray; this augmented the unrest and led to an India–Pakistan war in 1965 (see Dasgupta 1968).

The flames of discontent in Kashmir were fanned by Pakistan, which expected cooperation from the Muslims of the Valley. But it ended up being disappointed because the Kashmiri populace did not get involved in the war on a massive scale. The mindset of the Kashmiri people, which the Indian government had culpably ignored, was articulated by Prem Nath Bazaz ([1967] 2005: 99–100), who like Nehru, as I have mentioned in earlier chapters, was of Kashmiri Pandit descent and an eminent advocate of socialist democracy: "An overwhelming majority of them [Kashmiri Muslims] are not happy under the present political set-up, and desire to be done with it. But they are reluctant to bring about change through warfare and bloodshed." The nonaggressive and compliant attitude of the Kashmiris prior to the resurgence of violent secessionist movements in 1989 has been highlighted by other writers as well. Eminent political and social activists such as the aforementioned Prem Nath Bazaz, Jayaprakash Narayan, and others, conceded that India's image as a secular democracy had been tarnished by its repressively undemocratic tactics in the state (ibid.; see also, Akbar 1985).

The 1965 Indo–Pak war proved disastrous for both nation-states. In an attempt to save face, the two sides agreed to a UN-mediated ceasefire, which took place on 23 September 1965. In Tashkent, Russia, talks between Russian Premier Alexei Kosygin, Indian Premier Lal Bahadur Shastri, and Pakistani President Ayub Khan led to the ratification of an agreement, the Tashkent Declaration. Alastair Lamb (1991: 269) writes about the atmosphere, characterized by tact and diplomacy, in which the talks took place:

> In the era of Khrushchev the Soviet Union had publicly declared itself a supporter of the Indian stand on Kashmir. In 1962 a Russian veto had defeated a Security Council resolution on the plebiscite issue. By 1965, and after the fall of the Khrushchev regime, Russian attitudes were significantly modified. When President Ayub Khan visited Moscow in early April 1965, Aleksei Kosygin, the Soviet Prime Minister, showed himself far more flexible in outlook than Khrushchev had ever been. No doubt he was looking for some means to reduce Chinese support in Rawalpindi.

The Tashkent Declaration emphasized the resumption of dialogue between India and Pakistan through peaceful negotiations, and a rapprochement that would facilitate the development of amity between the two countries. In other words, the Kashmir conflict was consigned to a position of reduced political import. The declaration was perceived by the people of both India and Pakistan as a despicable act of evasion and was received with hostility by them: "Despite domestic opposition, both sides did respect the terms of the Declaration at least as far as practical measures were concerned. Prisoners of war were repatriated.... However, respecting the spirit of the Declaration (resolving disputes peacefully, promoting friendly relations) proved more difficult" (Malik 2002: 124–25). The disregard of the will of the people and the steady dissolution of democratic institutions caused colossal damage in the state of Indian-administered J & K, the effects of which came back to haunt India in 1989–1990.

Erosion of India's Democratic Façade, 1967

Despite the publicly voiced protestations by people who had access to the higher echelons of power, the 1967 elections in Indian-administered J & K did not bear testimony to India's democratic façade. Congress candidates supported by the Sadiq–Qasim faction of the NC won in 33 of the Valley's 42 constituencies, 27 of Jammu's 31 constituencies, and 1 of Ladakh's 2 constituencies—indubitably a large number. The draconian nature of the 1967 electoral process in Indian-administered J & K further entrenched corruption in the soil of the political culture, which is a yoke from which the people of the state, thus far, have not been able to free themselves. The official candidate from the southern Kashmir town of Anantnag was Khwaja Shamsuddin, who had been the prime minister of Indian-administered J & K for a few months in 1962–1963. Predictably, he was elected unopposed after papers filed by five other candidates were summarily invalidated. Of the 118 candidates whose papers were nullified, 55 were rejected because the candidates had declared their unwillingness to take the mandatory oath of allegiance to India. The government efficiently deployed the machinery and infrastructure available to it in order to ensure the victory of its political organization, winning 61 of the 75 seats (ibid.: 85; telephone conversation with Sheikh Nazir Ahmad, General Secretary of the NC, 12 January 2009). Clearly, India had left no stone unturned to ensure the victory of its cronies and the defeat of its ideological and political opponents. New Delhi's master of subterfuge greased the wheels of rampant deployment of governmental machinery to ease the path of the ruling party to victory and to delegitimize dissident politics (see Akhtar 2000 for further details about the corrupt practices that were legitimized during the 1967 assembly elections in Indian-administered J & K). The use of such discreditable methods enabled the Congress to create the semblance of a base for itself in the Valley, which, prior to these elections, had been nonexistent.

An unforeseen development that election year was the opposition of Bakshi Ghulam Mohammad, prime minister of Indian-administered J & K from 1953 to 1963, to the Congress parliamentary candidates Srinagar constituency candidate for the straggling faction of the NC. In an interesting reversal of political fortunes, Bakshi's faction of the NC won 7 seats in the Valley and 1 in Jammu that year. Not one to be easily slighted, the heretofore autocrat, known for his corrupt politics and brutal repression of dissent, proclaimed himself a Kashmir nationalist who was willing to fight tooth and nail against the centrist and integrative policies of New Delhi. This sudden and unexpected shift to regionalism and Kashmiri nationalism was Bakshi's ticket to the Indian Parliament. He was elected as the parliamentary representative from Srinagar (Lamb 1991: 209–10). The status of the ruling faction as a nonentity was reinforced when the brief release of Sheikh Mohammad Abdullah from incarceration in 1968 was greeted with overwhelming jubilation in the Valley. The "Lion of Kashmir" was welcomed by the people with such uninhibited exuberance and joy that the foundations of the Congress in the Valley were palpably shaken. Soon after his release, Abdullah addressed a mammoth gathering in Anantnag on 26 January 1968, in which he unhesitatingly voiced his dissident ideology. He made it clear that India's undemocratic and oppressive tactics would not inhibit the passionate desire of the Kashmiri people to be free. He also reminded India of its unfulfilled promise to hold a referendum in Kashmir and enable the people to exercise their right of self-determination. Sheikh Abdullah's disillusionment with Indian democracy created political and personal acrimony:

> Respect for the rule of law, the independence of the judiciary, the integrity of the electoral process—are all sought to be guaranteed by the Indian constitution. It is not surprising that many other countries have drawn upon this constitution, particularly the chapter on fundamental rights. Yet it must at all times be remembered that the constitution provides the framework, and it is for the men who work it to give it life and meaning. In many ways the provisions of the constitution have been flagrantly violated [in Kashmir] and the ideals it enshrines completely forgotten. Forces have arisen which threaten to carry this saddening and destructive process further still. (*Speeches and Interviews of Sher-e-Kashmir* 1968: 15–16; quoted in Bose 2003: 46)

In the wake of armed insurrection, genocide, extortions, exoduses, and state-sponsored atrocities, Abdullah's prediction has proved frighteningly accurate. His sharp delineation of India's antidemocratic strategies has proved to be the prognosis of a farsighted populist leader.

Attempts to Quell the Plebiscite Front (PF)

Regarding the role of women in the PF, illustrious journalist A.R. Nair observed in 1968: "The Plebiscite Front has done remarkable work among the village women who seem to be as enthusiastic as men in these gatherings." Highlighting the position of the woman in charge of the women's section of the PF, Nair went on to say, "She is the widow of a tonga-driver who was butchered along with 13 others who carried Hindu women and children from Srinagar to Jammu during the troublous days of 1947...." This woman, widow of the murdered tonga driver, is now an enthusiastic leader of the women's section of the PF, and she confronted me with an impressive array of challenging questions relating to the omissions and commissions of the Indian leadership toward Kashmir and the Kashmiri people. An illiterate woman for all practical purposes, she appeared saturated with the new ideas of self-determination and the popular will to achieve their ends at any cost. I deploy official and oral historiography, in chapter five, to further discuss the aftermath of this nationalistic awakening among the women of Kashmir.

But even the overwhelmingly popular response to Abdullah's politics did not discourage the then Congress central government headed by Jawaharlal Nehru's daughter, Indira Gandhi, from employing strategies that stifled greater autonomy for Indian-administered J & K. Some interesting political developments occurred in subsequent years. The PF, which had maintained its oppositional and dissident stance, proclaimed its intention to contest the parliamentary elections scheduled in 1971 and the legislative assembly elections scheduled in 1972. The PF had established itself in the Valley and made it its stronghold. As Syed Mir Qasim, Sadiq's successor as Indian-administered J & K's Congress chief minister anxiously predicted:

> I thought at this stage when the centre [central government] was to reopen talks with Sheikh Abdullah, the Plebiscite Front's participation in the elections would complicate matters. My reasons: if the elections

were free and fair, the victory of the Front was a foregone conclusion. And as a victorious party, the Front would certainly talk from the position of strength. (Qasim 1992: 132)

The regionalist and dissident policies of the PF had garnered overwhelming support, reducing the ruling elite to a caricature.

In January 1971, externment orders were served to the leaders of the Front, Sheikh Mohammad Abdullah, Mirza Afzal Beg, and Abdullah's older son-in-law, Ghulam Mohammad Shah. Beg was on his way to Kashmir from New Delhi by road, and Abdullah and Shah were planning to fly to the Valley from the capital. The flight that Abdullah and Shah should have been on was canceled because of a bomb hoax, and the same evening they were served with externment orders, preventing them from reentering J & K. Beg was stopped on his way to the Valley and told to turn back (author's conversations with political activists of the National Conference, 2007). In addition to the top brass of the PF being confined in New Delhi, a large number of members of the organization were arrested under the Preventive Detention Act.

Subsequent to the large-scale arrests of leaders and members of the Front, elections were held in the state in 1971–1972 in which the Congress orchestrated a landslide victory for itself, managing to acquire 5 out of 6 parliamentary seats and 56 out of 73 assembly seats. That year the Bharatiya Janata Party (BJP) gained visibility in the politically disputed state by garnering support to win 2 seats in Jammu. In an e-mail (dated 12 April 2008) to me, Ghulam Mohammad Shah, former chief minister of J & K and president of the Awami National Conference, a breakaway faction of the NC, wrote:

In the winter of 1970, my mother-in-law, Begum Akbar Jehan, my wife, Khalida, sister-in-law, Suraiya, and daughter, Aaliya, went to Delhi to spend some time with Sher-i-Kashmir [Lion of Kashmir]. In January 1971, after Sher-i-Kashmir Sheikh Mohammad Abdullah, Mirza Afzal Beg, Begum Akbar Jehan, and I were served with externment orders, workers of the PF came out in overwhelming numbers in the Valley and protested against the unconstitutional action of the government of India and the stooge government in Indian-administered J & K. We remained in externment for three and a half years. The revocation of the externment order in 1974 caused our supporters to celebrate with an unquenchable zeal, and our return to the Valley was observed with unfettered enthusiasm and rejoicing, manifesting a populist aversion to the despotic abuse of authority.

In another unforeseen and interesting development, a pro-Pakistan religious organization, Jamaat-i-Islami—which had insistently disavowed Kashmir's accession to India, and is currently a vocal opponent of elections held in Indian-administered J & K within the framework of the Constitution of India—in a tacit understanding with the Qasim regime, managed to get 5 representatives accommodated in the Legislative Assembly. In the parliamentary election, Bakshi Ghulam Mohammad again contested from Srinagar. Only this time he disavowed his Kashmiri nationalism and was patronized by the official regime with its unitary politics of Indian nationalism. Bakshi had once again engaged in a political volte-face with the ease of a carpetbagger. But unlike 1967 he was vanquished by a charismatic independent candidate tacitly backed by the PF, Shameem Ahmad Shameem, who won by an enormous margin.

Delhi Accord of 1975

Although the PF managed to gain such victories, Sheikh Mohammad Abdullah felt compelled to sever himself and his organization from their former credo of self-determination. Mirza Afzal Beg negotiated with the government of India for Abdullah's release from incarceration and for ensuring his position as head of government, and signed another "Delhi Accord" with the central government, which amounted to capitulating to the wishes of New Delhi and the Indian premier, Indira Gandhi. This Accord of 1975 reinforced the integration of J & K into the Indian Union, which had occurred in 1953. Although the central government proclaimed that the state would continue to be governed under Article 370, between 1954 and the mid-1970s New Delhi issued 28 constitutional orders ratifying the integration of J & K into the Indian Union, and 262 Union laws were implemented in the state, reducing its autonomy even further. In effect, the Congress central government made every attempt possible to render the state government defunct. Indira Gandhi's government condescended to allow Abdullah's state government to legislate on issues of culture, religion, and the Muslim personal law (Puri 1981: 151). The Delhi Accord was designed to divest Abdullah of his convictions, political platform, and strength. By that stage, Abdullah was decapacitated not just by age but by twenty-two years of incarceration as well. Also, after the 1971 Indo–Pak war India had become a force to contend with, and the ability of Pakistan to challenge that power had been greatly reduced.

The display of India's superior military strength and strategic dexterity during that war diminished Pakistan's stature. The Simla Agreement, ratified in 1972 by then Pakistani Prime Minister Zulfikar Ali Bhutto and Indian Prime Minister Indira Gandhi soon after the 1971 war, underlined the bilateral nature of the Kashmir issue; entrenched the cease-fire line, thereafter referred to as the Line of Control (LOC); reinforced the validity of the UN charter as governing relations between the two countries; and agreed to reaching a final settlement of the disputed area in the former princely state of J & K (Margolio 1999: 73–74). The common perception in India was that the Simla Agreement was a tacit acknowledgment of the Indian Union's claim over the state. This perception in politically influential circles seemed to give a much yearned after legitimacy to India's centrist policies.

In a strange turn of events, however, the Congress chief minister of J & K, Mir Qasim, stepped down of his own volition and asked Abdullah to replace him as head of government. Despite the dominance of the Congress party in the Legislative Assembly, Abdullah was elected leader of the house. New Delhi, consistent with its dubious record, had made every attempt to disempower Abdullah and his organization, but Abdullah's iconic status and the resurrection of the PF as the NC defeated its nefarious designs to eliminate oppositional politics in J & K. Sensing Abdullah's disregard of the emasculating conditions of the Delhi Accord, the Congress withdrew its support for him in 1977 and fresh elections were held. The 1977 elections were a landmark event in the history of Kashmir, with Abdullah's NC eradicating the Congress presence in the Valley and capturing an indisputable majority in the Legislative Assembly, 47 seats out of 75. The strength of the Congress was reduced to a mere 11 seats, greatly diminishing its hitherto fabricated larger-than-life presence in Indian-administered J & K. The political ideology of the Jamaat-i-Islami was unable to importune the electorate and secured just 1 seat. The fairness of the 1977 election has been highlighted by many political analysts: it offset the preposterous elections held in Indian-administered J & K between 1951 and 1972. Democratic elections, the installation of a representative government, and the forging of a political space that accommodated multiple ideologies contributed to the creation of a nonrepressive, relatively stable political atmosphere (Bose 2003: 90).

Sheikh Mohammad Abdullah addresses a mammoth gathering at the historic Lal Chowk in Srinagar, 1975. (*Courtesy*: The Archives of the National Conference, with the permission of the general secretary of the National Conference, Sheikh Nazir Ahmad)

Dynastic Politics within the National Conference

After this victory of magnified proportions, Abdullah remained in office until he died on 8 September 1982. In 1981, shortly before his death, Abdullah, contrary to his socialist politics, presided over the "coronation" of his oldest son, Farooq Abdullah, as president of the NC. This act perpetuated the subcontinental tradition of dynastic politics. The trauma of incarceration, political persecution, ill health, and age had substantially reduced the magnificence of the "Lion of Kashmir" when he assumed office in 1975. But his leonine stature and formidable roar intimidated New Delhi until the day he died and left an ineradicable mark on the political and cultural matrix of the state. Ian Copeland (1991: 246) articulates the political and cultural authority enjoyed by Abdullah in the state: "Despite the best efforts of the Pakistani authorities to discredit him before the UN, the Sheikh remained, in the world's eyes, the personification of Kashmiri nationalism, and in the end the Pakistanis had to come to terms with that fact."

Although the NC was founded on socialist principles, the centralization that occurred in the organization toward the late 1970s did not enable the engendering of a second generation of mature and responsible leadership. The "enthroning" of a new generation of leaders within the NC for whom the symbols of the 1930s were insignificant and who did not identify with Abdullah's rhetoric fueled an already explosive situation toward the end of the 1980s. Subsequent to Abdullah's death, even those who had vehemently condemned the political strategies that he had deployed during his three decades as the voice of Kashmiri self-determination assessed his politics applaudingly. An old associate of his who had migrated to Pakistan, Shahnawaz Khan Niazi, describes what he thought Abdullah symbolized:

> Sheikh Abdullah was a total idealist and his only interest was the best deal he could get for Kashmir and Kashmiris. His often repeated statement to me was that destiny had played an important role, that circumstances were such that they did not permit him to come to an understanding with Pakistan. Every small opportunity he got to make a point or establish the separate identity of Kashmiris he took. (Quoted in Taseer 1986: 67)

Despite the furious opposition of his detractors and the relentless efforts of the governments of India and Pakistan to delimit Abdullah's sphere of influence, and to dismantle the paradigmatic political and cultural structures built by him, his significance as the symbol of Kashmir's unique cultural identity and its stentorian demand for self-determination remains indelible.

Chapter Four

Militarization of Jammu and Kashmir

Sheikh Mohammad Abdullah's disillusionment with Indian democracy and his dismal reassessment of India's proclamation of republicanism, secularism, and democracy proved uncannily prophetic. After Abdullah's untimely death on 8 September 1982, the National Conference (NC) was led by his oldest son, Farooq Abdullah, until 2002, when he chose to step down as president of the party. In a curious turn of events since then, however, the NC nominated Farooq Abdullah as its chief ministerial candidate for the 2008 assembly elections. Subsequent to Sheikh Mohammad Abdullah's death, Farooq Abdullah took over as head of government and led the NC to a resounding victory in the assembly elections in 1983. At that point in India's political history, Indira Gandhi was attempting to bolster her political platform by making overt and covert appeals to Hindu majoritarianism against grossly exaggerated secessionist threats from Muslim and Sikh minorities (for a thorough discussion of Hindu majoritarianism, see Bose 1997). Indira Gandhi's mobilization of Hindu fanaticism worked wonders for the Congress in the Jammu region, where it won 22 out of 32 assembly seats. But the performance of the Congress in the Muslim-dominated Kashmir Valley was dismal, where it won just 3 seats, and 1 in Ladakh. The NC had another landslide victory in the Valley, winning 35 out of 41 assembly seats. The NC also won 7 seats in the Jammu region and 1 in Ladakh, enabling it to form the state government with the Congress as a large opposition. But Indira Gandhi did not accept the unambiguous verdict given by the people of Kashmir in a democratic fashion. Her ire was particularly provoked by the alliance that the NC formed with other Indian parties in an attempt to unify anti-Congress forces as preparation for the parliamentary elections in late 1984. By forging such a relationship with the opposition parties, Farooq was subverting a tacit clause in the 1975 Delhi agreement that had enabled Sheikh Mohammad Abdullah's release, according to which the NC would make no attempt to undermine Congress rule at the central government in exchange for the Congress government's noninterference in the political supremacy of the NC in Indian-administered J & K. In order to quell Farooq's declaration of autonomy, Indira Gandhi resorted to undemocratic and unconstitutional means as his government approached the end of its first year in 1984. The Congress government in New Delhi orchestrated the formation of a new political party, comprising twelve NC legislators who unconstitutionally quit their party and formed a new government with the support of the Congress legislators in the J & K Assembly. The leader of this break-away faction was Sheikh Mohammad Abdullah's older son-in-law, Ghulam Mohammad Shah, who had cast his lot with Abdullah in the heyday of the Plebiscite Front (PF).

Dismissal of the Farooq Government and Installation of the Shah Government

Ghulam Mohammad Shah, unlike Farooq, was not a political green-horn, and he had nurtured ambitions of being Abdullah's successor. Ministerships were bestowed on the twelve NC defectors in the new government. Farooq Abdullah wrote as follows about this plot hatched by the Congress prime minister of India, Indira Gandhi:

> ...the Congress high command decided to work for my downfall through disgruntled elements in my party [National Conference] who were already in league with Mrs G.M. Shah [Farooq's older sister]. The plan to overthrow my government was given final shape on 23 June 1984....The conspiracy had been hatched and the blueprint drawn up in 1 Safdarjang Road, New Delhi [Prime Minister Indira Gandhi's official residence]. The cast which performed as directed was presided over by Mrs Gandhi, who was the director and producer. (F. Abdullah 1985: 8)

As the old adage goes, those who forget history are condemned to repeat it, and Farooq had to pay a heavy price for having forgotten New Delhi's treatment of his father. The 1984 coup de grâce was reminiscent of the 1953 coup d'état. Farooq's appeal for fresh elections was denied by Indian-administered J & K's New Delhi–appointed governor, Jagmohan.

The dismissal of the Farooq government was perceived as a blow to the morale of the Kashmir people who had placed him on the political pedestal previously occupied by his father. I recall that divisive period as being a particularly difficult one for my maternal grandmother, Begum Akbar Jehan, and also for my mother, Suraiya Ali Matto.

They were devastated by the rift in the family and were painfully torn apart. In a society in which relationships are hierarchically structured and kinship ties determine loyalties, my maternal grandmother felt obligated to be loyal to her older son, the purportedly "legitimate" heir apparent despite his inefficacious administration. The protests that ensued in the Valley were brutally repressed by detachments of the Central Reserve Police Force (CRPF) and Indian paramilitary forces, which were flown surreptitiously from Delhi to Srinagar the night before the coup (conversations with the family in Kashmir, 2007). Salman Rushdie (1991: 43), in a display of political acumen, observed:

> The growth of Hindu fanaticism, as evidenced by the increasing strength of the RSS, the organization which was behind the assassination of Mahatma Gandhi, has been very worrying; and it has had its parallel...in the increased support for the Muslim extremist Jamaat Party in Kashmir—the support being, itself, the result of the toppling of Farooq Abdullah by the Centre [the central government], which seemed to legitimize the Jamaat's view that Muslims have no place in present-day India.

The beginning of representative government in Indian-administered J & K (in 1977) was summarily destroyed in 1984.

The shoddy dismissal of Farooq's government engineered by New Delhi's political bigwigs showed a callous disregard for the wishes and aspirations of the Kashmiri people, and brought political apathy in its wake. Later that year, India's parliamentary elections were held. Indira Gandhi's Congress, led by her older son Rajiv Gandhi, availed itself of the sympathy wave created in the wake of Indira's assassination by her two Sikh bodyguards on 31 October 1984, and won by an overwhelming majority. But all three parliamentary constituencies in the Kashmir Valley, Srinagar, Baramulla, and Anantnag, elected NC representatives with enormous majorities. The Congress won the two parliamentary seats from the Jammu region and one from Ladakh, but overall the NC made a wonderful recovery and a palpable dent in New Delhi's heinous designs (Akhtar 2000: 32). In 1986, the Congress government at the central government dismissed the G.M. Shah government and Governor Jagmohan took over as the representative of the central government and effective ruler of Indian-administered J & K. The rationale given by New Delhi to replace Shah with Jagmohan was the breakdown of the law and order machinery. This political move, in which Kashmiri politicians were shunted around like pawns, destroyed political autonomy and created institutional paralysis. During this election, the Farooq-led NC was ferociously opposed by Rajiv Gandhi's Congress. Quite a few writers on Kashmir have summarized the destructive effect of the policies deployed by New Delhi and India's political and military interference in the state during that fateful decade of the 1980s.

Ramifications of Despotic Gubernatorial Politics

Jagmohan, the governor imposed by New Delhi on the people of Indian-administered J & K, was adept at carrying out the oppressive policies of his patrons to a tee. He was responsible for the attempted extirpation of the secular Jammu and Kashmir Liberation Front (JKLF), which adhered to the ideology of an independent Kashmir. The incarceration and torture of its leader, Maqbool Bhat, occurred during Jagmohan's reign. Physical brutality began to be unapologetically employed as a tool for psychological degradation. Young Kashmiri men were arrested on suspicion and mercilessly tortured and killed by Indian soldiers. Kashmiri women, irrespective of age, were defiled and humiliated. This state-sponsored brutality boomeranged with young men subscribing to a form of militant nationalism and willy-nilly taking up arms to fight the Indian state (Ali 2003: 246). In late 1986 Farooq Abdullah conceded defeat by forging an alliance with the Congress party at the central government. The creation of this alliance was a death knell for regional political aspirations and cultural pride. Farooq's attempt to establish harmonious relationships with the Congress regime was met with contempt and derision by NC's popular base, but enabled his installation as head of government pending fresh assembly elections in March 1987. His capitulation to New Delhi created a deep rift between the NC and its mass following. Elections were held in Indian-administered J & K in 1987 in order to constitute a legislative assembly and a state government. By then the NC had managed to alienate its popular base and represented only the interests of a powerful political elite.

During the 1987 elections, the NC was opposed by an unwieldy coalition of nonmainstream, antiestablishment groups calling itself the Muslim United Front (MUF). It was a conglomerate that lacked structure and a unifying political ideology. However, as the newsmagazine *India Today* (31 March 1987: 26) observed during the campaign, the emergence of the MUF indicated that "the Valley is sharply divided between the party machine that brings out the traditional

vote for the NC, and hundreds of thousands who have entered politics as participants for the first time under the umbrella provided by
the MUF." As I mentioned previously, the MUF comprised several
political organizations. Its main component was the Jamaat-i-Islami,
chaired by Syed Ali Shah Geelani. Despite having participated in the
1972, 1977, and 1983 elections, and as part of the MUF conglomerate in the 1987 elections, the Jamaat had been unable to make a
mark on the political matrix of Indian-administered J & K. It had,
however, succeeded in making an impact in religious institutions
where young boys were indoctrinated by mullahs, which Sheikh
Mohammad Abdullah had attempted to quell by closing down places
of religious education (Verma 1994: 74). In addition, Abdul Ghani
Lone's People's Conference, G.M. Shah's breakaway NC faction, the
Awami National Conference, and Maulvi Farooq's Awami Action
Committee expressed unity of opinion, purpose, or interest with the
MUF. The ideological or experiential solidarity among a large number of opposition parties presented a formidable front. In the 1987
elections, the people of Kashmir unanimously expressed their wish
to elect a party that would redress their grievances and nurture their
aspirations (interview by the author with political activists of the
National Conference and independent candidates, Kashmir, 2007).
The emphasis laid by the MUF on Kashmiri nationalism and cultural
pride enabled it to woo a large number of Kashmiri youth. The MUF
underlined its ultimate objective of working toward Islamic unity
and disallowing political interference from the Indian government in
New Delhi (Verma 1994: 159). But New Delhi was not willing to let
antiestablishment organizations rule the roost in a state in which it
could exercise power only through proxy. As reported in *India Today*
(15 April 1987), the 1987 elections were characterized by heavy rig-
ging and booth capturing. The lower bureaucracy administering
the voting and counting processes worked brazenly in favor of the
Congress–NC alliance. The predictable outcome was the landslide
victory of this alliance, which won 63 seats and formed the state government without hindrance. This instance of the egregious erosion
of democratic processes and institutions worked to the advantage of
the Congress Party, which had been unable to form a mass base in
Kashmir and had traditionally been perceived as the arch opponent of
Kashmiri nationalism and cultural pride. There was an exponential
rise of fundamentalist forces in the Kashmir Valley during this period
(Balraj Puri, quoted in Verma 1994: 141). However, while the resurgence of religious fanaticism may have provided the disgruntled youth
of Indian-administered J & K with an ideological bastion, Islamist

organizations in the Valley were unable to convince Shah's Awami National Conference and Lone's People's Party of the viability of forming a theocratic state.

Faulty Electoral Processes

The 1987 elections tarnished the reputation of the Farooq-led NC and showcased it as a marionette that could be manipulated by New Delhi's seasoned puppeteers. The methods deployed in this election exacerbated the mood of sullenness and political apathy in the Valley. Farooq Abdullah's regional credibility was jeopardized by his willingness to kowtow to political strategists and gurus in New Delhi. Armed struggle gained impetus in the Kashmir Valley once the populace was disabused of the notions of regional integrity and autonomy it had once held. The subversive acts engineered by the JKLF in 1988 prognosticated political wreckage of extraordinary proportions. The disenchantment caused by dictats issued by the Indian government spawned resistance factions in various parts of Indian-administered J & K. "The JKLF, however, was singled out by the Indian authorities as being mainly responsible for the upsurge in internal disorder" (Schofield 2002: 140).

In the late 1980s, anti-India sentiments in the Kashmir Valley engendered uncritical support for Pakistan. While forty-one years of independence were being fervently celebrated in the rest of India on 15 August, the Valley resonated with sounds of lamentation about its fate: "Whereas in 1947 the Pakistanis were deemed the invaders whilst the Indians were greeted as the liberators, by 1988 in the minds of the militants the roles had been psychologically reversed" (ibid.). On 11 April 1988 in Ojhri in Pakistan, several people were killed in an ammunition dump that had been used as a depot for arms intended for Afghan rebels. In order to express their solidarity with Pakistan, zealous pro-Pakistanis in the Valley coerced shopkeepers to keep their shops shut for a day as a symbolic gesture of sympathy for those killed. This day of mourning was marked by instances of clashes with the police, vandalism, arson, and brandishing of pro-Pakistan feelings. In the wake of these events, Indian nationalist parties critical of the inefficacy of the Farooq-led government demanded his resignation (ibid.). Thus, as the decade of the 1990s dawned, the Kashmir Valley became a playground for Indian military and paramilitary forces, as well as for innumerable resistance factions that toed different ideological lines. The hitherto torpid Valley began to shake with a thunderous energy that would cause the complacency of the governments of India and Pakistan to teeter, and would expose their complicity in the neglect of the peoples of the former princely state of J & K.

Beginning of Armed Insurgency

The disillusionment and sense of disenfranchisement created by New Delhi's machinations and the collusion of Farooq's regime with it generated a new phenomenon. A large number of young men from various parts of the Kashmir Valley crossed the Line of Control (LOC) in search of ammunition and combat training. Sumantra Bose (2003) eloquently outlines the gist of the contemporary problem in Kashmir: a conflict driven by nationalistic and religious fervor, with each side pointing to the violence and injustice of the other, and each side pointing to its own suffering and sorrow. The distrust, paranoia, and neurosis permeating the relationship between a large number of people of Indian-administered J & K and the Indian Union had intensified the conflict. Kashmir, which to most outsiders was a becalming tourist haven, had been engulfed by the conflagration of armed insurgency. "The armed insurgency which gathered momentum after the 1987 election caught the rest of the world unawares" (Schofield 2002: 138).

The guerrilla war in the state has gone through a series of phases since 1990, but repressive military and political force remains the brutal reality, which cannot be superseded by seemingly abstract democratic aspirations (see Bose 2003). After the forces of separatism reared their heads in Indian-administered J & K, the Indian Union exacerbated the violence and disorder by deploying tactless means. For instance, on 1 October 1990, Indian paramilitary forces razed the bazaar of Handwara, a town located in the northwestern part of the Valley. This action, taken after a guerrilla attack, resulted in the indiscriminate killing of a large number of civilians. Ever since that reprehensible incident, the town has been garrisoned by Indian military and paramilitary troops. The landscape has been tarnished by shanty-like bunkers with firing positions adorned with Indian flags and nationalist slogans, underlining the brutal repression of regionalist and antiestablishment aspirations. Despite the conspicuous presence of Indian police and military forces, however, the dense forests of Handwara have provided a safe haven for the guerrilla fighters and have enabled them to wage a constant subversive war against the Indian army, which was heavily deployed in that area (ibid.: 138).

Unfortunately, systemic erosion of democratic rights in Indian-administered J & K has been the underlying theme of India's policy toward Kashmir since the dawn of independence in 1947.

While the popularity of the NC was steadily diminishing, a new phenomenon was emerging in Indian-administered J & K in 1988. A large number of young men had gone across the LOC, supposedly of their own volition, in order to acquire arms and combat training to fight for the cause of Kashmiri independence. On 31 July 1988, bomb explosions occurred outside Srinagar's central telegraph office and at the Srinagar Club, an establishment for the political and business elite of the state. Although the attacks were launched by young Kashmiri men trained across the LOC, they had been planned by Mohammad Rauf Kashmiri, a Pakistani member of the JKLF, an organization committed to regaining the independent status of J & K (conversation with political activists of the National Conference and the Congress, Kashmir Valley, 2007). To reinforce the point that I made earlier, events that were celebrated in the rest of India were overtly mourned in Kashmir: 15 August (the day India gained independence in 1947) and 26 January (India's Republic Day in 1950) were occasions that evoked a resentful and pain-filled response in the Valley, creating a paralysis of sorts.

Unfortunately, Farooq Abdullah's response to this new phenomenon and its ramifications was not particularly diplomatic. He resorted to belligerent tactics: invoking the political and economic support of New Delhi and antagonizing the Kashmiri people, who did not see a ray of hope in New Delhi (see Puri 1995). As the insurgency began to spread its tentacles, the authority of the Farooq-led government began to slacken and it experienced a progressive political decline. The hallmark of Farooq Abdullah's second term in office, which lasted until January 1990, was a sense of unaccountability. His behavior during this term was described as a virtual renunciation of authority vested in him (*India Today* 30 April 1990: 10). Veteran journalist and author of *Sheikh Mohammad Abdullah: Tragic Hero of Kashmir*, Ajit Bhattacharjea has critically analyzed Farooq's political prowess: "The last symbol of secular Kashmiriyat remained a lightweight given to helicopter sorties over the stricken Valley, to elitist projects to attract tourists, while basic facilities were ignored" (Bhattacharjea 1994: 257). Farooq gained the reputation of a sybarite and a connoisseur of luxury. His cabinet acquired a reputation for unaccountability.

In November 1989, another Indian parliamentary election was held in Indian-administered J & K, which the JKLF and other proindependence groups asked the populace to boycott. The electorate responded by abstaining, resulting in an overwhelming victory for the NC. The NC won unopposed in Srinagar, and in Baramulla and Anantnag, the other two parliamentary constituencies in the Valley, it won enormous victories. Although the NC ostensibly represented the Kashmir people and was accountable to them, a large proportion of the state's population was not just alienated but palpably antagonistic toward New Delhi: the political history of Indian-administered J & K is replete with examples of political dogmatism, repression, undemocratic methods, and state-sanctified brutality. Representative governments installed though democratic processes existed in J & K in 1947–1953 and 1977–1984. Otherwise the territory has been benighted by reprehensible misgovernance and trammeled by a militarized culture.

By the late 1990s the purportedly secular policies of the Congress had been replaced by the Hindu nationalist politics of the Bharatiya Janata Party (BJP). In the Kashmir Valley, Islamist groups mushroomed as Afghan mercenaries came across the border to perpetuate the reign of terror. The main rival organizations during that period were the homegrown Hizb-ul-Mujahideen (HM), the Pakistani-sponsored and abetted Lashkar-i-Taiba, and Harkat-ul-Mujahidin (interview with political activists of the National Conference and independent candidates, Kashmir, 2007). These groups assassinated each other's militants—HM and JKLF were belligerently opposed to each other, kidnapped Western tourists in order to extort money or for political mileage, harassed Kashmiri Pandits who had been an inextricable part of the region for centuries, took punitive action against Kashmiri Muslims who did not subscribe to their ideology, and organized subversive action against Indian forces and officials. Some contend that these groups did not target Kashmiri Pandits because of their religious affiliation or secular Muslims because of their ideological affiliation, but state agents. The factionalism in these groups enabled New Delhi to create gulfs between them, which disallowed them from joining hands in order to defeat the designs of the Indian administration and forces. Some of the Islamist groups in this region are the creation of Pakistani military intelligence (Ali 2003: 251). Governor Jagmohan employed ruthless measures to pulverize the support that these Islamist groups had managed to garner: nightlong house-to-house raids became the norm. Indian soldiers kidnapped young men at gunpoint only to barbarously torture and kill them in custody (ibid.: 247). Jagmohan's autocratic rule and the tyranny of the Afghan mercenaries resulted in the militarization of Kashmiri culture and the torture of hapless Kashmiri civilians. The sense of disenfranchisement in Kashmir was aggravated by New Delhi's rule, which lasted until 1996 when the Farooq Abdullah NC came back to power. But Farooq's collaboration with the Hindu fundamentalist BJP further eroded the mass base of the NC.

Indian-administered J & K is an example of a neocolonial territory manipulated by New Delhi in collusion with comprador governments unrepresentative of the populace, and reliant on the political and military prowess of their patrons. This policy appears to have been formulated to circumscribe anti-India and pro-Pakistan allegiances. This strategy, however, has had the adverse effect of stunting the development of democratic and civic structures conducive to suffrage and participatory procedures. The conscious policy of the Indian state to erode autonomy, populist measures, and democratic institutions in J & K has further alienated the people of the state from the "demonic" Indian Union (Bose 2003: 97–98). The erosion of political opposition in Indian-administered J & K has delegitimized the voice of dissent and radicalized antagonism toward state-sponsored institutions and organizations. The exposure of Indian democracy as a brutal façade has instigated disgruntlement and antipathy toward Indian democratic procedures and institutions in the state. The cause of the independence and/or autonomy of J & K has been thwarted by both India and Pakistan. Beijing is also worried about the ramifications that Kashmiri independence would have in Tibet. In India, the BJP has been deviously planning the balkanization of Indian-administered J & K along religioethnic lines, first propounded in 1950 by Sir Owen Dixon, the United Nations representative for India and Pakistan, which I have written about in chapter one.

In its initial years, Sheikh Mohammad Abdullah's NC enabled the emergence of a well-educated, politically aware generation of Kashmiris. But in the 1970s and the 1980s, Indira Gandhi's Congress regime characterized every demand for local empowerment as potentially insurgent, and discouraged the growth of a progressive generation of Kashmiris (Ganguly 1997: 84–85; Kohli 1997: 341–42; Rai 2004: 295). Sheikh Abdullah's strategic campaign to free the former princely state of J & K from the systemic violence perpetrated by the Dogra monarchy, which was launched in the early 1930s, had won strong support from the Kashmiri people, including the women. As Kashmiri historian Mohammad Ishaq Khan (1978: 192) is quick to point out, "13 July 1931 was a historic day in the annals of Srinagar. The 'dumb-driven cattle' raised the standard of revolt....Even the women joined the struggle and to them belongs the honor of facing cavalry charges in Srinagar's Maisuma bazaar." That political awareness manifested itself again in 1989–1990 when masses of women bolstered the JKLF's campaign to free J & K from Indian rule in the labyrinthine lanes of Srinagar city.

Militant Resistance to the Indian Administration

The rebellion that had been simmering in 1989–1990 soon erupted into a conflagration in 1990, in brutal resistance to Indian occupation in the Kashmir Valley. Assassinations of individuals suspected of being Indian spies occurred in large numbers toward the end of 1989. Such killings atrophied the government machinery and rendered its intelligence apparatus dysfunctional. Contrary to the belief in mainstream Indian political and civil circles, approximately three-fourths of the victims, comprising political or social bigwigs accused of collaborating with Indian forces, alleged spies, and local politicians who had either tacitly or overtly supported J & K's accession to India, were Muslims. The rest were Kashmiri Pandits, members of the privileged and comprador Hindu minority (Bose et al. 1991: 224–53). The parliamentary elections that were held in Indian-administered J & K in late November 1989 were boycotted by a large section of the population, rendering the process a sham.

In December 1989, Rubaiya, the daughter of Mufti Mohammad Sayeed, the Kashmiri Muslim Interior Affairs minister in India's federal cabinet and chief minister of Indian-administered J & K from 2002 until 2005, was kidnapped by militants of the JKLF. This incident manifested a growing malignancy in a culture that had prided itself on shielding its women from political and religious turbulence, and caused fear in the hearts and minds of young women all over the Valley. I recall the tangible tension and loaded silence in the examination hall at the Government College for Women where I was taking my British Literature examination the day after Rubaiya was kidnapped. Her captors demanded the release of six high-profile JKLF activists then in incarceration. Rubaiya Sayeed was kept in captivity until the government of India succumbed to the demands of her captors. The six JKLF activists who were released were welcomed by numerous Srinagar residents with happiness and triumph, undeterred by the Indian troops. The inability of the redoubtable government of India to work toward a resolution that did not require succumbing to political machinations and coercive force was incomprehensible, to say the least. Its choice to tread the path of least resistance bolstered the courage of organizations that deployed kidnappings, extortions, killings, and other violent methods as their modus operandi. In January 1990, Farooq Abdullah's defanged government resigned, citing a breakdown of civil order as the rationale.

Subsequently, J & K was brought under the direct rule of New Delhi. Jagmohan, who had played a treacherous role in J & K between 1984 and 1986, was sent back to Srinagar to govern with reinforced high-handedness and unaccountability (conversations with political activists and other civilians in Kashmir Valley, 2007). Huge demonstrations in support of independence surfaced in every part of the Valley. It was as if the unspoken urge for self-rule, lost among the debris of dismantled insurrectionist resolves, began to collect and cohere to form the certainty of this political demand. The cry for independence pierced the stifling atmosphere, and people marched with abandon along the uneven streets of various parts of the Valley. The rallying cry of independence galvanized people from all walks of life. In a gesture of defiance, adolescent boys and girls pelted stones at the well-equipped Indian military and paramilitary forces. The response of the Indian administration to the vociferous resurgence of this insurrectionary force was the implementation of bloodcurdling repressive measures. The state-sponsored violence in the Valley escalated between July and September 1990 after the Indian government legislated an Armed Forces Special Powers Act and a Disturbed Areas Act that reinforced the barbarism of Indian military and paramilitary troops, and legitimized the violence and reprisal unleashed by them.

> From our investigations...we found that the paramilitary forces and the Army jawans [soldiers] had no excuse of self-defence [*sic*] [as normally given when dealing with riotous mobs] when they fired indiscriminately upon what were crowds of unarmed demonstrators. A savage thirst for blood seemed to have gripped the CRPF, as evident from the calculated manner in which they went about pumping bullets into bodies of injured people in the Gow Kadal [Srinagar] area on 21 January 1990. The brutalities perpetrated by the Army jawans on 1 March 1990, call for serious disciplinary action against them. Attempts by the army authorities to justify their killing of bus passengers at Tengpora [Kashmir] on that day by inventing a false story, are a further blot on the country's defense forces who are required to be highly disciplined cadre dedicated to the task of protecting our people. (Bose et al. 1991: 233)

The attempt of the Indian administration to represent the Kashmiri as a fanatical terrorist is indicative of political and military discourses of exclusion that rely on tightly drawn boundaries to maintain the "authenticity," or purity, of their respective discourse. The Kashmiri, by his or her status as a secessionist traitor, served to reaffirm draconian authority that required opposition in order to assert itself.

Initially, the insurgent demand for autonomy resonated just through the Kashmir Valley, reminiscent of the 1930s and 1940s when the Valley had been festooned with the pennants of the NC, streaking the sky with the color of liberation. The political rebellion of these two organizations was forcefully reiterated by the JKLF in the early 1990s in the Valley. The JKLF's unwavering commitment to the discourse of an independent state antagonized the Pakistani military's Inter-Services Intelligence (ISI), which abruptly withdrew its economic and political support to the organization (for the secular formation of the separatist group JKLF, see Khan 1970). As a retaliatory measure, the ISI patronized and facilitated the establishment of two pro-Pakistan organizations, Al-Umar Mujahideen and Ikhwan-ul-Muslimeen, which deployed guerrilla tactics to perpetrate a reign of assassinations and unbridled terror. The ISI also enabled the entrenchment of bigoted Islamic groups such as Harkat-ul-Ansar and Hizb-ul-Mujahideen (HM) in the Valley (interview with political activists of the National Conference and People's Democratic Party, Srinagar, 2007). The strategies employed by these organizations and their pro-Pakistan leanings created a generation of trigger-happy youth, engendering a malignant gun culture in the Valley. The fanaticism of the HM led to an upsurge of violence in the Valley. The rising strength of pro-Pakistani guerrilla outfits caused marginalization of the JKLF. Sporadic disagreements leading to violent clashes between the JKLF and the HM occurred in 1991 and 1992 in various parts of the Valley. The HM had an uncontested dominance over the Islamist and pro-Pakistan outfits in the Kashmir Valley. In the early part of the insurgency, the HM claimed that its employment of guerrilla strategies would render Indian-administered J & K impregnable for the Indian military and paramilitary forces, intern the Indian forces in their restrictive camps, and make them vulnerable. This spurious claim impaired the credibility of the HM, particularly after the increasing factionalism within the organization (ibid.). In the early part of 1992, the JKLF made an assiduous attempt to regain lost ground by organizing a march to the LOC to underscore the unity between Indian-administered J & K and Pakistani-administered J & K. The march was dispersed by Pakistani border troops who, firing indiscriminately, killed twenty-one marchers. This incident created a wave of sympathy for the JKLF, and 60,000 people convened at the Hazratbal shrine to express condemnation of the unwarranted show of strength by Pakistani forces, marking an overwhelming political victory for the JKLF (*India Today*, 31 March 1993: 27).

In 1993, over thirty political organizations joined hands to form a coalition group known as the All Parties Hurriyat Conference (APHC). The conglomerate comprised Syed Ali Shah Geelani of the Jamaat-e-Islami, Abdul Ghani Lone of the People's Conference, Maulvi Abbas Ansari of the Liberation Council, and Professor Abdul Ghani Bhat of the Muslim Conference (MC), and was headed by the then teen-aged religious leader of the Awami Action Committee, Maulvi Omar Farooq. The commonality that bound these politicians and religious leaders of disparate ideologies was the necessity to give the people of J & K the right of self-determination. The various components of the APHC were at loggerheads about whether independence was the most desirable solution for the troubled state, or whether unification with Pakistan was the better alternative. "The Hurriyat Conference gave the militants a united political platform through which they could voice their grievances, but their demands did not permit them to consider a solution which lay within the existing framework of the Indian Union" (Schofield 2002: 60). The APHC has since been joined by the leader of a breakaway faction of the JKLF, Yasin Malik. While most of the other components of the conglomerate lean toward unification with Pakistan, Malik tenaciously adheres to JKLF's ideology of independence for the former princely state. A leader of one of the core groups of the APHC, Abdul Ghani Lone was assassinated in 2002 by the Lashkar-i-Taiba. Another unyielding Islamist member of the organization, Syed Ali Shah Geelani, severed ties with the APHC after Maulvi Omar Farooq seemed to do a volte-face by beseeching the militant factions to adopt a more reconciliatory approach. It is necessary to point out here that Geelani was a member of the J & K Legislative Assembly from 1972 to 1977, 1977 to 1982, and 1987 to 1990. During his three tenures as a member of the assembly, Geelani was not quite as vociferous about the illegitimacy of the accession of J & K to the Indian Union, nor did he publicly prioritize the autonomy of the state. The Omar Farooq-led APHC has been vacillating about its political stance vis-à-vis the status of the state, equivocating between reversion to the pre-1953 autonomous status of Indian-administered J & K within the Constitution of India as the most expedient solution to the Kashmir conflict, and the unacceptability of any solution within the said Constitution. Despite the participation of its leadership in various international forums, the seemingly bona fide intentions of the organization have come under severe scrutiny, and political analysts as well as laypeople have leveled allegations of corruption and complicity with the law-enforcing agencies of both India and Pakistan.

Pakistan's attempt to chart the course of the insurrection created paranoia in the Valley and was resented by JKLF supporters. By the mid-1990s, the HM had become notorious for targeting not just JKLF's proindependence supporters, but also members of nondescript militant groups. Many ex-militants, renegades or *baaghee*, and their families sought security—physical, financial, and otherwise—through collaboration with Indian counterinsurgency forces. The emergence of such collaborators, who were incorporated into the Special Task Force (STF)—a militia group comprising renegades that I have written about in chapter five—bolstered India's military and political campaign against Kashmiri insurgents and Pakistani infiltrators. Although the government of Pakistan did not explicitly avow the legitimacy of insurgency in Indian-administered J & K in terms of acknowledging its financial and military support in the armed conflict, the perception in India was that Pakistan supported the insurgency through its formidable intelligence agency, the ISI. This common perception was created by the recognition of the centrality of the Kashmir issue to the theocratic and nationalistic identity of Pakistan (Desmond 1995: 15).

Communal Turn of the Insurgency

The communal turn taken by the insurgency in the state was exacerbated with the grisly murder of sixteen Hindu men who were taken off a bus on their way to Jammu and killed at point-blank range in August 1993. In September 1989, a Kashmiri Pandit, Tikka Lal Taploo, was brutally killed; he was an advocate of the High Court and a leader of the Hindu nationalist BJP. Soon after this incident, another Kashmiri Pandit, Neel Ganth Ganju, was remorselessly killed. Ganju was a retired sessions judge who had passed the death sentence on the iconicized founder of the JKLF, Maqbool Bhat (Schofield 2002: 144). Reports of the desecration of women by militants did much to besmirch their image. In 1990, a Kashmiri Pandit nurse at the Sher-i-Kashmir Institute of Medical Sciences, Srinagar, Sarla Bhat, was reportedly raped and killed by JKLF militants for having informed the police/state authorities about injured militants at the Medical Institute. Rita Manchanda, whose politics are ambiguous, quotes Kashmiri Pandit sources, according to whom Sarla Bhat had the acronym "JKLF" inscribed on her naked torso ("Guns and Burqaa," 2001: 62). Asia Watch reported that while it was unclear that militant leaders willfully permitted such abuses, there was little indication that they had taken substantive action to prevent such gruesome incidents. Some of the victims and their families were accused of being police informers, and the brutal humiliation of these women was a tool wielded to wreak revenge and silence the detractors of militant organizations (Asia Watch 1993: 98). In 1995, a group of Western tourists was kidnapped by an obscure militant outfit, Al-Farhan. One of the tourists, a Norwegian, was decapitated; one of the Americans in the group surreptitiously escaped; and the whereabouts of the other three are unknown to date. Proindependence and proautonomy organizations in the Valley are of the opinion that this gruesome incident, like the mass exodus of Kashmiri Pandits, was orchestrated by the Indian government to tarnish the insurrection in J & K, and to pigeonhole it as zealot and talibanized. By 1996–1997, the coercive tactics employed by Indian counterinsurgency forces had successfully emasculated most of the guerrilla outfits and rendered the JKLF a moribund organization.

In 2000 the HM restored its damaged organizational ethos by engineering and executing a series of attacks reminiscent of the guerrilla tactics used by them in the 1990s, but with escalating violence. These attacks were clearly designed to instigate communal dissension in Indian-administered J & K and to maintain the tenuousness of the India–Pakistan rapprochement. The chilling and horrifying phenomenon of suicide bombing had surfaced in the state in 1999 and mounted in hostility in the early 2000s. The first suicide attack occurred in August 1999 when militants of the Lashkar-i-Taiba, a group purportedly consisting of ultraorthodox Muslims from Pakistan but believed by many Kashmiri locals to be working in collusion with Indian paramilitary forces, stormed a Border Security Force (BSF) post in the Kupwara district. The official estimate is that since then fifty suicide attacks have occurred in the Kashmir Valley, of which twenty-nine took place in 2001. While most of the attacks have occurred in the Valley, the suicide bombers have made their mark in the Jammu region and in Delhi as well. A suicide squad of the Lashkar-i-Taiba launched a bloody attack on an army garrison positioned inside the Red Fort in Delhi on 22 December 2001 (Ramachandran 2002). The demand for autonomy made a foray into the Jammu region in the 1990s. In August 2002, an army colonel supervising counterinsurgency operations was killed in a mine blast in the Doda district in Jammu. This attack was attributed to HM operatives in the area (*Kashmir Times*, 20 August 2002).

Toward the end of 2002 the Indian government, tarnished by the widespread and condemnable allegations of human rights abuses by its military and paramilitary forces, organized assembly elections in the state in order to form a new state government. I was in the Kashmir Valley a couple of months before that election, in which the NC suffered a miserable and humiliating defeat. The first phase of the elections covered constituencies in Baramullah and Kupwara in the Kashmir Valley, Rajouri and Poonch in Jammu, and Leh and Kargil in Ladakh; the second phase covered constituencies in Srinagar and Badgam in Kashmir Valley and Jammu; the third phase covered constituencies in Pulwama and Anantnag in the Kashmir Valley, and Udumpur and Kathua in Jammu; and the fourth phase of the elections covered constituencies in Doda in the Jammu division. The voter turnout in most constituencies was dismal, and demonstrations in favor of autonomy and against integration into the Indian Union were held at several places. The NC performed poorly, winning 9 out of 37 assembly seats in Jammu, 18 out of 46 seats in the Kashmir Valley and 1 out of 4 seats in Ladakh. The Congress secured 15 seats in Jammu and 5 in the Valley. In a curious turn of events, the Hindu nationalist BJP was able to secure just 1 seat in the predominantly Hindu Jammu province. National and local newspapers reported despicable attempts at intimidation and coercion by Indian paramilitary troops. According to a rather dubious claim by Indian authorities, voter turnout was 42.97 percent in Baramullah district, 54.57 percent in Kupwara district, 35.57 percent in Poonch, 44.94 percent in Rajouri, 76.89 percent in Kargil, 43.82 percent in Badgam, 12.83 percent in Srinagar, 60.19 percent in Jammu, 29.45 percent in Pulwama, 24.43 percent in Anantnag, 59.82 percent in Udumpur, 62.35 percent in Kathua, and 53.24 percent in Doda. These figures, however, included voters who were coerced to exercise their franchise. Interestingly, almost a million and a half citizens entitled to vote were just not registered and were therefore not included when estimating these figures. Apparently women did not participate either, in large numbers or enthusiastically (interview with observers of the electoral process in Kashmir, 2007). There were districts, however, in which the voting was impartially carried out. The politicization that was palpable in Kashmiri-speaking areas had not occurred in the predominantly Gujjar or Ladakhi constituencies, which did not harbor the antipathy toward the Indian state and its institutions that a large section of the Kashmiri Muslim population did.

Terrors of Counterinsurgency

More than a decade later, in 2010, the Valley remains the hub of counterinsurgent activity. In March 2008, for example, Farooq Ahmad Sheikh, resident of Sopur, Kashmir, was coercively detained by a cohort of policemen in civilian clothes. Fearing police savagery, his family made frenetic inquiries about his whereabouts. They were callously informed that he had drowned.

His wife had been mercilessly widowed and his once mollycoddled son was now a waif. The incessant wails heard in Farooq's house, begging salvation, the ineluctable disarray in the lives of his wife and child, plunged any democratic process in the Kashmir Valley into an unfathomable abyss (*Greater Kashmir*, 25 March 2008). In another incident in Sopur, Kashmir, students of the Sopur Degree College protested against the killing of a fellow student, Mohammad Ramzan Shah, by soldiers of the Indian army in an allegedly fake encounter. The police deployed unwarranted force to quell the protests and in the resulting violence, thirty people were injured (*Greater Kashmir*, 13 September 2007). In September 2007, twenty-five people were brutally beaten by Indian soldiers when they voiced their resentment against the reign of terror unleashed by Indian military and paramilitary forces in Graw Gund Kulpora, Pulwama, in south Kashmir. Residents of that area lamented the inhumane treatment meted out to them by the police and military personnel (*Greater Kashmir*, 13 September 2007).

In an unprecedented move, G.M. Shah's Awami NC petitioned the government of J & K to make substantive attempts to redress the violation of human rights and liberties in the state. Shah (president of the Awami NC) e-mailed the petition to me (2 April 2008), and I take the liberty of reproducing portions of it:

> The state of Jammu and Kashmir is in turmoil since 1989. People are mentally tormented and unsure of their future. Deeply humiliated by the excesses, human rights violations, unwarranted killings, kidnappings, rapes, and other inhuman atrocities under state terrorism through its police force and security agencies in the name of rule of law, peace and security, the people are at the receiving end. The people are witness to the on-going spectacle of deception and manipulation which has given rise to confusion, insecurity and cynicism. The situation is fraught with immense danger to the welfare of the state, its people and their identity. This situation has left hundreds of thousands of youth and others dead, displaced sections of the populace as refugees, and thousands are languishing in jails away from their homes. The anarchy and non-governance in the state should not lull

the government into further inaction. The present regime, instead of pulling the state out of its hopeless condition of violence and destruction has miserably failed in discharging its obligations toward lay people. The present chief minister of the state is avoiding his moral responsibility and obligations toward the people of the state by letting them suffer tyranny, anarchy and annihilation at the hand of police forces, security and other paramilitary agencies endowed with draconian authority. Kashmiris find themselves embroiled in a cruel and heartless campaign to make Kashmir an expendable pawn in the game of world politics. No worthwhile effort has been made to address the genuine grievances and just demands of the people. It is unbelievable that people of the subcontinent and the world once considered Kashmir as "heaven on earth." The place lies in shambles and the survival of the people at large has been jeopardized. Human rights abuses in the state have reached their peak and the security agencies have been given unbridled powers to deal with the populace in an arbitrary manner. These agencies are unaccountable for the acts which they have been carrying out since 1989 in Indian-administered J & K, as a result of which approximately one lakh people have lost their lives, thousands of crores worth of property has been destroyed, thousands of custodial deaths and rapes have taken place. Some details about human rights abuses which have occurred recently, are given below. On 27 Sept. 2007 Colonel Sharma and Major Azad of Rashtriya Rifles 33, along with a huge force, plundered the Magam, Kashmir, police station, snatched weapons, broke furniture, manhandled the local police personnel, and decamped with 20,000 rupees belonging to the state police. On 27 September 2007 Bilal Ahmad Bhat in Pulwama, Kashmir, was shot in cold blood after his refusal to hand over a box of apples to a Central Reserve Police Force trooper. On 14 October 2007 Abdul Rashid Mir, a teacher at Rehbar-i-Taleem in Rawatpora Kupwara, Kashmir, was killed while trying to protect a female colleague from being molested by army personnel. On 14 October 2007 a fifteen-year-old mentally retarded boy, Aqeel Ahmad Mir, was shot dead by the army in Watlab Sopore, Kashmir, for no fault of his. On 17 November 2007 Riyaz Ahmad Sofi was shot dead in Damal Hanjipora, Kashmir, by nine soldiers of the Rashtriya Rifles without any cause. Sofi leaves behind his widow and three children. On 16 December 2007 Imtiaz Ahmad and Mohammad Amin of the Special Operations Group tried to raze a house to the ground. After protests from local residents, they opened fire injuring scores of people and killing Ghulam Mohammad Lone on the spot. On 15 December 2007 Zahoor Ahmad Mir was killed when the police opened fire on peaceful demonstrators demanding establishment of a degree college in Magam, Kashmir.

Rights relating to life, liberty and dignity of the people, guaranteed by the Constitution, embodied in the fundamental covenants and enforceable by courts of law, are being gravely violated. It is respectfully requested that the recent killings brought to the notice of the honorable Human Rights Commission be investigated/enquired into through some impartial and credible agencies, subject to the direction and control of the Commission, under Section 15 (1&2) of the J & K Protection of Human Rights Act 1997. We further request the members of the Commission to visit jails and detention centers where thousands of innocent persons are languishing and make recommendations thereof. Considering the unified command consists of various police, security, military and paramilitary wings, including the Task Force, Central Reserve Police Force, Border Security Force, their respective commanders are collectively and individually responsible and legally liable for the gross violations, killings and all other human rights abuses committed against the people en masses. We request the Human Rights Commission to initiate appropriate criminal prosecution against persons found connected, directly or indirectly, or in abetment of the above crimes. ("Petition under Jammu and Kashmir Protection of Human Rights Act 1997, Chapter no. 111, Section 13")

Despite the sectarian and ethnic violence in Indian-administered J & K, the cultural syncretism of the state has managed to garner the strength of conviction to survive.

In 2002, a large number of Kashmiri Pandits participated in a festival held at a Hindu shrine, Khir Bhawani, in a village close to Srinagar, where they enjoyed the hospitality and protection of the Muslims in the area. This occasion marked the return of many migrant Pandits to the Kashmir Valley. This celebration was held after a pain-filled hiatus of eighteen years, and was conducted in a convivial atmosphere (Fazili *Tribune News Service* 2000). The representative organization of dislocated Kashmiri Pandits, Panun Kashmir Movement, which is riven by factionalism as well, now acknowledges that the exodus of their community in 1990 was orchestrated by the government of India (*Greater Kashmir*, 12 November 2007).

The administrators of India and Pakistan cannot remain steadily indifferent to requests from human rights organizations to probe into the instances of carnage that have been occurring in J & K since 1989–1990. How long will the blaring trumpet of "war on terror" sanctify the gauche attempts of the governments of India and Pakistan to blame every calamitous occurrence on foreign mercenaries?

Chapter Five

Negotiating the Boundaries of Gender, Community, and Nationhood

What are the traditional freedoms and prerogatives of Kashmiri women in the land of a spiritual luminary like Lalla-Ded? Is there any history of a substantive indigenous or modern feminist movement in Kashmir? Although, traditionally, women's experiences in situations of state-sponsored violence, armed insurgency, and counterinsurgency have been negated in narratives of dominant history, the recollection and interpretation of the lived experiences of the women I talked with in conflict-torn Indian-administered J & K showcase the nuances of women's narratives in these situations.

Militarization of Kashmiri Culture

Over the years, tremendous political and social turmoil has been generated in the state by the forces of religious fundamentalism and by exclusionary nationalism that seek to erode the cultural syncretism that is part of the ethos of J & K. These forces are responsible for the shutting down of dissenters who voice cultural critiques for the repression of women, for political anarchy, economic deprivation, lack of infrastructure, and for the mass displacements that have been occasioned by these events. Since 1949, the United Nations and Pakistan have consistently demanded that a plebiscite be held in order to determine the wishes of the Kashmiri people (for more information on the provisional accession of the former princely state of J & K to India, (see "Appendix A" 175–178). India has denied this wish for fear of losing the vote in the predominantly Muslim Kashmir Valley. India uses Pakistan's reluctance to withdraw its forces and the decision of the U.S. government to supply arms to Pakistan in 1954 to justify its denial (Ganguly 1997: 43–57; Rahman 1996: 4). Nearly 400,000 Indian army and paramilitary forces have been deployed in the state to date, in India's most beefed-up counterinsurgency operation. Financing these operations has taken an enormous toll on the annual administrative budget of the state (Ganguly 1997: 1–2).

Since the inception of the secessionist movement in 1989, more than 50,000 Kashmiris have been brutally murdered by the Indian forces, 100,000 Pandits have migrated to Jammu and other parts of India for fear of persecution, a large number of women (over 5,000 according to a conservative estimate) have been violated, and innumerable people have been incarcerated and held incommunicado. UN experts on extrajudicial, summary, and arbitrary executions have not been invited to Kashmir, and international human rights monitoring organizations have been prevented from entering the state (Amnesty International, "India Must Prevent Torture," 2005). In such a conflict situation, the law and order machinery is rendered dysfunctional, increasing the vulnerability of women and children. The counterinsurgency operations in Indian-administered J & K have been brutal—not just militarily, but politically and economically as well. Has J & K now been reduced to a garrison state?

The unpleasant reality in which J & K lives—one of Indian and Pakistani dominance—is marked by the overwhelming presence of paramilitary troops, barbed wire, and invasive searches; dispossessed youths trained in Pakistani training camps to unleash a reign of misguided terror; custodial killings in detention centers, and mothers whose faces tell tales of woe waiting outside those gloomy centers to catch a glimpse of their unfortunate sons (an exercise in futility); and *burqa*-clad women living in fear of the wrath of fundamentalist groups as well as paramilitary forces bent on undercutting their self-respect. The military has carte blanche under the Jammu and Kashmir Public Safety Act of 1978 and the Terrorist and Disruptive Activities (Prevention) Act of 1987 (for a discussion of the draconian laws in J & K, see Puri 1995; Widmalm 2002; Wirsing 2002). The traditional communal harmony in Kashmir has been eroded by Pakistan's sponsorship of terrorism in the state, India's repression of every demand for local autonomy and shelving of self-determination for the people of the state, and the eruption of ethnoreligious fervor as a result of the central government disregarding democratic institutions in Indian-administered J & K (Ganguly 1997: 14–20). The anarchy that pervades the cultural and political fabric of Indian-administered J & K has been stoked by government-sponsored militants and foreign mercenaries. Such an unwieldy situation has rendered women psychologically incarcerated (ibid.), and does not enable an autonomous life, devoid of the pressures that people of the state have been subjected to since 1947. The brutalization of the culture has been rendered more lethal by the socialization of Kashmiri boys and men into a military culture. Within such a masculinist discourse and praxis, the rigidly entrenched hierarchical relationship between men and women is inextricably linked with sexualized violence. Although I consider her agenda questionable and am skeptical about her scholarship, there is an element of truth to Rita Manchanda's observation that "the conservative patriarchal ideology of the Kashmir struggle cast women as symbols—Grieving Mother, Martyr's Mother and Raped Woman. It developed an instrumental relationship with women as the frontline of the propaganda war over human rights violations by the Indian state and undervalued their activism, dismissing it as accidental" ("Guns and Burqaa," 2001: 43).

For instance, numerous cases of rape are reported to have been committed by Indian security forces in the state since the inception of the secessionist movement in 1989 (Prasad 1999). A number of women have been ruthlessly violated by members of the paramilitary troops deployed in Indian-administered J & K as a tool to avenge themselves, and indelibly scathe the consciousness of a culture that dared to raise its insurgent head against the two mammoth nuclear powers on the subcontinent. Although rape was construed as a weapon of war in the then burgeoning discourse of armed insurgency evoking a submerged nationalist identity and the corollary discourse of human rights violations, "dishonored" women retained their status as familial and cultural chattels lacking control over their own bodies. Furthermore, custodial disappearances, custodial deaths, and bestial interrogation methods have indelibly scarred the psyche of the Kashmiri people. In a highly brutalized culture can women assume hitherto unexplored agential roles?[1]

Mobilization of Women

Association of Parents of Disappeared Persons (APDP)

Parveena Ahangar is one of many unfortunate mothers whose son was a victim of custodial disappearance. Her son, Javed Ahmad,

---

[1] I consider it important to underline my assiduous attempt not to hinder or obstruct the various testimonies that I listened to with foregone conclusions or unfounded biases. The women I spoke with were not testifying simply to empirical data but to the profundity of survival and resistance to the pervasive "culture of silence" in which they were bearing witness to the traumas they had lived through (see Felman and Laub 1992 for insights on trauma theory).

was picked up by the National Security Guards (NSG) in Batmaloo, Srinagar, on 18 August 1990, and taken to one of the interrogation centers that have emerged all over the Valley. Javed was a school-going adolescent when the NSG, suspecting him of being affiliated with a militant organization, brusquely picked him up without a substantial rationale for questioning. I met Parveena at her house in July 2006, and she graciously spent a couple of hours explaining to me the plight of ordinary Kashmiris who do not have access to the echelons of power, and therefore live anonymously in the fortresses of ruthless militarism until they are buried in the catacombs of history. Parveena, a courageous and forthright woman, chose to shed the veil and the inhibitions imposed by her cultural mores in order to verbalize the agony of a wounded mother. Instead of lamenting voicelessly behind the closed portals of her cultural and societal standards, she formed an organization called the Association of Parents of Disappeared Persons (APDP), comprising bereaved mothers whose sons had been victims of custodial disappearances or deaths. Politicians at the helm of affairs in the Valley have only managed to turn the groans of these mothers into screams that cut through the air, laden with pain and longing for their children. In early 1999, Amnesty International ("If They Are Dead, Tell Us") estimated that since 1990 over 800 people have been victims of custodial disappearances; in August 2002, *Kashmir Times* ("Militancy in Kashmir Valley Completes Fourteen Years"), a local English daily, estimated the figure to be 3,500. Members of the APDP mobilize women on the basis of the concept of protecting the dignity and rights of nonpartisan citizens who do not have vested political interests. It is an apolitical organization that does not receive funding from any regional or national political organization, and is not patronized by either the establishment or by the opposition. Parveena succeeded in assembling the relatives of persons who had been subjected to torture, death, solitary confinement, and other brutal methods while in the custody of the police or military forces in various parts of the Valley. In the course of foregrounding their trials and tribulations, she participated in conferences on human rights violations in the Philippines, Thailand, and Indonesia and organized peaceful demonstrations in the backyard of India's political gurus and masters, New Delhi. She stuck to her conviction in the midst of forceful antagonism, refusing even the monetary compensation that was offered to her to forget "the unfortunate incident."

Parveena and other mothers like her seek to know the fate of their children who disappeared in the abyss of political and military oppression before life had a chance to beckon them. The unknown fate of their children is a constant presence in their lives, like a leaden sky whose clouds are getting lower and lower. The lack of closure in their lives makes their existence unbearable. Their stories evoke tragic destinies, unredeemed by justice. "There are many families of disappeared persons who are deprived of the basic necessities of life. There are hundreds of half-widows [grass widows], who have been rendered destitute and don't know whether to await the return of their spouses or move on," says Parveena (conversation with the author, Srinagar, 2006). Although the APDP relies on the cultural and moral authority of the mother, which is religiously sanctioned, members of the organization have carved a niche for themselves in the public space. It is as bereaved mothers that the members of this organization can challenge the apathy and complacency of the political and bureaucratic machinery.

On the other hand, women like Farida Dar also emerged within the fractured fabric of insurgency. Farida shelved her maternal role and did not avail herself of the discourse that sanctified the dignity of the mother. In 1996, she along with Farooq Ahmad Dar was incarcerated as a co-accused in the Lajpat Nagar, New Delhi, bomb blast. After having founded the Students Liberation Front, Farida became an operative of the outlawed militant organization Ikhwan-ul-Muslimeen. When I spoke with Farida, she told me that although her complicity in the Lajpat Nagar, New Delhi, bomb blast case has yet to be proven, she was mercilessly interrogated by Special Operations Group personnel, the heinous role of which I have written about in a later section, at the infamous *Papa II* interrogation center in Srinagar after her arrest. Subsequently, she was transferred to the impregnable fortress of Tihar jail, which is Asia's biggest prison complex, located in New Delhi. Farida was confined to ignominious preventive detention for five years, during which, she claims, she did not buckle under pressure or wilt in the ignominy of an imposed invisibility. When I asked Farida about her stance vis-à-vis a feasible solution to the Kashmir conflict, she ruled out self-determination and emphasized tripartite talks, in which India, Pakistan, and Kashmir would engage in security-related dialogues in order to make changes in areas of security policy, such as military doctrines or new political agreements (telephone conversation with the author, 2009). But how much credence would those involved in bilateral or multilateral negotiation processes in order to discuss conflict resolution give to the opinion of a nonstate actor like Farida?

Ethnographer Sharon Pickering, in her study of women in Northern Ireland, theorizes that historically, political analysts and social scientists have not considered the experiences of those coerced and tortured by state violence as relevant to their studies (Pickering 2001: 490). But the unflinching courage of marginalized women like Parveena in their fight for justice symbolizes the self-actualization and intervention of Kashmiri women in patriarchal national history by speaking from their locations about the current political realities. J.P. Hewitt's theorization of identity is relevant to the situation of women like Parveena: "As the definition of a situation is first disrupted and then reconstituted, people carve out new roles for themselves, and in locating themselves within these new perspectives they acquire new identities" (1989: 162). Recently, the APDP broke the walls of silence when its researchers found the graves of 1,000 unidentified corpses, unceremoniously dug in graveyards across Uri, the de facto frontier region that divides Indian- and Pakistani-controlled Kashmir. Despite its meager sources and the uphill climb ahead, the APDP has made "a strong case for an independent international scientific investigation" (*Greater Kashmir*, 31 March 2008). Such an investigation would facilitate the creation of a climate of accountability, curb the carte blanche given to the Indian paramilitary forces, and provide civilians with recourse to legal procedures. The resolve of the members of the APDP to make their voices heard validates their experiences and their perception as a centrifugal force that vehemently calls into question the coercive power of the state. It is the peripheralized, of whom women form a large portion, that are concerned about structural changes that would enable transformations within entrenched structures and appropriate the peace-building mission from the elitist national security constituency.

"Dukhtaran-e-Milat" (Daughters of the Nation)

In contemporary Kashmiri society, the question of the role of women in the nationalist scenario remains a vexed one. As Ann McClintock observes about the role of the subaltern woman in "third-world" societies: "Excluded from direct action as national citizens, women are subsumed symbolically into the national body politic as its boundary and metaphoric limit" (McClintock 1997: 345). I reinforce that in Kashmir there has been a dearth of secular women's organizations working toward structural change that would enable gender equity. For instance, the only reactionary women's organization in Kashmir, the *Dukhtaran-e-Milat* (DM), claims that the image of woman as a burqa-clad, faceless and voiceless cultural icon, devoid of the agency to pave a path of her own choosing, is sanctioned by the interpretations of religious scriptures that this vigilante group subscribes to, and reinforces her strength and courage of conviction to sacrifice for the family. This group uses intimidating and questionable tactics to raid houses that allegedly have been converted into brothels, and brutally censors romantic liaisons between college-going boys and girls. The members of DM would perhaps never identify the modern Kashmiri woman with the liberated woman of secular discourse. On the contrary, they make a facile attempt to reconstruct historical and cultural discourses in order to inspire the kind of cultural nationalism that fundamentalist politics requires. Krishna Misri, former principal of Government College for Women, Nawakadal, Srinagar (1975–1982) and Maulana Azad Government College for Women, Srinagar, Kashmir (1982–1991), wrote to me in an e-mail (dated 5 April 2008), that

> the imposition of a dress code by authoritarian organizations such as the DM signaled dangerous portents for the right of women to make their own choices. I was shocked that barring a few, most of the Muslim women staff members were clad in "burqas" when the Maulana Azad College for Women reopened in March 1990. I thought the day of reckoning had come and we had surrendered. The college had a rich history. I could recollect only the past, while the present and the future looked blurred.

Such organizations advocate the creation of a homogeneous culture devoid of the freedoms that Kashmiri women have traditionally enjoyed. Their draconian methods to enforce the *purdah* reinforce a patriarchal structure in which an unaccompanied woman is rendered vulnerable, and curtail the mobility of the tech-savvy youth in an attempt to Arabize the syncretic ethos of Kashmir.

There seems to be an insensitivity in such reactionary organizations, as well as in former and current regional and national administrations—such as the Congress and People's Democratic Party (PDP) coalition government in the state and the centralizing regimes of the Congress, the Bharatiya Janata Party (BJP), and the National Democratic Front in the central government—toward the diverse interpretations of religious laws regarding the institutions of marriage, divorce, inheritance rights, and so on, and to the rich heterogeneity of cultural traditions and the paradoxes within them. The vociferous members of the DM would better serve the female population of the state by campaigning for quotas for women in the legislative assembly, legislative council, parliament, and the judiciary. An increase in the female representation in these institutions of authority would facilitate a cultural shift in terms of gender role expectations, legitimizing a defiance of the normative structure. The intrusion of women into traditionally male domains would cause perceptible erosion in the structural determinants of sexualized violence. Such a form of empowerment would "frame and facilitate the struggle for social justice and women's equality through a transformation of economic, social and political structures" (Bisnath and Elson 2002). In the present scenario, no thought is given either by the state authorities or by the insurgent groups to women who have been victims of the paramilitary forces and/or militant organizations. In the late 1990s the brutalization of the culture became further horrifying with reports of "unidentified gunmen" intruding into the sanctum sanctorum of women and shooting them without an iota of compunction. For example, on 28 August 1998 a well-reputed local English daily, the *Kashmir Times* (Jammu), reported that in Poonch district two women, Latifa and Khatija, who were allegedly moles, were shot in cold blood by "unknown assassins," alias renegade militants, mercenaries, and paramilitary forces.

The women of Kashmir have borne the brunt of the violence. In the absence of their menfolk, hapless women have been negotiating with officials and military personnel, both materially and sexually. Unfortunately, the innate conservatism of Kashmiri society disables them from overtly describing and condemning sexual exploitation. Kashmiri women are further dehumanized because of the self-denigration that accompanies physical defilement. There is no statistical data of rapes and molestations in the state because of the secrecy with which such acts are shrouded. I asked a *Gujjar* matriarch, Pathani Begum, about the political awareness of women in her native village, Mahiyan, and neighboring rural areas in the Valley. I asked her if she was familiar with the ideology of the DM. Pathani, who did not pursue a formal education for fear of being ostracized, claimed that she and her ilk had not heard about the DM and its political agenda. Her concern was the inability of rural women to retaliate against the harassment they are subjected to by militia groups such as the Special Task Force (STF) and the Indian paramilitary forces. The molestation of three women by members of the STF in Pathani's village had marked the ebb of youthfulness and stanched the blooming atmosphere (Pathani Begum in conversation with the author, July 2006).

The validity of these fears was established by a recent study, which reported that "There can be no two opinions that the women of Kashmir during the past two decades have been in the vanguard and have been fighting battles against all kinds of injustices and crimes against humanity committed by the State and by some dubious non-state actors" (Kashmir Human Rights Site 2005). A large proportion of rape victims and war widows are afflicted with post-traumatic stress disorder, and are prone to suicidal tendencies (ibid.).

Negotiating Political, Cultural, and Social Spaces

In order to explore women's empowerment in some of the rural areas of Kashmir ravaged by militancy, I traveled to the villages of Mahiyan and Qazipora in July 2005. These villages are in Tangmarg, a revenue *tehsil* (revenue unit) of Kashmir bordering Pakistan. The Kashmiri and *Gujjar* women I met with there belong to predominantly agricultural communities, and are workhorses on the lands they cultivate, but they lack the tools with which to critically understand their reality and the causes underlying structural poverty. While conducting my research, I found myself constantly beleaguered by the following question: is the version of events of women absent from the official records relegated to the archives of memory and history? While conducting my research, I found myself constantly beleaguered by the following question: Is the rich complexity in the social and cultural positions of "native women" ignored in order to retain the remnants of colonialist power-knowledge in "[the] appropriation and codification of 'scholarship' and 'knowledge' about women in the third world by particular analytic categories…"? (Mohanty 196).

My research enabled me to realize that despite being unable to understand or overturn the structural determinants of their oppression, these Kashmiri and *Gujjar* women are able to negotiate in small spaces. The importance of context must be understood and used to identify items within each boundary appropriate to local circumstances. None of them had qualms about functioning as the main socializing agents for their children, and considered the constitution of the mother–son relationship as the nexus of every social relationship in their culture. With their faces turned away from the camera and controlling their shy laughter after being berated by their mother-in-law, the feisty Haneefa Begum, Hafeeza Begum, Fareeda Akhtar, and Rifat Ara sang a medley of folk songs for me in the intimacy of their hut. The songs, which were translated for me by Shabeer Ahmad, a *Gujjar* lawyer, were a doleful rendition of the self-abnegation and loneliness of a young bride who is severed from everything familiar to her and finds herself being ruthlessly molded to fit a new environment. The most articulate of the group was Shabeer's mother, who was content to understand historical and social events within the explanatory frameworks of religious and filial obligation. Her stance vis-à-vis the contexts that formed her identity displayed a capacity to act upon the social boundaries that "define fields of action for all actors" (Hayward 1998: 27). The ostensibly compliant attitude of these women seems to be a strategy of survival in a social setting in which relationships are hierarchically structured, maintaining social and political stasis. The notion of uncompassionate in-laws is a part of their folklore. But it might be easier to imagine the survival strategies that women deploy in that environment if we think of power "not as instruments powerful agents use to prevent the powerless from acting freely, but rather as social boundaries that, together, define fields of action for all actors" (ibid.).

Subsequent to the dismantling of the feudal economic and social structure in Kashmir in the early 1950s, feudal clans and the emasculated nobility clung to their decadent traditions with unparalleled ferocity. Educated Kashmiri women like Dr. Hameeda Naeem, professor at the University of Kashmir, are unable to relate to the ideologies of such dethroned feudal clans and of the DM as well. Hameeda Naeem articulately delineated the brutal human rights violations occurring in Indian-administered J & K at the United Nations Conference in Geneva in 1996, after which the government of India impounded her passport until 2005, rendering it impossible for her to speak at other international conferences during that period. In an enlightening conversation with Hameeda at my parents' house in Srinagar (in July 2006), she described the DM as self-styled custodians of the Islamic faith who had caricaturized Islam by reducing it to the veil. She categorically stated that the DM did not represent all Kashmiri women and lacked the authority to enforce a code of conduct. I asked her how sixteen years of armed insurgency and counterinsurgency had pervaded the social fabric, and what measures, if any, had been taken to redress the grievances of women adversely affected by militancy. Hameeda expressed an adverse judgment on the government of Indian-administered J & K for having facilitated the psychological, sexual, economic, and emotional violation of women, particularly in the insulated rural areas. The law of the jungle that prevails in those areas leaves no scope for rehabilitation of the victims of violence. The desecration of the political, social, and cultural landscape looms large over the lovely face of nature in its pure majesty. The grievances of these lacerated hearts are, inevitably, not redressed. The unalloyed purity of nature and the spiritual illumination it inspires have, therefore, been indelibly tarnished.

Hameeda's unequivocal censure of Indian military and paramilitary forces was echoed by Shamim Firdous. Shamim was a member of the Legislative Council of J & K from 1999 to 2005, and is now the president of the women's wing of the National Conference (NC) and a member of the newly elected Legislative Assembly of J & K (2008). She is responsible for having opened vocational centers in her constituency, Habbakadal, for illiterate and semiliterate women who lack financial autonomy. Despite being well educated and well spoken, Shamim was relegated to the background in the prestigious halls of the Legislative Council. In response to my question (during a discussion in Srinagar, in July 2006) about whether she had adequately represented the people of her constituency in the Legislative Council, she was critical of the treatment meted out to women legislators, who are not deemed worthy of consulting on matters of governmental policy. Although they are permitted to voice their opinions, their claims or objections are pooh-poohed. The strident machismo of the male legislators in the council enables the reductive objectification of the women members. Although educated women desire full participation in professional and political life in Kashmir, the nexus between patriarchy and militarism has insidiously indoctrinated women, to the extent of making a virtue of helplessness and destitution. Shamim expressed her resentment at the complicity of women in fortifying existing political and social structures.

Women in Kashmir now live in an unendurable atmosphere created by the acrimonious implementation of draconian laws. Indian paramilitary forces, militants, and mercenaries have unleashed indiscriminate violence in the state, which has metamorphosed the legendary beauty of Kashmir into an intolerable inferno of molten bodies and bottomless perdition.

Brutalization of Women in the Conflict Zone

Horrifying narratives of women and adolescent girls being humiliated and brutally interrogated in remote villages are absent from the official records, and are fearfully voiced in the atmosphere of paranoia that pervades the Valley. For instance, in 1991, more than 800 soldiers of the Fourth Rajput Regiment raped between 23 and 60 women in the course of one night in the village of Kunan Pohpura in Kashmir. These soldiers raided the village on the pretext of interrogating the local men who were allegedly insurgents. Another gruesome incident of a similar nature occurred in Handawara village in 2004, where a mother and her minor daughter were sadistically violated by a major of the Rashtriya Rifles (RR). In Mattan in south Kashmir, an Indian army subedar and his bodyguard of the Seven Rashtriya Rifles were involved in a chilling rape case against which the necessary governmental action is yet to be taken (interview with human rights activists in the Kashmir Valley, June 2004; Kashmiri Women's Initiative for Peace and Disarmament 2004).

The rape of a pristine young bride, Mubeena Bano of Lissar Chowgam, on her way to her marital home is particularly disturbing. In anticipation of her marriage to Abdul Rashid Malik on 18 May 1990, Mubeena had been weaving youthful dreams of creating a romantic life away from the trials and tribulations of her militant-infested village. Her family had gone to great lengths to give their home a festive, bridal air. Despite threats from militants who were opposed to celebrations of any kind, Mubeena and her relatives had managed to create an atmosphere of laughter and happiness. Little did Mubeena's family know that their precious daughter, whom they had sheltered from the turbulent waves of life, was not destined to be indulged by the affection of her husband and in-laws. While on her way to her husband's home along with his entourage of relatives and friends, *baratis*, the virgin bride was horrendously violated by a bestial group of paramilitary personnel. The groom, Malik, and some members of his entourage were brutally shot at without provocation at Bodhasgam crossing. The pain-filled screams of the young bride, who had given her heart and soul to her groom, would have pierced the hardest of hearts. She had been defiled and her beautiful innocence had ended. She felt abandoned with no one to turn to. Had God forsaken her? Would she be saved by a messiah or would she be left at the mercy of these satanic creatures? Was this a nightmare that would vanish at the break of dawn? Would she wake up to find herself in the bridal chamber, anxiously awaiting the sound of her husband's footsteps? Mubeena's mind was so numbed that she could not remember a single Quranic verse that she had been taught to recite when in danger. Her husband, who had hitherto carried himself with dignity, was incapacitated for a while after this horrendous incident. I met Mubeena and Abdul Rashid Malik on 25 July 2008, at Sarnal. Mubeena is now an emaciated woman who is plowing a lonely furrow. Subsequent to the violence unleashed on 18 May 1990 at Bodhasgam crossing, Mubeena was ostracized by her in-laws. They were unwilling to forgive her for having been brutally raped by paramilitary personnel. Despite the indelible scar on her psyche and her humiliation, Mubeena had the resilience to cope with the buffets that fate had dealt her. Her husband's unflinching support helped to strengthen her. Abdul Rashid, unlike a lot of men raised in a patriarchal culture, was sympathetic to his wife's physical pain and psychological crippling. He made the firm decision to defy everyone who cast aspersions on Mubeena and who chose to shun her. Abdul Rashid realized that he could have been in the same plight as Mubeena. With the pervasion of the culture of violence and humiliation of the dominated, there has been an increase of such dishonorable and shameful incidents. Mubeena is now the mother of three spirited and courageous children who know about the reprehensible atrocities inflicted on their parents. Her children have the strength to protect their mother's dignity with aplomb. Her younger son gave me the First Information Report (FIR) that his parents had filed soon after the incident of 18 May 1990. That FIR, like many others filed by people who lacked the armor of clout or money, was buried under the detritus of law and order. Mubeena's husband, Abdul Rashid, like a lot of young and able-bodied Kashmiri men, is unemployed, exacerbating his sense of impotence. Will the grievances of such wounded and powerless people ever be redressed? Will the violated women of Kashmir ever have the satisfaction of knowing that those who wronged them did not go unpunished?

In order to further my research, in June 2009 I asked the director of the Psychiatric Diseases Hospital, Dr. Margoob, to allow me to sit in on a couple of his sessions with militancy related trauma patients. Dr. Margoob was magnanimous enough to permit me to observe some of these patients carefully. It was heart-wrenching to see despondent women with hopelessness entrenched in their atrophied looks and minds. Orphaned, widowed, improvident; socially marginalized and left to their own devices; unsought by those with the means to help; each sigh bespoke a grief that knew no bounds and had no hope of respite. These repositories of communal values and cultural traditions were unable to find a support system in a community that had experienced the trauma of state formation at its expense. The political turbulence in Indian-administered J & K has taken its toll on such people and has left them stone-faced with a stoicism that expects no recompense. Does the state give any thought to the economic and emotional rehabilitation of such people? Dr. Margoob lends a sympathetic ear to his patients; provides them with fatherly care; boosts their morale; is quick to provide them with the necessary medical care; and is doing groundbreaking work in a culture in which people don't mention psychiatric ills without fear of being stigmatized. It was enlightening to see young men and women seeking psychiatric care of their own volition. I was pleasantly surprised to see a peasant from a rural area take his grandson to the child psychologist and beseech his grandson to conceal nothing from the psychologist. But we still have a long way to go in recognizing the dire consequences of trauma brought on by political turmoil, military brutality, and psychosis of fear created by such happenings. There are people who do not have recourse to the judicial and administrative machinery. Prabal Mahato found in an independent survey of the Psychiatric Diseases Hospital in Srinagar, conducted July–August 1999, that post-traumatic stress disorders increased from 1,700 in 1990 to 17,000 in 1993 and to 30,000 in 1998 (Mahato 1999). It is unfortunate that the more unaccountable state-sponsored agencies have become in Indian-administered J & K, the more aloof and gluttonous the bureaucratic, military, and administrative machinery has become. The culture of impunity has grown around India and Pakistan unabated. Women and children are in a miserable plight because of the lack of not just physical infrastructure but from a deficit in gynecological, obstetric, welfare, and economically rehabilitative services as well.

I met three female patients of Dr. Margoob who were traumatized after the loss of their male heads of the households. Two of the women had been widowed and the third orphaned because of the frenetic violence at the apex of insurgency and counterinsurgency in Indian-administered J & K. Their counseling sessions with Dr. Margoob were enabling them to redefine their life experiences as contributing to the depression and suicidal ideation in their adult lives; work through the discourse of victimhood was developing into the construction of their identities as survivors; they were clearly working toward accepting their life circumstances and tentatively attempting to redefine them within clear conceptual frameworks (see Warner and Feltey 1999: 161–174, for details about traumatized women and identity reconstruction). Do such patients have access to a community perspective, or a reference group, or avenues for rehabilitation (Shibutani 1961)?

Women representatives of the then ruling PDP and those of its ally, the Congress Party, were quick to make visits accompanied by their entourages to isolated villages or towns in which the Indian army had trammeled upon the sensibilities of the female population. The PDP, while in opposition, raised the issue of human rights abuses, which, until then, had not been given much credence by the NC government. But they were unable to advocate reforms that were specific to women, and no stringent and timely measures were taken to redress those wrongs. In effect, the Kashmiri woman is constructed as a parchment on which the discourses of religious nationalism, secular nationalism, and ethnic nationalism are inscribed, and the most barbaric acts are justified by the Indian paramilitary forces as means to rein in separatist forces and by militant organizations as means to restore the lost dignity of the "woman."

Construction of Kashmiri Womanhood by Ethnonationalists

Secular as well as ethnonationalists assert that as long as the inner or spiritual distinctiveness of the culture is retained, an autonomous "nation" of Indian administered J & K can equip itself to cope with a globalized world without losing its essential identity. This nationalist discourse creates the dichotomy of the inner/outer in order to make the inviolability of the inner domain look traditional. For example, ethnonationalists assert that a native woman of Indian-administered J & K who marries a non-Kashmiri, non-Dogra, or non-Ladakhi loses her legal right to inherit, own, or buy immoveable property in the state. To them, by inhabiting the metaphoric inner domain, the native woman of J & K embodies the virginal purity of their culture and ethnicity, and these would get tainted by her stepping over the cultural threshold.

As a strategy to maintain the inviolability of the cultural sanctum sanctorum, ethnonationalists problematize the law concerning state subjects that was promulgated in J & K on 20 April 1927 by Maharaja Hari Singh. This injunction was meant to protect the interests of the local landed class and the peasantry against wealthy people from outside the state who had the wherewithal to buy the locals out of hearth and home. In 1957 the new constitution of the state changed "state subject" to "permanent resident," and permanent resident status was accorded to individuals who had been living in the state for at least a decade before 14 May 1957. On 25 March 1969, the state government issued an injunction requiring deputy commissioners to issue certificates of permanent residence to women of Indian-administered J & K (Kashmiri, Dogra, Ladakhi, and *Gujjar*), with the stipulation that the status was valid only till marriage. After that, women who married permanent residents would need to get their certificates reissued, and those who married outside the state would automatically lose their permanent resident status; on the other hand, a male permanent resident would have the privilege of endowing his nonstate subject spouse with the ability to own and inherit property in the state as long as she did not leave the state for permanent residence elsewhere (for a clearer delineation, see Abdullah 1993; Zutshi 2004).

In 2002, the High Court declared that this proviso had no legislative sanction because it violated the gender equality clause of the constitution of the state as well as of India. The court held that the proviso relied on Section 10 of the British law, which had governed pre-partition India and which had itself been amended (see Bhagat 2005; Puri 2004). The bench quoted Section 4 of the Sri Pratap Consolidation Law Act to declare that the only legislative prohibition was that the property inherited by a woman permanent resident who married a nonpermanent resident could not be sold to a nonstate subject. But this decision of the court created a furor, with the then opposition NC asserting that the earlier proviso invalidating the permanent resident status of women who married outside the state as outmoded was an attempt to erode the distinctive cultural identity of the state. The NC accused the then ruling PDP of having made a compromise by withdrawing its appeal from the Supreme Court against the judgment of the state High Court. The angst of power caused the PDP, including its women members, to immediately draft a Permanent Resident Bill reinforcing the earlier stipulation. The High Court's decision was supported by the PDP's coalition partner, the Congress. The issue of permanent residence was hijacked by Hindu fundamentalist organizations, the BJP and the Rashtriya Swayamsevak Sangh (RSS), to inflame regional divisiveness; they condemned the opposition of the NC and the PDP to the High Court's decision as acts of Muslim secession, which excluded the predominantly Hindu Jammu. Representatives of the NC and the PDP in the Legislative Assembly and Legislative Council opposed the decision of the High Court that declared the earlier proviso archaic and outmoded, and the Congress and the BJP supported them (Puri 2004). In effect, thus, women were deployed as a political tool not just by regional political organizations, but also by national political parties.

Women politicians in the Legislative Assembly and Legislative Council played the role of tokens, bolstering the social, cultural, and moral institutions that maintain a male-dominated power structure (Amnesty International, "India," 2005; Kashmiri Women's Initiative for Peace and Disarmament 2004). Even those with access to the echelons of power refused to engage "more effectively with the politics of affiliation, and the currently calamitous dispensations of power" (McClintock 1997: 396). Despite its firm promise, the then coalition government comprising the PDP and the Congress was unable to entirely incorporate the Special Operations Group (SOG), a paramilitary division of the police accused of heinous human rights violations, into the regular police force. The SOG continues to run amok and functions as an entity that only obeys the law of the jungle. Alongside the SOG, the Special Task Force (STF), a militia group comprising renegade militants, was incorporated into the regular police force but was not disbanded, in contravention of a promise made by the PDP government at the time of its installation in office. These forces were deployed to handle extrajudicial matters in arbitrary ways, and were responsible for gross misdemeanors against women (Amnesty International, "India," 2005).

Women as Repositories of Communal Values and Cultural Traditions

Why is gender violence such a consistent feature of the insurgency and counterinsurgency that have wrenched apart the Indian subcontinent for decades? The equation of the native woman to the motherland in nationalist rhetoric has, in recent times, become more forceful. In effect, the native woman is constructed as a trough within which male aspirations are nurtured, and the most barbaric acts are justified as means to restore the lost dignity of women.

The story of the partition of India in 1947 into two separate nation-states, India and Pakistan, is replete with instances of fathers slaughtering their daughters in order to prevent them from being violated by the enemy, and of women resorting to mass suicide to preserve the "honor" of the community (for further discussion of gendering and structural determinants of gender violence, see Kaul 1999; Kumari and Kidwai 1998; Jayawardena 1986; Ray 2000). If a woman's body belongs not to herself but to her community, then the violation of that body purportedly signifies an attack upon the honor (*izzat*) of the whole community.

In one instance, the crime of a boy from a lower social caste against a woman from a higher upper caste in Meerawala village in the central province of Punjab, Pakistan, in 2002, was punished in a revealing way by the "sagacious" tribal jury. After days of thoughtful consideration, the jury gave the verdict that the culprit's teenage sister, Mai, should be gang-raped by goons from the wronged social group. The tribal jury ruled that to save the honor of the upper-caste Mastoi clan, Mai's brother, Shakoor, should marry the woman with whom he was accused of having an illicit relationship, while Mai was to be given away in marriage to a Mastoi man. The prosecution said that when she rejected the decision she was gang-raped by four Mastoi men and made to walk home seminaked in front of hundreds of people. The lawyer for one of the accused argued the rape charge was invalid because Mai was technically married to the defendant at the time of the incident (Reuters 2002).

Such acts of violence that occur on the Indian subcontinent bear testimony to the intersecting notions of nation, family, and community. The horrific stories of women, in most instances attributed to folklore, underscore the complicity of official and nationalist historiography in perpetuating these notions. I might add that the feminization of the "homeland" as the "motherland," for which Indian soldiers and Kashmiri nationalists in Indian-administered Kashmir and in Pakistan-administered Kashmir are willing to lay down their lives, serves in effect to preserve the native woman in pristine retardation. Although this essentialist portrayal of the Kashmiri woman in J & K is clearly suspect, it is embedded more deeply in the quasi-feudal culture of Pakistan-administered Kashmir. Pakistan-administered Kashmir has been a fiefdom of feudal lords whose only concern is with the impregnability of their authority and the replenishment of their coffers. Tribal women in Azad (Free) Kashmir are still circumscribed within the parameters created by the paternalistic feudal culture that disallows the creation of a space for distinct subjectivities; see discussions about the creation of Pakistan in Cohen 2004; Talbot 1998).

Conceptualization and Crystallization of Women's Agency

My attempt to theorize women's empowerment in terms that allow the creation of a space for distinct subjectivities involves framing the concept with regard to its cognitive, psychological, economic, and political aspects. I borrow eminent educationist Nelly Stromquist's assertion regarding agency, which involves taking decisions that deconstruct cultural and social norms, and beliefs that structure seemingly intransigent traditional gender ideologies; the psychological aspect refers to developing self-esteem, for which some form of financial autonomy is a basis; the political aspect involves the ability to organize and mobilize for social change, which requires the creation of awareness not just at the individual level but at the collective level as well (Stromquist 1995: 12–22). For me, empowerment is a process that enables the marginalized to make strategic life-choices regarding education, livelihood, marriage, childbirth, sexuality, and so forth—choices that are critical for people to lead the sort of lives they wish to lead and that constitute life's defining parameters (Kabeer 1999: 437). It is important to keep in mind, however, that women are constrained by and grapple with the normative structures through which societies create gender roles.

I was raised in a secular Muslim home where we were encouraged to speak of the "liberation of women" and of a culturally syncretic society. I was taught that Islam provides women with social, political, and economic rights, however invisible those rights are in our society. It was instilled in me that Islam gives women property rights (the right of Mrs. Ghulam Kabra, a Kashmiri state subject, to inherit the property to which she was the legal heir was challenged as early as 1939 because she had married a nonstate subject, but the High Court legislated that she could inherit the property bequeathed to her by her parents); the right to interrogate totalizing social and cultural institutions; the right to hold political office (Khalida Zia and Sheikh Hasina in Bangladesh, Benazir Bhutto in Pakistan, Najma Heptullah and Mohsina Kidwai in India, and my maternal grandmother, Begum Akbar Jehan, in Kashmir [who represented the Srinagar and Anantnag constituencies of J & K in the Indian parliament from 1977 to 1979 and 1984 to 1989, respectively, and was the first president of the J & K Red Cross Society, from 1947 to 1951; see Lok Sabha 2000]); the right to assert their agency in matters of social and political import; and the right to lead a dignified existence in which they can voice their opinions and desires so as to "act upon the boundaries that constrain and enable social action by, for example, changing their shape or direction" (Hayward 1998: 271).

Renowned historian Tariq Ali, among many others, has written about Begum Akbar Jehan's enormous political and social contribution:

> She threw herself into the struggle for a new Kashmir. She raised money to build schools for poor children and encouraged adult education in a state where the bulk of the population was illiterate. She also, crucially, gave support and advice to her husband, alerting him, for example, to the dangers of succumbing to Nehru's charm and thus compromising his own standing in Kashmir. (Ali 2003: 230–31)

Begum Akbar Jehan established an organization, the *Jammu and Kashmir Markazi Behboodi Khwateen*, in 1975, for the purpose of providing women from the downtrodden sections of society with

Begum Akbar Jehan Abdullah and Lady Edwina Mountbatten, wife of the last viceroy of British India, with a Kashmiri peasant woman, 1947. (*Courtesy*: The Archives of the National Conference, with the permission of the general secretary of the National Conference, Sheikh Nazir Ahmad)

functional literacy, training in arts and crafts, health care, and social security. Once economically empowered, these women would gain self-respect, be able to protect their rights, and lead purposeful existences. The organization was registered under the Societies Registration Act of 1998. Its current vice chairperson, Suraiya Ali Matto, provided illuminating information (e-mail dated 10 April 2008 about the aims and objectives of the *Behboodi Khwateen*:

> to impart intensive training to women in various arts and crafts which would become a source of livelihood for them, enabling them to become better citizens and homemakers, and work for the betterment of society; to run homes for destitute women and disenfranchised orphans; to provide supplementary nutrition to preschool children in ghettoized areas; to provide accommodation for working women from rural areas.

In order to highlight the groundbreaking work accomplished by local agencies, cadres, and social networks in Kashmir, the distinction between traditional praxes that conscript the role of women and progressive roles prescribed for women within Islamic norms needs to be underscored by responsible scholarship and social work. The Western preoccupation with empirical observation has led to an inaccurate conflation of Islamic norms with practices. Western feminist epistemologies can impair the research paradigms, hypotheses, and field work on women in Islamic societies.

I would emphasize that the articulation of the fervent patriotism of Kashmiri women, which manifested itself in their emboldened presence in 1931, 1947, 1950, and 1975 until the dawn of insurgency and counterinsurgency in 1989–1990, requires research that gives as much credence to the path-paving work of women within religious, familial, and communal frameworks as to the work of those women who deconstructed established frameworks in order to lead subaltern movements; motivate minority education as opposed to state-controlled education; and recognize culture and history as sites of struggle.

Reminiscences about Women's Agential Roles or Lack Thereof, 1947 and 1989

Do women's multiple narratives reveal a capacity for alternative ways of negotiating the construction of conflictual identities? Does the assumption of agential roles by traditional women in a patriarchal culture cause an identity conflict crisis that can be resolved through a firm commitment to specific values and goals? While reminiscing about Begum Akbar Jehan's and other women's significant roles in 1947, Krishna Misri writes about the formation of the National Militia and Women's Defense Corps—volunteer forces of men and women organized under the leadership of Sheikh Mohammad Abdullah—to ward off the onslaught that occurred on 22 October 1947 when hordes of tribesmen from the Northwest Frontier Province, under the patronage of the Pakistani army, crossed the border of the princely state of J & K in order to coercively annex the region:

In the absence of a competent civil authority, volunteers of the National Militia filled the void. They patrolled the city day and night with arms, kept vigil, guarded strategic bridges, approaches to the city, banks, offices, etc. With preliminary training in weapons, some of them were deployed with army detachments to fight the enemy at the war front. With its multi-faceted and radical activities, Women's Self Defense Corps (WSDC) was a harbinger of social change. It provided a forum where women steeped in centuries-old traditions, abysmal ignorance, poverty and superstition could discuss their issues. Attired in traditional Kashmiri clothes and carrying a gun around her shoulders, Zoon *Gujjari* symbolized the WSDC. A milk vendor's charismatic daughter, hailing from a conservative Muslim family that lived in downtown Srinagar, she received well-deserved media coverage. My elder brother, Pushkar Zadoo, joined the National Militia, while I along with my sisters, Kamla and Indu, became volunteers of WSDC. We were first initiated into physical fitness and then divided into smaller groups where weapons' training was imparted. It was essential to follow the instructions given by our instructor, an ex-army serviceman to a tee. Soon we understood the operational details of loading and unloading a gun, taking aim, and finally pressing the trigger. To get acclimatized to shooting the 303 rifle, sten-gun, bren gun and pistol, practice drills were organized in an open area, known as "Chandmari." The initial nervousness soon gave way to confidence and we would hit the target when ordered. For all parades including "ceremonial guards" and "guard of honor," the practice was that men's contingents were followed by women's contingents.

During that invasion of 1947, Begum Akbar Jehan undertook exhaustive relief work to rehabilitate displaced and dispossessed villagers. She addressed the volunteers on political issues to raise their political consciousness. Miss Mahmuda Ahmad Shah, a pioneering educationist and champion of women's empowerment, along with other women, was in the forefront of WSDC. Begum Zainab was a grass-root level leader. She took charge of the political dimension of WSDC. Shouldering a gun, she was in the forefront, leading women's contingents. Sajjada Zameer Ahmad, Taj Begum Renzu, Shanta Kaul, and Khurshid Jala-u-Din joined the "Cultural Front" and worked with Radio Kashmir as anchors, announcers, and actors. Several women writers and poets emerged on the literary scene and contributed to the cultural renaissance that followed down the decades. (E-mail to author 5 April 2008)

Women, as evidenced by the work of constructive and rehabilitative work undertaken by political and social women activists in the former princely state during both turbulent and peaceful times, have more or less power depending on their specific situation, and they can be relatively submissive in one situation and relatively assertive in another. Assessing women's agency requires identifying and mapping power relations, the room to maneuver within each pigeonhole, and the intransigence of boundaries (Hayward 1998: 29). The level of a woman's empowerment also varies according to factors such as class, caste, ethnicity, economic status, age, family position, and so on. Also, structural supports that some women have access to bolster their commitment to action. In 1950, the government of J & K developed educational institutions for women on a large scale, including the first Government College for Women. This institution provided an emancipatory forum for the women of Kashmir, broadening their horizons and opportunities within established political and social spheres. Higher education in the state received a greater impetus with the establishment of the Jammu and Kashmir University (Misri 2002: 25–26). The mobilization of women from various socioeconomic classes meant that they could avail themselves of educational opportunities, enhance their professional skills, and attempt to reform existing structures so as to accommodate more women. The educational methods employed in these institutions were revisionist in nature, not revolutionary. But the militarization of the political and cultural discourse in the state in 1989–1990 marginalized developmental issues and negated the plurality of ideologies through a nonnegotiable value system. In her e-mail to me (5 April 2008), Misri wrote about the gory landscape of 1989:

> In 1989, Kashmiris were caught between the terrorists and state terrorism, two sides of the same coin. Women bore the brunt of the suffering since, ironically, the two forces wielding power shared a patriarchal mindset that views women as symbols of individual and collective "honor." As has been the case throughout history, women's bodies in Kashmir became sites of war irrespective of their class, caste, religion, region or ethnicity. Physical violations of women became common and were used to challenge the collective honor of the community. Rape, gang-rape, abductions, kidnappings, naked corpses with amputated limbs hanging from tree-tops, were visible manifestations of the grim reality that gripped women's lives in the Valley. In addition were the hordes of panic-stricken people on the run, uprooted from their moorings, bereft of their home, history and identity. They had become refugees in their own land. For women, the new reality was in part reflected

in the new identities they assumed: rape victims, abducted women, widows, grass widows, migrants and so on. The United Nations Declaration on Elimination of Violence against Women states that pervasive violence against women is a product of "unequal power relations" between men and women, which characterizes gender relations in all parts of the world. Violence is built into patriarchal structures and it is practiced during peace as well as war. Kashmiri women have gone through immense turbulence and torture in the last two decades, and reconstituting their devastated lives is a formidable challenge. Given the urgency of the problem, what they need is empowerment. However, much of the discourse in the last two decades has focused on women either as victims/losers or welfare beneficiaries. Scant attention has been paid to their attempts to reconstitute their lives and to face the struggles of everyday existence. One of the ways in which victimized and displaced Kashmiri women are rebuilding and creating meaning in their lives is by taking up agency-oriented roles. The resourcefulness of underprivileged women in becoming part of a larger reconstitution and conflict-mitigation process is to be commended. For example, Parveena Ahangar's untiring search for her son culminated in the creation of the Association of Parents of Disappeared Persons. This association has become a rallying forum for parents and relatives in search of missing kith and kin. Others have set up self-help groups that deal with specific issues pertaining to widows, grass-widows and orphans. Still others have become involved in large-scale social work and/or social activism.

Agency-oriented roles are highly visible in the political participation and mobilization of women. Outnumbering men at times, they have made their presence felt in a big way in protest rallies and dangerous political missions. Women are organized under several political organizations that are affiliated to their male counterparts. *Dukhtara-e-Milat* ("Daughters of the Nation") is affiliated to a radical Islamist group and advocates restrictive codes of conduct for women. They even condone the use of coercive methods to enforce their agenda. Those aligned with moderate militant groups, on the other hand, have less restrictive codes and refrain from the use of coercive methods. At the other end of the continuum is Daughters of Vitasta (Daughters of the Jhelum, a river that is the lifeblood of Kashmir), the women's wing of *Panun Kashmir* ("Our Own Kashmir"), mainly operating from Jammu and Delhi. They seek resolution of the problems of internally displaced Kashmiri Pandits in terms of a separate homeland within the geographical space of the Valley. Despite their varying perceptions, all the women's organizations in India-administered J & K share some common traits: they are based on a radical politicization of religious identities and their agendas exemplify their exclusionary ideologies. Though these women have served in the lower and middle tiers of their respective organizations, they have to date been excluded from the upper echelons. Some of these organizations have expressed deep reservations about including women in the top tier, and none of them has a plan of action for women. How women perceive their future after struggle in a regressive discourse is unclear. It appears that they look at issues from the lens of their patriarchies and believe in an illusionary post-conflict resolution. While women have gained some "agentive moments," these gains are flawed as their agendas stem from an insulated world-view.

I agree with Misri's passionate articulation of the merciless forms of oppression that Kashmiri women now confront: "The focus has shifted from empowerment of women to the brutal politics of intimidation and coercion symbolized by attempts to enforce a dress code on them.... The burden of the new adjustments has disproportionately fallen on women" (Misri 2002: 26).

Realizing the significance of oral historiography and the importance of preserving it for posterity, I touched base with Sajjida Zameer, a dedicated member of the WSDC in 1947 and former director of the Education Department, J & K. I also wanted to delve into the politicosocial activism of women like Begum Akbar Jehan, Sajjida Zameer, Krishna Misri, and Mehmooda Ahmad Ali Shah in order to study their transition from keepers of home and hearth to people who saw themselves as a social force to be reckoned with. Within the confines of nationalist discourse they claimed the right to define themselves. Sajjida was in the forefront of the cultural movement, designed to awaken and hone a political consciousness through mass media:

In the early 1930s Sheikh Mohammad Abdullah spearheaded the struggle for a socialist, democratic government under the banner of the Muslim Conference. He had a very clear vision for Kashmir. Maharaja Hari Singh's rule hadn't done anything for the masses. While select courtiers and those who enjoyed royal patronage became richer, the poor led a truly miserable existence. Sheikh Mohammad Abdullah wanted the support of Indian leaders and masses to gain freedom from the Maharaja. While the rest of India chanted "Quit India" to the British, we in Kashmir chanted "*Kashmir Chhod Do*" ("Quit Kashmir") to the Maharaja's government. I was very impressed by the fervor to build a new Kashmir. The slogan was, "*Kashmiriyon utho, yeh jang hai apne aap ho banana ki*" ("Wake up Kashmiris, this is a battle to create yourself anew"). On 3 September 1947, under Operation Gulmarg, Pakistan initiated its raid across the state borders. The state administration was in shambles and the unending stream of refugees from Pakistan created many problems for the ruler. The Maharaja fled to Jammu, leaving Kashmiris to be brutally killed by the intruders. At this stage it was Abdullah who took charge and enlisted the help of civil society to save human lives. Even before Indian troops landed in Srinagar, the citizens of Kashmir had organized themselves into a militia to protect the land from raiders. Young men who had never seen a gun, let alone handled one, volunteered to join the militia. The women's militia was formed simultaneously in 1947. The slogan that inspired us was "*Kadam kadam bhadayenge hum, mahaz pe ladenge hum*" ("We will advance step by step to fight on the front"). Women, men and children were infused with a sense of patriotism. It was with this spirit that the people of Kashmir lived without salt for six months. Food items were to be supplied by Pakistan under the Standstill Agreement, but Pakistan withheld supplies of essential commodities in an attempt to force the issue of accession. The common Kashmiri puts a pinch of salt even in his/her tea. Yet people did not complain. There was a unifying bond of nationalism, a feeling that we could overcome all hurdles. Men and women joined together to form committees to prepare the people of the former princely state to fight against marauding raiders. I was able to follow the battles fought by the army due to my involvement in the women's militia. My husband, who was in the men's militia, kept me posted with all the details. I was an active volunteer in the militia. We were trained in the use of firearms by Indian army officers. Often firing competitions were held at Badami Bagh cantonment. At one competition I fired on target. General Cariappa, who was the chief guest, asked me to fire again to ensure that the bull's eye was not a mere fluke. I fired bang on target again, to win the "Brigadier Lakhinder silver Cup." I went to hospitals to visit the soldiers with homegrown fruits and vegetables. Some of them were so young and were away from their families. But their cheerful courage was heart-rending. For the first time I realized that war is initiated by Machiavellian politicians, but soldiers lose their lives and the masses are put through untold misery. Many army officers stand out in my memory for the way they carried out their duties. War was thrust upon India when Pakistan sent tribal irregulars and its soldiers into the former princely state of Jammu and Kashmir. Even as the situation in the Kashmir Valley was stabilized, the threat continued to be serious in the Jammu region. On 3 November 1947 the raiders reached Badgam a few miles from the Srinagar airfield. Major Somnath Sharma was sent to Badgam. Being outnumbered by seven to one, Sharma immediately sent a request to Brigadier Sen for reinforcements. He knew that if the enemy advanced any further, the airport would be lost and Kashmir would become a province of Pakistan; the airfield was the only lifeline between the Kashmir Valley and the rest of India. His last wireless message stated that they would fight to the last man and the last bullet. Soon after, Somnath Sharma was killed by a mortar. In November, I remember there was absolute panic because 3,000 enemy troops were on the outskirts of Srinagar in Shalateng, just four miles from the city centre, preparing to attack the city. In a brilliantly planned and executed operation, Colonel Harbaksh Singh attacked Shalateng on 22 November and routed the Pakistani raiders. Finally, Brigadier Sen was able to lure the raiders into the net of Indian forces, near Shalateng. The raiders were defeated and the threat to Srinagar was over. If the capital city had fallen, it would have been one of the greatest disasters for the people of Kashmir. Today, there would have been no talk of self-determination for Kashmir. We would have been administered stringently like a poor cousin of Pakistan, similar to Pakistan-administered Kashmir. I wonder how many Kashmiris realize this. The militia worked with the army, guiding them through unfamiliar terrain, gathering vital information and giving details of the raiders' movement. The women's militia played a substantive role in repulsing the raiders. Zoon *Gujjari* of Nawakadal, Srinagar, Jana Begum of Amrikadal, Srinagar, and Mohuan Kaur, a refugee from Baramullah, Kashmir, were active participants in the women's movement. Kashmiris from all walks of life, irrespective of religion or race, actively participated in the various activities of the Cultural Front of the militia. Prominent among the Kashmiri participants were Mahjoor, a very famous poet who wrote poems about Kashmir, its freedom and secular traditions. Other well-known indigenous poets in the movement were Noor Mohammed Roshan Arif Beigh, Premnath Pardesi, Pushkar Baan, Mohanlal Aima, Ghulam Mohammed Rah, and Abdul Sattar. Lending his voice to their verses was Abdul Ghani Namtahali (from Wathura Budgam, Kashmir). I must also mention Ghulam Qadir, a small-time businessman who would partake in the activities.

I joined the cultural front due to a crisis situation that arose when the leading lady, Ms. Usha Kashyap, in the play *Kashmir Yeh Hai (This is Kashmir)* had to leave due to some pressing personal problem. Pandit Jawaharlal Nehru, first Prime Minister of independent India, and other dignitaries were due to arrive to watch the play written by Professor Mehmood Hashmi, a refugee from Jammu who had fled to Srinagar. All the members of the Cultural Front pleaded with me to take over Kashyap's role. I had just a few days to prepare for the grand event. However, the play was a huge success and it moved the audience to tears. We staged another play during that time, *Shaheed Sherwani (Martyr Sherwani)*, written by Prem Nath Pardase whose illustrious son Som Nath Sadhu, along with Pushkar Bhan, later aired a very popular program, "*Zoon Dab*," on Radio Kashmir. I also worked for Radio Kashmir whenever required sans remuneration. Also, I vividly remember the role played by Sumitra Lakhwara and her sisters who worked relentlessly round the clock with the women's militia. Members of the women's militia hoisted the flag of Indian-administered Jammu and Kashmir when Abdullah was sworn in as prime minister of the state in 1948. Sumitra, her sister and I passionately sang the anthem of the state, "*Leheraaye Kashmir ke Jhanday*" ("The flag of Kashmir is unfurled and flies high"), at the ceremony.

After the attack by Pakistani raiders was successfully repulsed, the men's militia was amalgamated into the Indian army as the Jammu and Kashmir Light Brigade. The amalgamation, however, was not with retrospective effect, from the day the militia was formed, but from a later date. This affected the seniority of the officers and soldiers of the Jammu and Kashmir Light Brigade. The fact that the amalgamation came into effect from a date later than the actual formation of the militia was construed as the Government of India's attempt to discriminate against Kashmiris. (E-mail from Sajjida Zameer to author, 1 April 2008)

Ironically, women in J & K have not yet found niches in the upper echelons of decision-making bodies—political, religious, or social. Asymmetrical gender hierarchies legitimized by the forceful dissemination of fundamentalist and militarized discourses portend the debasement and prostration of women.

Kashmiri society needs to recognize the terror caused by such predatory discourses that swoop down on the vulnerable, devouring their ideological and experiential strengths. The retrieval of the strength that nurtured the rich experiential content of the teachings of mystic poet Lalla-Ded, the conviction of the women volunteers of WSDC, the vision of women activists who were harbingers of change in the sociopolitical and cultural realms, would facilitate the recomposition of women's roles in the significant process of nation building. Do women embody the history of a culture and community only as it is remembered in the murky corridors of officialdom? The inception of the militant separatist movement in J & K in 1989 scorched the landscape, particularly the headway that had been made in providing women with educational and economic opportunities. The ongoing story of the trouble-torn state is replete with instances of fathers forcing their daughters to live in marital unions of psychological, sexual, and material frustration, to prevent them from being violated by the paramilitary forces or by trigger-happy militants; of women accepting physical and emotional torture in their marital homes to preserve the "honor" of the family and the community; and of women who were "dishonored," either by being violated or by asserting their political and sexual agency, being shunned by their families (Amnesty International, "India," 2005; Kashmiri Women's Initiative for Peace and Disarmament 2004). Consider Gayatri Chakravorty Spivak's delineation of the contexts in which the politics of representation renders mute the figure of the "third-world woman," which would apply to the situation in Kashmir:

> Between patriarchy and imperialism, subject-constitution and object-formation, the figure of the woman disappears, not into a pristine nothingness, but a violent shuttling which is the displaced figuration of the "third-world woman" caught between tradition and modernization. (Spivak 1999: 304)

Power relations within the prevalent discourses of patriarchy and fundamentalism mediate the Kashmiri woman's identity. The valorization of her subordination is underwritten by praxes that legitimize gender identities, which are necessary to patriarchal and fundamentalist dominance.

Despite the political mobilization of Kashmiri women during the upheaval in 1931 and the politically volcanic "Quit Kashmir" movement of 1946, they have now reverted from the public sphere to the private realm. The onslaught of despotism in 1931 unleashed by Maharaja Hari Singh awakened Kashmiri women from their slumber

Kashmiri women protesting against the atrocities inflicted by police and paramilitary troops, Srinagar, Kashmir. (*Courtesy*: The collection of Shuaib Masoodi/*Rising Kashmir*)

and induced them to rattle the confining bars of the monarchical cage. Remarkably, the illiterate women of Srinagar, Kashmir, were initiated into political activism and it was they who heralded the political participation of educated women (Khan 1978: 115). The "Quit Kashmir" movement of 1946–1947 saw the evolution of women into well-informed and articulate protestors, assuming leadership roles in the quest for a Kashmiri identity: "When male leadership was put behind bars or driven underground, women leaders took charge and gave a new direction to the struggle" (Misri 2002: 19). But this consciousness of the women, which could have produced women cadres, was diluted by the reversion to normative gender roles. Attempts to drown the voices of progressive women into oblivion became more frequent with the onset of militancy in 1989–1990. Can women step out of their ascribed gender roles, once again, to significantly impact sociopolitical developments in J & K? Can the political and social exigencies of the women of J & K be addressed in more nuanced and purposeful ways?

Delineation of Concrete Measures

In November 2007, an intra-Kashmir women's conference, "Connecting Women across the Line of Control (LOC)," was organized in Srinagar by the Delhi-based Centre for Dialogue and Reconciliation (CDR), in collaboration with the Women's Studies programs at the Universities of Kashmir and Jammu. Women delegates from both sides of the LOC participated in the conference to productively discuss concrete methods of rehabilitating victims of violence, either state-sponsored or militancy related. Women from Indian- and Pakistani-administered J & K discussed the socioeconomic hardships, psychological neuroses, and political marginalization caused by dislocation, dispossession, and disenfranchisement. Delegates at the conference sought mobilization of women for effective change in political and social structures. They vehemently endorsed diplomacy and peaceful negotiations in order to further the India–Pakistan peace process; withdrawal of forces from both sides of the LOC; decommissioning of militants; rehabilitation of Kashmiri Pandits to rebuild the syncretic fabric of Kashmiri society; and rehabilitation of detainees (Barve 2008). Some of the strategies delineated at the conference may seem utopian, but it highlighted the ability to imagine confidence-building measures that grapple with normative structures and underscore the decisive role that women can play in raising consciousness, not just at the individual but at the collective level as well, giving the marginalized a vision with which to redefine life's constituting parameters.

Historically, cultural, societal, and market constraints have denied women access to information about the outside world. But the sort of advocacy concretized by the intra-Kashmir women's conference could overturn the historical seclusion of women and provide them with routes to make forays into mainstream cultural and socioeconomic institutions. Perhaps the mobilization of women at the collective level would enable a metamorphosis, fostering the skills and ability of women to make informed decisions about issues in the nondomestic sphere. The conference provided a forum where women's experiences were contextualized, theorized, and politicized. Culture inscribes a wide range of experiences that centralizing institutions attempt to render invisible and homogeneous. But women in J & K, as in other postcolonial countries, are positioned in relation to their own class and cultural realities; their own histories; their sensitivity to the diversity of cultural traditions and to the questions and conflicts within them; the legacies of Sufi Islam; their own struggles not just with the devastating effects of Indian occupation and Pakistani infiltration, but also with the discourses of cultural nationalism and religious fundamentalism; their own relations to the West; their interpretations of religious law; their beliefs in the different schools of Islamic and Hindu thought; and their concepts of the role of women in contemporary societies.

Conclusion

Complexity of the Kashmir Issue

The people of Kashmir have tried, time and again, to translate themselves from passive recipients of violence, legitimated by legislations of the physically and psychologically removed parliaments of India and Pakistan, into subjects who recognize that they can exercise agency and command their own destinies. They march forward with a refusal to allow history to be imposed on them, and they attempt to take charge of their own social and political fortunes. The confluence of religious nationalism, secular nationalism, and ethnic nationalism create the complexity of the Kashmir issue.

Over the years, successive Congress governments of the Indian Union may have made attempts to highlight the purported illegitimacy of Article 370, but they have taken no serious measures to revoke it from the Constitution of India. Surprisingly, even the Hindu right-wing BJP, when it assumed power in New Delhi, avoided succumbing to the pressure put on it by its more fanatical cohorts to eradicate the special status enjoyed by the Muslim-dominated Indian-administered state of J & K. India's policy vis-à-vis Kashmir was influenced by other variables. Pakistan's formal political alignment with the United States motivated the Soviet Union, in the 1950s, to overtly support the Indian stance toward Kashmir. The Soviet premier Khrushchev made explicit his government's pro-India position on Kashmir in 1955, when he belligerently declared in Srinagar, the heartland of the Kashmir Valley:

> The people of Jammu and Kashmir want to work for the well-being of their beloved country—the Republic of India. The people of Kashmir do not want to become toys in the hands of imperialist powers. This is exactly what some powers are trying to do by supporting Pakistan on the so-called Kashmir question. It made us very sad when imperialist powers succeeded in bringing about the partition of India....That Kashmir is one of the States of the Republic of India has already been decided by the people of Kashmir. (Jain 1979: 15–20)

The explicit political support of the Soviet Union in the Cold War era bolstered Jawaharlal Nehru's courage, and, in 1956, Nehru reneged on his earlier "international commitments" on the floor of the Indian parliament.

He proclaimed the legitimacy of the accession of Kashmir to India in 1947, which ostensibly had been ratified by the Constituent Assembly of J & K in 1954. Nehru's well-thought-out strategy was deployed in full measure when the Soviet Union vetoed the demand for a plebiscite in Kashmir made at a meeting of the UN Security Council convened at Pakistan's behest (see Dasgupta 1968). It was in 1953 that Pakistan initiated negotiations with the United States for military assistance. Bakshi protested that "America might arm Pakistan or help her in any other way but Kashmir will never form part of Pakistan" (*The Hindu Weekly Review* 1953). Nehru vehemently warned Pakistan and the United States that, "it is not open [to Pakistan] to do anything on Kashmir territory, least of all to give bases" (*Indiagram* 1953). He expressly declared that the agreement between him and Pakistani Premier Liaquat Ali Khan regarding the Kashmir issue would change if Pakistan received U.S. military aid (Speech, House of the People, 29 December 1953).

Subsequent to the disintegration of the Soviet Union, India lost its powerful ally (Kodikara 1993). India's relations with the United States reeked of distrust and paranoia at the time. This worsened when senior officials in the first Clinton administration questioned the legality of the status of Kashmir as a part of the Indian Union (Battye 1993). The nonproliferation agenda of the United States in South Asia actively undermined India's proliferation strategy in the early and mid-1990s (Perkovich 1999: 318–403). Washington's agenda was propelled by the fear that South Asia had burgeoning potential for a nuclear war in the future (see Kelly 2008). Pakistan's overt policy of abetting fanatical Islamic elements in Kashmir and Afghanistan led to its political insularity and seemingly legitimized India's proactive approach. The United States adopted the policy of persuading both India and Pakistan to actively participate in the nonproliferation regime by agreeing to comply with the Comprehensive Test Ban Treaty (CTBT) and to an interim cap on fissile-material production (Talbott 1998).

Human Rights Violations during the Insurgency

The insurgency in J & K, which has extracted an enormous price from the people of the state, was generated by the systemic erosion of democratic and human rights, discrimination against the Muslims of the Valley, socioeconomic marginalization, relegation of the right to self-determination to the background, and so on. While the rebellion may have been incited by India's political, social, and economic tactlessness, it has been sustained by military, political, and economic support from Pakistan. Proponents of the independence of the state of J & K are just as stridently opposed to Pakistan's administration of Azad (Free) Kashmir as they are to India's administration of J & K. During the ongoing insurgency, the Indian military has been granted carte blanche without an iota of accountability. In a telephone conversation (21 April 2008) with the chairman of the breakaway faction of the Jammu and Kashmir Liberation Front (JKLF), Yaseen Malik reiterated his commitment to an independent J & K. Speaking in favor of an ideology of nonviolence, in a tenor that was radically different from the violent rebellion he had espoused in 1988–1990, Malik was forthright in condemning the irreverence of the Indian Union toward the aspirations of the people of J & K. He pointed out that Sheikh Mohammad Abdullah had led a nonviolent struggle for self-determination from 1953 to 1975, to no avail. During that period, the Indian Union treacherously employed its institutional powers to gradually defang Abdullah so that his struggle of mammoth proportions could be pummeled into a much-weakened substitute. In the spirit of Kashmiri nationalism, the JKLF keeps the revolutionary flames of the Plebiscite Front (PF) alive, the movement spearheaded by Abdullah and Mirza Afzal Beg, Malik said. (I have discussed the formation and the credo of the PF in chapter three.) Foregrounding the ugly side of Indian democracy, Malik pointed out that his espousal of nonviolence has only won him more brickbats from the purported upholders of democratic processes in the Indian Union. Although he declared a unilateral cease-fire in June 1994, he and his comrades have been persistently harassed, tortured, and brutalized. He observed that from 1988 onward the political sentiment of the majority of Kashmiris has been concretized through immeasurable sacrifices made by the people. Most families in the Valley have lost at least one member and have been uprooted or dispossessed.

Custodial disappearances and deaths continue, and official orders regarding the protection of detainees are brazenly rubbished. While condemning the impunity with which paramilitary forces and the police conceal the illegal, malicious, or premeditated killing of a detainee, the acting chairperson of the State Human Rights Commission observed:

> The growing incidences of torture and death in police custody have been a disturbing factor. Experience shows that the worst violations of

human rights take place during the course of investigation, when the police, with a view to secure evidence or confession, often resort to third-degree methods including torture. It [the police] hides arrest either by not recording the arrest, or terming the deprivation of liberty merely as a prolonged interrogation. (*Greater Kashmir*, 20 March 2008)

A particularly draconian decree, the Jammu and Kashmir Public Safety Act (1978), permits law-enforcing agencies to detain a person for up to a period of two years on grounds of vaguely defined suspicion. The act originally stipulated that a detainee could be kept in custody for up to a year without being formally charged if public order was in jeopardy and for up to two years if the security of the state was jeopardized. A modification to the act in 1990 made it non-obligatory for the authorities to provide the detainee with reasons for his or her arrest. The International Commission of Jurists, in its report, has drawn the inference that victims of the aforementioned act have undergone terrible trauma. The discriminatory nature of this act undermines efforts to discover the whereabouts of such persons (*Human Rights in Kashmir* 1994).

Another equally stringent measure was the Terrorist and Disruptive Activities (Prevention) Act of 1987, which was designed to quash terrorist acts. In the zeal of the moment, the act defined disruptive activities in the following words:

any action, whether by act or by speech or through any other media or in any other manner, which questions, disrupts the sovereignty or territorial integrity of India, or which is intended to bring about or supports any claim for the cession of any part of India or the secession of any part of India from the Union. (Section 4, as quoted in *Human Rights in Kashmir* 1994)

This rather high-handed definition was a violation of the freedom of speech. Under the act, two special courts were established, in Srinagar and Jammu, to try arrested persons.

The Armed Forces (Jammu and Kashmir) Special Powers Act was enacted in 1990, giving the Union government in New Delhi and its representative in the state, the governor, the authority to arbitrarily declare parts of J & K "disturbed areas" in which the military could be willfully deployed to quell legitimate political activity. The military was entitled to shoot to kill, which involved "a potential infringement of the right to life" (ibid.). The introduction of other severe laws by the government of India has made it further nonobligatory to provide for any measure of accountability in the military and political proceedings in the state. Despite these highly discriminatory and unpopular measures, the support enjoyed by some of the militant organizations in the early 1990s abated by the mid-1990s. Balraj Puri (1995: 78) points out that the mushrooming of militant organizations, the disarray within their ranks, disagreements regarding their ultimate objective, and Pakistan's vacillating attitude toward the insurgents contributed to the steady decrease in their verve and influence.

Human Rights Violations in Areas under Pakistani Control

While strongly conveying its disapprobation of the treatment meted out to the Northern Areas by the government of Pakistan, the Human Rights Commission of Pakistan reported, in its monthly newsletter in January 1994, that:

> The government of Pakistan governs the Northern Areas (NA) through the Kashmir and Northern Areas Division (KANA). Authority behind KANA has remained vague. The executive head is the chief commissioner appointed by KANA and only answerable to it. The place is totally under bureaucratic rule. There is no industry in NA. The Judicial Commissioner does not have writ jurisdiction and, as the people of the NA do not have any fundamental rights, the Judicial Commissioner does not have jurisdiction to enforce them. The Judicial Commissioner has no say in the appointments and the transfers of subordinate court judges, which are done by the KANA division. The people of the NA have no say in what laws should govern them. The KANA exercises the powers of the provincial government for the NA, and by notification extends laws of Pakistan and such amendments as it thinks fit to the NA. Entrusting such absolute legislative powers to a government functionary is not without its share of hardships. By a notification, Order 39 of the Civil Procedure Code was amended, taking away the powers of the civil courts to grant temporary injunctions against the government. By another notification, the Speedy Trial Courts Act, 1992 was made applicable to the NA with the amendment that in appeals from the trial court, any differences of opinion between the two judges of the Appellate court will be settled by the chairman of the court. Such arbitrary application of laws is particularly unfair because not only do the people have no forum to protest against or amend these laws, but

also because the courts have no writ jurisdiction, nor do the people have any fundamental rights. Thus such laws cannot be tested for their legality and reasonableness for violation of fundamental rights. The Northern Areas Council is headed by the minister of KANA and meets whenever called by the minister. The members cannot convene a meeting. The orders require that a meeting of a Council should be called every two and half months, but in practice the minister does not convene one for months. The Council in any case has no power. It cannot form a government, cannot legislate, and has no say in the administration. It cannot suggest development schemes. The main function of the Councilors, as a cynic said, is receiving dignitaries from Pakistan. The police in the NA has no prosecution of crime branch nor a forensic laboratory. No newspaper is published within the NA. There are few local language weeklies and monthlies, but they are printed elsewhere. It has even given rise to the occasional rumor that the government itself pays the Ulema [Islamic clergy] to start the clashes. With very low literacy, extreme poverty and no organized political activity, it is not surprising that the Ulema have acquired such a strong hold over the people. No judicial enquiry has been held into the clashes in 1992, and no compensation paid to the heirs of the person killed or for properties damaged.

The remorseless militarization of the region, ecological and economic plunder, negation of legal procedures, lack of infrastructure, and virtual erasure has fueled the hitherto restrained resentment and anger in the NA. It is ironic that pro-Pakistan separatist groups in the Kashmir Valley gloss over the arbitrary exercise of authority in the NA, and glibly declare that these areas chose their geographical and political affiliation, legitimizing the lack of fundamental rights and the unaccountable authority of the KANA.

Military Crises and Diplomatic Rapprochements

During the last decade, each military crisis between India and Pakistan has been followed by attempts at diplomatic rapprochement, which have turned out to be fiascos. The two countries go through sporadic peacemaking efforts, characterized by negotiations. For instance, in January 2004, the then Indian prime minister, Atal Bihari Vajpayee, and the Pakistani president, General Pervez Musharraf, agreed "to the resumption of a composite dialogue" on all issues "including Jammu and Kashmir, to the satisfaction of both sides." Musharraf assured the Indian government that he would not permit "any territory under

Pakistan's control to be used to support terrorism in any manner" (*The Hindu*, 6 January 2004). But this joint statement could not mitigate the existing skepticism:

> Many observers have interpreted the joint statement as a tacit admission of Pakistan's past support for the LOC in Kashmir and an indication of its resolve to finally end military confrontation over the dispute. However, there is also considerable skepticism in India on the nature of change in Pakistan's policy: is it tactical or strategic? Similarly, the Pakistani government fears that India is taking unfair advantage of Islamabad's restraint to consolidate its political and military grip over Kashmir. (Kampani 2005: 179)

Pakistan has won the disapprobation of international powers by adopting the policy of fighting proxy wars through radical Islamist groups, which has reinforced New Delhi's confidence that the internationalization of the Kashmir dispute would not get unwieldy. India also believes that the restraint it exercised during the 1998 nuclear tests has given it the reputation of a responsible nuclear power.

Despite international pressure, the India–Pakistan crisis has not been defused; on the contrary, it is highly volatile. Given their interests in South Asia, Russia and China have expressed concern about the brinksmanship between the two countries. In order to facilitate a rapprochement, President Vladimir Putin of Russia offered to play the role of mediator between Indian Prime Minister Vajpayee and Pakistani President Musharraf at the scheduled regional summit conference in Almaty, Kazakhistan. Both Putin and the Chinese president, Jiang Zemin, held talks with Vajpayee and Musharraf in order to create a space for political negotiations. But the two heads of state continued to remain aloof and uncompromisingly condemned each other's belligerence. The one positive outcome of the summit talks, however, was the proposal of the Indian government for joint patrolling of the Line of Control (LOC) by Indian and Pakistani forces. But the Pakistani government was quick to reject this proposal and expressed the requirement for building a third-party force instead. Subsequently, the lethal and hitherto readily adopted practice of maneuvering a dangerous situation to the limits of tolerance mellowed, due to Vajpayee's and Musharraf's judicious approach to nuclear warfare. But the simmering grievances between India and Pakistan, and the distress of the Kashmiri people, remained unredressed (Schofield 2002: 242).

Indian Militarism and Pakistani Infiltration

Senior research associate at Proliferation Research and Assessment Program, Monterey Institute of International Studies, Gaurav Kampani's (2005) assessment of Indian militarism and Pakistani infiltration seems of particular relevance: valid concerns about the disastrous repercussions of a large-scale conventional war and the menace of nuclear escalation looming large on the horizon have deterred India from launching full-scale attacks on training camps, insurgent strongholds, and permeable routes in Pakistan-controlled territories that precipitate infiltration (ibid.: 166). Pakistan has been successful in aiding and abetting insurgents in Kashmir, in providing a red herring to divert the attention of the Indian military from insurgency and counterinsurgency operations in the Valley, and in underlining the internationalization of the Kashmir dispute. Pakistan has carefully wooed the United States by making the argument that nuclear disarmament can be achieved in South Asia only if the Kashmir crisis is resolved (Iqbal 1993). Again, I turn to Kampani's interesting inference regarding Pakistan's strategic rationale for its nuclear capability and its constant attempts to foreground the Kashmir issue: "the political linkage between regional nuclear disarmament and the resolution of the Kashmir dispute appears to be an opportunistic attempt on the part of Islamabad to create nonproliferation incentives for US policymakers to intervene in the Kashmir conflict" (Kampani 2005: 167; also see Chadha 2005). The Pakistani military reinforced Western concerns regarding nuclear proliferation in South Asia. In reaction to Pakistan's aggressive transgression of the LOC, India exercised political tact and restraint, winning international support for its diplomacy. Washington's political volte-face became apparent when it explicitly demanded that Islamabad withdraw from occupied Indian positions and maintain the legitimacy of the LOC in Kashmir. It was implicit in this demand that it saw Pakistan as the egregious aggressor.

The attempt by the United States to mitigate Pakistan's aggression also implied that it would not reinforce the status quo in Kashmir (Kampani 2005: 171). Washington's incrimination of Pakistani aggression mitigated New Delhi's fear that internationalization of the Kashmir dispute would spell unambiguous victory for Pakistan. India's strategy of diplomacy and restraint increased the international pressure on Pakistan to withdraw its forces from Indian territory. India took recourse to limited conventional war under nuclear conditions, prior to President Clinton's March 2000 visit to New Delhi. At this point in time, proliferation was relegated to the background in Indo–U.S. relations. In an e-mail to me (dated 10 April 2008), senior advocate of the Supreme Court of India, the late P.N. Duda, wrote:

> The US has a morbid syndrome of commune-phobia. After the end of the World War I, Palestine was brought under the mandate of the UK, and on releasing it for freedom, an enclave in the heart of Palestine, Israel, was created as landing, stacking and attacking base to all West Asian states. Now the sole superpower and its conclave are interested in creating another Israel to artfully manage the former Soviet Union, China, Mongolia and Afghanistan in South Asia. There cannot be a better place for that than India.

Stephen P. Cohen and Sunil Dasgupta underline the further recession of this issue to the background during the Bush administration. The neoconservatives in that administration zeroed in on India as a country in the Asia–Pacific region that would offset China's burgeoning economy, which I see as an attempt to reconstruct the Cold War paradigm ("U.S.–South Asia: Relations under Bush," 2001).

U.S. strategic ties with New Delhi were further consolidated in the wake of 11 September 2001, when the links between militant Islamic groups and Pakistan's military and militia forces were underscored. As one of the consequences of the decision of the Bush administration to eliminate Al-Qaeda and its supporters in Afghanistan, Pakistan's General Pervez Musharaff found himself with no option but to sever ties with the Taliban. Following this drastically changed policy decision to withdraw political and military support from Al-Qaeda and the Taliban, Islamabad found itself unable to draw a clear line of distinction between "terrorists" in Afghanistan and "freedom fighters" in Kashmir. Islamabad's quandary proved New Delhi's trump card (Chaudhuri 2001). New Delhi was able to justify its military stance vis-à-vis Pakistan in the wake of the terrorist attacks on the J & K State Assembly in the summer capital, Srinagar, in October 2001, and then the attacks on the Indian Parliament, New Delhi, a month later. New Delhi's strategy was validated by U.S. military operations in Afghanistan and the deployment of U.S. forces in and around Pakistan to restrain Pakistani aggression. India was assured by the United States that it would stall any attempt by Pakistan to extend the Kashmir dispute beyond local borders, which might disrupt its operations against Al-Qaeda and the Taliban. Also, deployment of the U.S. military in Pakistani air bases strengthened New Delhi's confidence that Islamabad would hesitate to initiate nuclear weapons use (Kampani 2002). The result of India's policy of coercive diplomacy was that the Musharraf regime was pressured by the United States to take strict military action against the mercenary and militant Islamic groups bolstering the insurgency in Kashmir (Armitage 2002). New Delhi was successful in getting Islamabad to both privately and publicly renounce its support of insurgents in J & K.

The Indian administration decided that in the event deterrence measures failed, the Indian army would have to fight a limited conventional war under nuclear conditions. The possibility of fighting a war has driven the Indian government to contemplate a nuclear response to Pakistan's deployment of nuclear weapons (see Chengappa 2000). But Indian leaders have threatened Islamabad with punitive measures if Pakistan resorts to nuclear weapons use (Tellis 2001: 251–475). India and Pakistan routinely brandish their nuclear capabilities to intimidate each other. The two countries have also resorted to direct nuclear signaling through ballistic-missile tests. Such strategies emphasize the military and political volatility in South Asia (*Dawn*, 27 December 2001). Pakistan's nuclear arsenal has given its military the prowess it requires to exploit the disgruntlement of the Muslim population of the Kashmir Valley. Kampani makes an intelligent assessment about the growing nuclear capabilities of both India and Pakistan, and the role they have played in deterring a large-scale conventional war. Pakistan's military leaders are privately convinced that its daunting nuclear arsenal has dissuaded India from embarking upon a large-scale war. India's cautious stance is, however, dictated by multiple factors. Its primary concern is that a limited war will not enable it to accomplish substantive political or military objectives; that such a war might spin out of control and would be impossible to cease according to the wishes of the administration and the military; that India might find itself in disfavor with and spurned by the international community; and that a war might beef up nuclear armament. The impending menace of precipitative nuclearization has been one of the many factors underlining the necessity to maintain a quasi-stable regime in the South Asian region (Kampani 2005: 177). In effect, one of the ramifications of India and Pakistan climbing the ladder of nuclear proliferation has been a tottering stability, maintained amidst the continuing conflict in Kashmir. However, the overt support that the Pakistani government has lent to the insurgents in Kashmir has enabled India to tarnish Pakistan's reputation by labeling it a terrorist state.

Pakistan's explicit aiding and abetting of insurgents in Kashmir has created misgivings about its strategies and enabled India to prevent UN mediation. New Delhi managed to diminish the threat of internationalization of the Kashmir dispute in 2001–2002 by threatening a nuclear exchange unless the United States intervened to prevent Pakistan from fomenting cross-border terrorism (ibid.: 178). The ideological and power rivalry between India and Pakistan, however, transcend the Kashmir dispute (Tellis 2001: 8–11). Regardless of the possibility of nuclear restraint in South Asia, a resolution of the Kashmir dispute would put a monkey wrench in the drive in both countries to beef up their nuclear arsenals.

Groping for Concrete Resolutions to the Conflict

Disenchanted by the intractable political positions taken by India and Pakistan vis-à-vis the former princely state of J & K, there are organizations, political leaders, insurrectionists, intellectuals, and social activists on both sides of the LOC that propagate politically workable solutions for a resolution of the complex Kashmir issue. For example, the late G.M. Shah, political veteran and older son-in-law of Sheikh Mohammad Abdullah, also former chief minister of J & K and president of the Awami National Conference, took an initiative of providing a broad-based forum for masses, leaders, and intellectuals of all hues and faiths to come together and deliberate upon the intricate Kashmir tangle. His desire was to generate practically workable and politically feasible recommendations for coming out of the imbroglio. Toward this objective he had proposed a two-day conference, "J & K Conference—In Search of Peace and Solution," in Jammu on 17–18 March 2001 to enable the "power of dialogue" to reassert itself in the former princely state of Jammu and Kashmir;

> to enable, for the first time in fifty years, political leaders, protagonists of the armed struggle, social activists, intellectuals, technocrats and eminent citizens from both sides of the Line of Control to meet and interact; to enable the supporters of diverse political solutions and thoughts to sit face to face and exchange views on the political, ethnic and social dimensions with the people of all regions of the state; to enable detailed discussions on all aspects and complexities of different proposals put forth over the past fifty years by various personages and political opinions for the resolution of the Kashmir issue. (E-mail to the author from G.M. Shah dated 2 April 2008)

The objective of this conference was to generate ideas, proposals, and recommendations for a broad-based resolution to the conflict, which would be acceptable to the people of the state. Shah's well-publicized willingness to undertake this initiative awakened eager interest in Gilgit, Baltistan, and Skardu as well. But the turmoil in Indian-administered J & K and rumblings of discontent in Balawaristan, unfortunately, created an atmosphere distended with misgivings and paranoia. The governments of India and Pakistan, impaired by the travails of political instability and military belligerence, did not allow the conference to be held in 2001.

I do not question the bona fide intentions that might have propelled Shah's organization to propose an intra-Kashmir conference. But, rather than hypothetical ideas, the deescalation of violence in the former princely state requires decentralization of power. Decentralized autonomy in the entire region might prove a feasible solution to the political upheaval in the state. A well-constructed autonomy proposal, observes ex-foreign secretary of India Jagat S. Mehta, would require Pakistan to terminate its policy of infiltration and abetment of the insurgency in J & K. The political legitimacy of the state and its autonomous status would be established by the retention of Article 370 of the Indian Constitution. The separate identities of Jammu and Ladakh would be accommodated in the aforementioned policy of decentralization, and not through divisions along ethnoreligious lines. The LOC would be converted into the de facto international border, facilitating travel and economic exchanges while maintaining the political status quo of India and Pakistan. Free and fair elections in a democratic setup would need to be held simultaneously in both Indian- and Pakistani-administered J & K, after which the two elected governments would establish contact with each other in order to encourage economic and cultural exchanges between the two parts of the former princely state. Mehta's proposal stipulates that a final resolution of the Kashmir issue would be shelved for an agreed upon period, during which Pakistan would refrain from demanding internationalization of the issue or from holding a partial or state-wide plebiscite under UN auspices (Mehta 1992: 388–409, quoted in Wirsing 1994: 225–28).

In an e-mail exchange (dated 14 April 2008) that I had with a source at the Pakistan chapter of the All Parties Hurriyat Conference (APHC), the source observed that:

> the turbulence in Indian-administered Jammu and Kashmir has had a terrible fall-out on the political, economic and social life. Today, our politics is rough, vulgar, vengeful and materialistic. The economy of the state is devastated, and the social fabric has broken with disparity and unemployment amongst the lower sections of society. Moral values are trembling, and exploitation of weaker sections such as women,

widows and orphans is common. Islam is used merely as a political slogan and not as the most peaceful code of conduct and civilization. A viable solution to the conflict is to create a neutral, independent and federal democratic state of Jammu and Kashmir after complete demilitarization of the state. Let the right of self-determination of Kashmiris be supreme. Both India and Pakistan should respect the free will of the people of the state [former princely state]. There is a profound truth in the statement of Sir Morrice James, British High Commissioner to Pakistan in 1961–66, who, before his death in November 1989, said that, "if Kashmiris had inhabited an area of Sub-Saharan Africa or an island in the Indian Ocean instead of a key area of the Himalayas, their flag would long since have been hoisted along with those of other states—outside the United Nations building in New York."

Rather than demand pulverization of the insurgency and cessation of infiltration, the people of Indian- and Pakistani-administered Kashmir would favor resumption of dialogue with the militant groups in the state.

In order to protect the autonomy of the state, Article 370, which (as I have shown in chapter three) has undergone steady erosion, would need to be bolstered. Once the LOC is converted into a de facto international border, the Kashmir issue would be relegated to the catacombs of history. What substantive measures would sustained contact between the democratically elected governments of the two halves of the former princely state achieve? Is Mehta's insistence on Pakistan's renunciation of its demand for a plebiscite under UN auspices a surreptitious way of India ensconcing itself in a no future negotiations position? Does this proposal take the ethnic divisions in the former princely state into account?

Policy analyst and veteran journalist B.G. Verghese advocates a solution that would allow for conversion of the LOC into a soft, demilitarized international border. He proposes the creation of an overarching, transnational administration that would facilitate periodic meetings on matters of common interest, such as trade and tourism, economic exchange, environmental concerns, and so on (Verghese 1993, quoted in Wirsing 1994: 229). The efficacy of such an administration is not, however, developed by Verghese beyond its nascent appeal. The autonomy option is a lot more complex than it is made out to be by the plethora of proposals laid out by the Indian intelligentsia. As opposed to the various autonomy proposals, the notion of independence for either part or all of the former princely state is derided as impractical, economically destructive, and dangerous in terms of arousing the monstrous passion of communalism in the rest of the Indian subcontinent.

Robert G. Wirsing (1994: 231) sums up the repugnance toward independence for part or all of J & K in both India and Pakistan: "Kashmiri self-determination...has never meant for Pakistanis that Kashmiris had a right to any more than a bifold choice of destinies. The seeming unpopularity of the independence option among both Indians and Pakistanis leaves the Kashmiri Muslims as its only consistent advocate." Will such seemingly nonnegotiable antipathy expressed by politically and militarily powerful players allow for the implementation of UN resolutions by holding a free, fair, and internationally monitored plebiscite in the state?

Historical Omissions and Repressions

P.N. Duda wrote to me (e-mail dated 15 April 2008) about the turmoil in the state in an amusingly perceptive manner:

> I think I should stop reading newspapers. They make me sick with disgust. It has become common in the world of public media that the government of India will continue army siege of Kashmir till terrorism does not die, and in Kashmir making generous offer of line of control being converted to international border of Kashmir—India's commonplace political refrain! Or, Pakistan generously participating in bilateral talks with India from section officers' to secretaries' levels. That conveys nothing more than dogs in rings, moving at tremendous speed and stopping precisely at the point wherefrom they started. I fear both India & Pakistan have gone totally mad. The export wealth of G-7 is conventional arms and ammunitions. Under USA foreign affairs strategies currently, there are around four hundred big and small armed conflicts going on at intra or inter third world countries, USA in main and other G-7 giants graciously providing toys of killing in exchange for surrendering their options for development to breaking tariffs for flooding their markets with lifestyle junk. Their hundred percent occupations are: for one, occupying Kashmir without meaning it; the other, maintaining it as a state under siege. For both it is a God-given gift to both rape people's minds with animus against the other, for seeking support for their underworld politics that has taken the most dominant place in both. Not surprisingly, both tacitly being armed to their fingertips to be engaged in a Kilkenny Cat fight till rendered into lifeless bleeding tails.

The insurgency in Kashmir, India and Pakistan's ideological differences, and their political intransigence could result in the eruption of a future crisis.

The atmosphere of paranoia and mistrust is exacerbated by the frightening attempts of Hindu fundamentalist groups to rewrite Indian history and the recasting of Pakistani history by Islamist organizations: efforts to radically redefine Indian and Pakistani societies in the light of ritualistic Hinduism and Islam, respectively. Writing about this antihistorical attitude, Kai Friese reported in the *New York Times* that in November 2002, the National Council of Education Research and Training, which is the central government organization in India that finalizes the national curriculum and supervises education of high school students, circulated a new textbook for the social sciences and history. The textbook conveniently overlooks the embarrassing fact that the architect of Indian independence, Mohandas Karamchand Gandhi, was assassinated by a Hindu nationalist in 1948, a year after the proclamation of independence. Friese also points out that Indian history has been embellished with some interesting fabrications, one of which is the erasure of the Indus Valley civilization and the conjuring up of a mythical "Indus–Saraswati" civilization in its stead. This is a strategic maneuver to transform a historical civilization into a mythical one. The chapter on the Vedic civilization in the history textbook lacks important dates and is inundated with uncorroborated "facts," such as: "India itself was the original home of the Aryans. The Aryans were an indigenous race and the creators of the Vedas" (Friese 2002). Similarly, mainstream Pakistani history portrays the movement for the creation of the nation-state of Pakistan as a movement for an Islamic state, the carving out of which became a historic inevitability with the first Muslim invasion of the subcontinent. This version of Pakistani history establishes the Islamic clergy as the protagonists of the movement for the creation of a theocratic state (Hoodbhoy and Nayyar 1985: 164–77). Such propaganda to further narrow agendas makes it impossible to hold informed debates on issues of political and religious import. Jingoistic textbooks and biased interpretations negate the possibility of reaching a national consensus regarding Kashmir.

In the wake of Benazir Bhutto's assassination in December 2007, the politically chaotic climate of Pakistan, the belligerence of the military, and the tenacious control of fundamentalist forces basking in the glories of a misplaced religious fervor stoked by a besmirched leadership, can India and Pakistan produce visionary leaders capable of looking beyond the expediency of warfare, conventional or otherwise? Will the emerging leadership in Pakistan seek to douse the flames that threaten to annihilate the entire region by shelving the issue for future generations to resolve? Preparing to lead the new coalition government in Pakistan, cochairperson of the Pakistan People's Party and Benazir's widower, Asif Ali Zardari, condemned the distrustful atmosphere created in the Indian subcontinent by the Kashmir imbroglio. While underwriting the importance of fostering amicable relations between the two countries, Zardari said that the Kashmir conflict could be placed in a state of temporary suspension, for future generations to resolve (*Greater Kashmir*, 22 March 2008). Will the besieged populace of the state of the former princely state of J & K remain beholden to a leadership that doles out crumbs to them while dividing the spoils among themselves?

There is a dearth of responsible leaders in Indian-administered J & K: "Admittedly, there is no Sheikh Abdullah now, no single leader who authoritatively embodies the aspirations of his people" (Guha 2004: 15). Unlike the Machiavellian actors in current subcontinental politics, as Dr. Wahid, retired chair of the Department of Internal Medicine, Sher-e-Kashmir Institute for Medical Sciences, Srinagar, eloquently observed,

> every one of the founders of the freedom struggle who assembled in 1931 against the autocratic Dogra rule knew that this rebellion would mean death, torture, imprisonment and what not. Their ultimate aim was not to win an assembly seat. They were not electoral politicians. They all were a gift from God, who were destined to lead a tough struggle. They were all young and were not familiar with political machinations and maneuvering. They all had a sentiment and har-bored a purpose. In spite of having interpersonal misgivings and distrust, they all were great and the nation owes a lot to them. Nobody is perfect. They all had a deficiency here and there. But every great person can have such deficiencies. This does not make him small. Every one of them thought that his ideology was correct. Some of our intel-lectuals try to belittle their greatness and nobility. It is ironic that both India and Pakistan tried to demolish Sheikh Mohammad Abdullah but they did not succeed. Our tragedy is that we are never objective and carry with us malice and hatred based on false and ill-fed propaganda. (E-mail to the author dated 25 March 2008)

Within the wide political spectrum in the state, one does not even come close to a representative body willing to forge a reasonable dialogue. Duda, too, lamented the leadership vacuum in the Indian subcontinent, made more glaring by the insidious political culture in India and Pakistan. Before he passed away in December 2009, he was working on a *Causative History of Kashmir Politics since Partition* with Dr. Pushpesh Pant of the Department of International

Relations, Jawaharlal Nehru University, New Delhi. Duda wrote (in an e-mail to the author dated 6 April 2008):

> For four and a half decades, your grandfather, Sheikh Mohammad Abdullah, played the same role in politics which Noor-ud-Din Wali and Lalla Arifa played in religion. I look upon him as the greatest secular leader South Asia has produced. And when I say that I have in mind Nehru and Gandhi too, who didn't come close to him in secular and humane politics. The Kashmir matter calls for two voices: problem exists; no solution seems plausible. These leaders have come to be carrying a price-tag; almost the entire leadership is a commodity for sale and purchase; there is no idealism; no patriotism; people of Kashmir (India-occupied) will suffer if Pakistan gets control over them because they might be looked upon as apostates and suffer worse; Kashmir on boil is providing to both India and Pakistan a blood-stained bowl for begging that provides access to easy money. The material problems and ambitions will continue to be rewarding in multiples if the movement continues with slaughter, death and rape of a few to seek notice and attention. Some time back I read a gossip column that an army officer from Uri, near the de facto Pakistan border, revealed that when some insurgents were trying to cross over from across the border, a bargain took place: five were killed (for a pat on the back from Army headquarters), twelve were permitted to enter (for booty-sharing of sizeable degree in US dollars). The Muslim leadership in Kashmir has reached an abysmally degenerate stage of the political marketplace where they sell the interest and honor of Kashmir to political mafiosos of India. The way the Hindu fundamentalist leadership is behaving is metaphorically spitting on the faces of Sheikh Mohammad Abdullah, Mahatma Gandhi and Jawaharlal Nehru, manifesting the fast-depleting traces of secularism.

Efficacy of the Discourse of International Conferences on Local Realities

In an attempt to create a congenial atmosphere for rational dialogue, the globally known nonprofit organization Pugwash organized a two-day seminar on the Kashmir conflict, in the capital city of Pakistan, Islamabad, on 29–30 March 2008. The purpose of the Pugwash conference was to facilitate a convention of public figures and intellectuals from India, J & K, Pakistani-administered J & K, and political and scholarly persons of international repute, in order to define conflict-mitigating strategies in South Asia. The governmental and military representatives at the conference discussed stability in the state of J & K; initiatives to promote peace and cooperation between India and Pakistan; volatility of the situation in Afghanistan and measures to counter the instability in that region; and the impact of the changed Pakistani political scenario on the South Asian region (*Daily Etalaat*, 3 April 2008).

Such conferences are held on a regular basis but the propositions discussed have failed to make a substantive impact on the fragile Kashmir issue. Although representatives from both sides of the LOC make regular appearances at these venues, the prevalent discourse is rather elitist in nature and the woes of the marginalized remain unheard. Participants at the 2008 Pugwash conference in Pakistan were those with access to the higher echelons of power who prefer to toe the line of totalitarian political and cultural institutions, and who to date have not outlined a meaningful plan for conflict resolution and rehabilitation of the dispossessed in the fractious political sphere of J & K. A global discourse that is generated at international forums, such as the recent Kashmir Summit Meet in Brussels, Belgium, held on 1 April 2008, can do little to formulate constructive programs for the ethnic and religious minorities in the bellicose nation-states of India and Pakistan unless the bona fide effort is to demilitarize the region and rehabilitate the disenfranchised—those who have been languishing in Indian and Pakistani jails without a cause, militancy affected people, and victims of counterinsurgency repression. At times it seems that such summits, organized by the hegemonic powers, and their privileged participants would not willingly allow the dilution of their raison d'être, namely, conflict situations.

A feasible solution to the conflict in Kashmir must fulfill the conditions delineated decades ago by Sheikh Mohammad Abdullah. It should not be designed to assuage the insecurities of either India or Pakistan. But it must, unconditionally, allay the fears of ethnic and religious minorities in both countries, and it must be in accordance with the wishes of the people of the state. International legal scholar Gidon Gottlieb, in his discussion of the changing world order, underlines the need to deconstruct old notions of sovereignty and, instead, construct a transnational community that would endow stateless peoples with citizenship and territorial and security guarantees:

> Nations and peoples that have no state of their own can be recognized as such and endowed with an international legal status. Those that are politically organized could be given the right to be a party to different types of treaties and to take part in the work of international organizations. (Gottlieb 1993, quoted in Wirsing 1994: 233)

But the solution outlined by Gottlieb is unrealistic and rather utopian. It is predicated on the nullification of national identity, cultural integrity intertwined with attachment to territory, and is clearly a politically vexed issue for the people of the former princely state, who, as I have underlined in the introduction, would stop being altogether in the absence of a body politic built on national pride. A solution of this sort could lead to further balkanization in the South Asian region, depleting national resources.

The Indian Union is on the verge of becoming an insuperable economic power. In order to enhance its economic and political clout in the South Asian region, it requires stability. Can it begin the process of establishing itself as a stable political force by initiating a serious political process in Kashmir in which the people of the state have a substantive say (telephone conversation with Yaseen Malik, chairman of the breakaway faction of the JKLF, on 21 April 2008)? A political package short of autonomy for the entire state is viewed with suspicion by Kashmiris. Can the governments of India and Pakistan make a smooth transition into the globalized world by shelving the politics of duplicity and recognizing the autonomous status of the former princely state? I do not pretend to know the answers to these questions. I do not know if the brand of treacherous politics that pervades not just the Indian subcontinent, but also Western vested interests will undergo a transformation in the years to come. Will the international community recognize the poignancy of the countless sacrifices made by the people of Kashmir over the last eighteen years?

In a post 9/11 world, political and cultural edifices that have been entrenched by imperial discourse have sanctified the convenient "first world–third world" dichotomy. Institutional politics have facilitated the construction of the "third world" subject as an eternally feral being whose essential savagery is not amenable to sociocultural conditioning. The rationale provided for the invasion of Iraq and Afghanistan, for example, is those territories' purportedly dehumanized condition that cries out for enlightenment, underscoring the constructed bestiality of non-Western, other cultures. The rhetoric of hate and destruction rent the air and engender a mass hysteria, inciting communal riots and human rights violations, as evidenced, for example, by the reprehensible negligence of human rights in J & K and the relentless persecution of Muslims in the Indian state of Gujarat in 2002.

The construction of the "first world–third world" dichotomy has befouled institutionalized politics and cultures, and vitiated progressive political and social change. In such a scenario, I, as a feminist activist–scholar, have sought to reinterpret the repressive frameworks of military occupation, nationalism, religious fundamentalism, and an ethnoreligious nationalism that developed unevenly among the social classes and regions of J& K. I have written this book specifically with the goal that it be useful in getting a broader picture of the Kashmir issue. I, uncharacteristically, have consigned theory to an obscure position, no matter how sophisticated, if I thought it did not have a practical application to the real lives of real people in J & K.

As I revise this conclusion to my book, the 2008 J & K Assembly election results have were declared in December 2008 and an NC–Congress coalition government was installed in January 2009. As the results of the assembly elections show, none of the mainstream political parties elicited a particularly ecstatic or loyal response from the electorate. Out of 46 assembly seats in the Kashmir Valley, the NC won 20, the PDP won 19, and the Congress secured 3 seats. Out of 37 assembly seats in Jammu, the NC won 6, the PDP won 2, the Congress made quite a showing by securing 13, and the Hindu right-wing BJP performed incredibly well by winning 11—a tremendous leap from the 1 seat it had won in Jammu in the 2002 assembly elections. In Ladakh, the NC won 2 out of 4 assembly seats, the Congress won 1 seat, and the PDP and BJP were nonexistent in that region. In a replay of history, the Congress with a total of 17 assembly seats and the NC with a total of 28 assembly seats, the same number it had in 2002 when it shunned the possibility of power-sharing and chose to sit in the opposition in all probability because neither Farooq nor his son, Omar, had a chance of heading the government as the former had not contested the election and the latter lost by a big margin to an obscure green horn. It could have been politically fatal for Omar to allow anybody else in the NC to taste blood. The same holds true for the PDP where the father-daughter duo would not want anyone else in their party to taste blood either, both parties contributing to the installation of democratic monarchy. This brings to my mind a couplet of the celebrated poet-philosopher Allama Iqbal: *Hum ney Khud-Shahi ko pehnaya hey jumjoori libas, jab zara adam hua hay khus shinas-o khud nigar.* (We have adorned our royal selves with a democratic attire, the moment man gained self-confidence and political sagacity). The Congress and the NC have now formed a coalition government headed by Farooq Abdullah's son, Omar Abdullah. The NC has managed to regain its lost dominance in the urban areas of the Kashmir Valley, whereas the authority of the PDP has remained unchallenged in the rural areas of the Valley. The BJP continues to be a political pariah in both the predominantly Muslim Valley and the predominantly Buddhist Ladakh, evidenced by its inability to win a single seat in either. The PDP, which has donned the robe of messiah of the rural populace of the Valley, also was unable to cut a figure in Ladakh. The Awami National Conference, which participated in polls after a hiatus of twenty-two years, was unable to make inroads into a single constituency in J & K. It remains to be seen if the increase in female representation in the 2008 assembly elections will facilitate the creation of a well-defined position for women in decision-making bodies in the national scenario (conversation with observers of the electoral process, 2008). The outcome of the election has reinforced the religious, regional, and provincial ruptures in the political fabric of the state. The dominance of the Congress has been buttressed by the fractured verdict and the zealous overtures made to it by the two mainstream regional parties, the NC and the PDP.

Subsequent to the declaration of the election results, the significance of the collective will of the people was undermined by the anxious appeals made to the Congress by regional parties to forge a jagged coalition government with them. It was interesting to watch the politicians rush to New Delhi in order to humbly submit their petitions to the Congress "High Command," which observed the political developments in J & K from its minaret in the citadel of quasi-secular politics. The yearning with which J & K politicians awaited "positive signals" from New Delhi about which party the Congress would choose to tie the proverbial knot with does not bode well for those who were hoping for a well-orchestrated fight for an independent, or at the least autonomous, J & K and a sincere attempt to protect "Kashmiriyat."

Has a veil been drawn over the wishes and aspirations of the people of the state? Have two decades of insurgency and counterinsurgency been made insignificant by the facile claim of mainstream politicians and separatist leaders that there is a clear line of demarcation between elections within the Constitution of India and the struggle for self-determination? Is the boundary between the two truly that well delineated?

The process of nationalist self-imagining is likely to remain in a nebulous state so long as the destiny of mainstream Kashmiri politicians is etched by the pen of the calligrapher in New Delhi and determined by maneuvers in the murky den of subcontinental politics. Can J & K politicians rise above their myopic aspiration to willy-nilly grab the throne and scepter? The obvious lack of self-reflexivity in regional parties shows a glaring inability to carefully consider the stakes. I wanted to end my book on a hopeful note but, sadly, the reins of J & K are yet again in the hands of New Delhi. The powers that be can pull those reins in any direction they deem fit. The two mainstream regional parties—the NC and the PDP—are pawns in a game of chess in which the odds are in favor of the Congress. A mere case of one-upmanship or power by "hook or by crook."

J & K in the current political context is a house divided. It is paradoxical to watch political bigwigs, bureaucrats, and civilian and paramilitary officers preening and gearing up to celebrate India's Independence Day, 15 August, while many Kashmiris continue to remain in the abyss of socioeconomic deprivation and political marginalization. J & K is a palimpsest that has been inscribed upon two or three times, yet the previous texts have been imperfectly erased and, therefore, remain partially visible. A history of unfulfilled pledges, broken promises, political deception, military oppression, illegal political detentions, a scathing human rights record, sterile political alliances, mass exodus, and New Delhi's malignant interference have created a gangrenous body politic that hasn't even started to heal. The various political, religious, and cultural discourses written on the palimpsest of the state may have created alternative epistemologies but without an epicenter.

On the one hand, lavish sartorial and epicurean preparations are annually made for Independence Day; on the other hand, there is a legitimately disgruntled segment of the populace that really hasn't experienced the trickle-down effect of India's burgeoning economy or flourishing democracy. August fifteenth has been a day of mourning for the marginalized, the disenfranchised, silenced, and invisible people of J & K. It is my hope that political actors of various hues in the state do not inter the victims of military and police brutality to the catacombs of history in their ardent desire to ingratiate themselves with the puppeteers in New Delhi and Islamabad who are adept at manipulating marionette regional representatives. August fifteenth is entrenched in world history as the day the nation-state of India gained independence and ousted the British colonial master, but in J & K it remains a day that reinforces the fragility of an ill-defined democracy and is blurred by the incessantly flowing tears of widows, orphans, dispossessed people, and despondent mothers.

After the first edition of *Islam, Women, and Violence in Kashmir: Between India and Pakistan*, published in June 2009, was reviewed by several Kashmiri academics, it was pointed out to me that autonomy was an inadequate solution. The intractability of the Kashmir conflict has made advocates of conflict resolution rather wary of applying a seemingly workable but facile solution to the complex political conflict. Mainstream media, intellectuals housed in academic institutions, formulators of public policy, and members of think tanks are quick to point out that regardless of the bloody and seemingly infinite nature of a political, ethnic, or racial conflict, a viable solution can always be found to dilute the fierceness of a conflictual situation. But one is cautioned against glibly advocating a kitsch solution to the Kashmir conundrum by the complexity of the Kashmir conflict, which embodies the brutalities of nation building devoid of myth or self-infatuation. The unruliness of the Kashmir conflict has led many to confuse the idea of nation with the power and brute force of the nation-states of India and Pakistan. Although the idea of self-determination collides with military oppression on the contentious site of nationalism, political accommodation can lead a war-weary people out of the colonnade of duplicitous rhetoric, political domination, and forceful imposition. The debate among political thinkers, scholars, and policy makers about finding viable ways to placate marginalized ethnic minorities in J & K has been infinite. Since the advent of independence, New Delhi's self-deluding and self-serving "democratic" approach has been to allow the disaffected people of J & K to voice their "seditious" opinions within the existing political framework legitimized by governmental rhetoric. The reasonableness of the autonomy solution advocated by mainstream political parties in J & K may seem axiomatic, but what is the likelihood of its being adopted in an undiluted form to metamorphose Kashmir's political, cultural, or territorial circumstances?

Both India and Pakistan have a long history of deploying rhetorical strategies to skirt the issue of plebiscite or complete secession of the former princely state of J & K. When feeling particularly belligerent, Pakistan cries itself hoarse declaring the legitimacy of plebiscite held under UN auspices in J & K; India responds just as aggressively by demanding the complete withdrawal of Pakistani troops from the territory of pre-partition J & K; or, in a moment of neighborly solicitude, for conversion of the LOC to a permanent international border. Which of these solutions is the most viable? Currently, mainstream political parties in Indian-administered J & K have jumped on the autonomy bandwagon. Although these terms are often used interchangeably, the differences between them are not insignificant. New Delhi asserts, time and again, that a revitalized Indian federalism will accommodate Kashmiri demands for an autonomous existence. But, historically, federalism hasn't always adequately redressed the grievances of disaffected ethnic minorities. Here, I concur with Robert G. Wirsing's observation that, "while autonomy seems to imply less

self-rule than does the term *confederalism*, for instance, it is generally understood to imply greater self-rule than *federalism*, which as in
the American case, need not cater to ethnic group minorities at all"
(2003: 199).

Given Kashmir's treacherous political climate and the rampant
political factionalism in that region, the appeal of an ambiguous
"autonomy" remains intact for some groups but for others, as has
been forcefully pointed out to me by a couple of political scientists,
it is a wrong narrative to establish in the case of Kashmir. Sadly, the
Kashmir conflict is no longer just about establishing the pristine
legitimacy of the right of self-determination of the people of J & K,
the former princely state. Rather, prolonging the conflictual situation
works in the interests of some of the actors, state as well as nonstate,
on both sides of the LOC. Some civil and military officials—Indian,
Pakistani, and Kashmiri—have been beneficiaries of the militarization of Kashmir and the business of the "war on terror." Also, some
militants, armed and unarmed, have cashed in on the political instability in the state to establish lucrative careers. For such individuals
and groups self-determination and autonomy work well as hollow
slogans stripped of any substantive content. The dismal truth is that
the wish to establish the legitimacy of self-determination or autonomy
vis-à-vis J & K is not universal. The current political discourse in the
state has strayed far from home.

Negotiating Necrophilia: An Afterword

Ashis Nandy

Kashmir overwrites almost everything that is written about it. Not because of its unique culture, its geopolitical significance, or its breathtaking natural beauty but because of its pain. Like Palestine and Northern Ireland, Kashmir is a typically twentieth century problem that has gate-crashed into the twenty-first century. All three places are beneficiaries of partitions mindlessly implemented by a tired imperial power and all are associated with gory, repetitious, gratuitous violence that wear out outside observers and analysts, but not those who participate in the violence.

State formation and nation building have an ugly record the world over. The subsequent humanization of many states and nations cannot wipe off that record, for the earlier memories are immortalized as part of a myth of origin that includes the idea of an unavoidable birth trauma. The sufferings experienced and the sufferings inflicted blend in that myth. Under the lofty rhetoric of today lie the persistent fears, bitterness, and anxieties of the past, even when the past has become distant. Every nation-state, thus, is permanently on guard. So are its detractors, enemies, and critics. That is because the myth of origin never fades or dates. Each generation rediscovers it, sometimes with even more passion than the earlier generation did.

Sadly, Kashmir has been captive, during the past sixty years, in the making of the myths of origin of India and Pakistan. Even more sadly, it now seems unable to resist the birth of a new creation myth of its own, which promises to replicate the efforts of its tormentors faithfully. Once a community experiences the trauma of state formation at its expense, its capacity to envision a different kind of political arrangement weakens. Happily, the myth may not have yet gelled in Kashmir. This is where Nyla Ali Khan comes in.

The main issues in Kashmir, as the officialdoms would have it, center around national interest, strategic significance, territorial contest, and security implications. Only ordinary Kashmiris trying to live ordinary lives in extraordinary times—Muslims, Hindus, and Buddhists—sense that the problem of Kashmir has to do with survival, clash of death machines, and the collapse of social ethics, that the pain of communities and families, however unfashionable and out-dated the idea may sound in the security community and policy elite, is the central reality in the land. To the experts and professionals, who man higher rungs of a state apparatus, and increasingly to the mainstream media, things like trauma and suffering are artifacts that have little to do with realpolitik, diplomacy, and public policy. They want to solve the problem of Kashmir the way such problems are usually sought to be solved—very scientifically, very dispassionately, and very professionally—backed by the coercive machineries of the states involved. They would rather not solve the problem if the solu-tion involves going beyond their known world.

In the meanwhile, Kashmir is becoming a haunted land where tens of thousands of dead haunt the landscape and question the living on the meaning and purpose of their deaths. The living cannot answer, because their melancholia has no place left anymore for lofty ideas and ideologies. At some level they know that the dead have died in vain, whether they have died resisting the Indian army or fighting militant Islam or Pakistan's territorial ambitions. Because Kashmir's own creation myth is not yet fully formed and functional, the rhetoric of martyrdom fails to compensate for the sense of loss. Kashmiris know that the death machines have done their job; that both sides can now only hope to say if they win, in the language of Yudhisthira in the Shanti Parva of the Mahabharata, "This, our victory is inter-twined with defeat."

The high casualties of violence in a small community only three million strong leaves no one untouched. Neither the official figures nor the unofficial estimates of human rights groups include the perma-nently maimed, those whose lives have been cut short by the trauma of uprooting, bereavement, or psychosomatic ailments. Everyone is bereaved and everyone is a mourner. The casualties include not merely the official and unofficial dead and the incapacitated, but also those who have disappeared without a trace. Family and kinship ties are strong in South Asia and the death of a distant cousin or an aunt can be a shattering personal tragedy. There is in Kashmir a miasma of depression that touches everyone except the ubiquitous tourist deter-mined to consume Kashmir's unearthly beauty. For decades, I am told, Srinagar's only medical college has had two beds for psychi-atric patients. Sometimes they seemed insufficient but usually they sufficed. Now some psychiatrists and psychotherapists estimate that the college requires the facilities to treat at least fifteen thousand at a time.

There are also the invisible victims of Kashmir, in Kashmir and outside. Thousands have died fighting for Kashmir; others have died in Kashmir, fighting for India or Pakistan. But there are even more humble victims, invisible and inaudible. I once met a few Kashmiri Muslim families, staying on the banks of Yamuna at Delhi in an impromptu slum. Someone took me to meet them because no one even wanted to listen to them. I listened to them but could not find out why they were there; they gave contradictory, often incoherent reasons for their plight. Were they simply looking for jobs in the plains pretending to be uprooted? Were they the victims of the militants for real or imaginary collaboration with security forces? Were they victims of suspicious security forces for their connections with the militants? I still do not know, but it seemed to me at the time that the political upheavals in the valley had created new kinds of refugees who had fallen through the black holes of the history of South Asia. They constitute parts of the flotsam and jetsam of our times.

One tragic instance of such uprooting are the Kashmiri Pandits. Ancient inhabitants of the Kashmir Valley, almost all of them have been driven out of the Valley to become invisible refugees. Even human rights groups look at their uprooting either as a case of minor collateral damage or an instance of foolish, self-induced trauma. Was the community really seduced by Governor Jagmohan's advice to them to leave their ancestral home? Do people leave a place where they have lived for centuries just because one bureaucrat, however important and powerful, single-handedly goads or invites them to implement the world's only known case of self-induced ethnic cleansing? Were there no genuine reasons at all for them to fear for their security? After their ouster from the Valley, some of the Pandits in their bitterness have organized themselves into a cacophonous, Hindu nationalist political group, further arousing the disdain of most human rights activists trying to be politically correct. Indeed, militant Kashmiri leaders have spoken to me about the Pandits with more compassion than have most scions of progressivism and radicalism.

During the last sixty years, Kashmir has emerged as the ultimate litmus test for the two largest South Asian states of their commitment to the ideas of a humane, democratic state and political imagination. Nyla Ali Khan spends much time in this book detailing the dishonesty, chicanery, inhumanity, and sheer cruelty that have characterized the behavior of the Indian and Pakistani states, the former claiming to be the world's largest democracy committed to global peace and Gandhian values, the latter continuously and noisily claiming to be an upholder of Islamic virtues. However well intentioned Khan's efforts, she has probably wasted her time. For this part of the story is by now well known to all except rabid nationalists and the cocooned bureaucracies and foreign policy elite of the two countries. What is less known is how, in the process, the problem of Kashmir has strengthened some of the worst trends in the political cultures of the two countries that comprise nearly three-fourth of South Asia.

The most noticeable of these trends is the growth of a culture of impunity around the two states. As they have intermittently unleashed their army, police, and paramilitary forces against the local populations in Kashmir, Nagaland, Balochistan, and Manipur in the name of territorial nationalism or Islamic solidarity, strangely, they have succeeded in debasing both the languages of nationalism and political Islam and discrediting the armies and the police. Indeed, many of the technologies South Asian states have deployed to fight secession and armed dissent are now being routinely deployed to crush dissent and abridge freedom, even in normal situations and normal times—such as state-sanctioned, fake-encounter deaths sometimes for reasons as trivial as bravery medals or businessmen facing threats from local thugs; large-scale use of third-degree methods during interrogation, an official euphemism for torture; and proliferating cults of violence. People have been subjected to aerial bombing in South Asia for aggressively articulating their grievances against the state. Entire villages have been burned down and women raped in the wake of army operations against secessionist movements. The large-scale degeneration and dehumanization in the state sector in the region finds expression not merely in normal pathologies of the security sector such as multimillion dollar scams in defense deals and the emergence of the region's own arms dealers with vested interest in war and conflict, but also in the triumph of the culture of nuclearization (which encourages the Left in India, backed by the silence of the First-World Left, to demand not the denuclearization of the country, but the full sovereignty for India's nuclear weapons program), and the growing culture of secrecy, censorship, and surveillance.

But nowhere have the two most populous states of South Asia faced such stubborn, recalcitrant people unwilling to turn docile, obedient citizens, safely integrated into either the world's largest democracy or the world's only nuclear-armed Islamic country. And the resistance has been more exasperating because of the passive-aggressive style that has often characterized it. A clue to this unequal battle lies probably in Kashmir's unique version of Sufism, with its distinctive touch of the androgynous. Kashmiris were officially seen by the British-Indian state—and, following it, by the court of the erstwhile maharaja and the successor regimes—as a nonmartial race, mired in passive, life-denying *sufiana*, ever unwilling to aggressively confront their political authorities. They were underrated by the rulers of India and Pakistan, the way the latter had underrated the nonmartial, poetry-chopping Bengalis in East Pakistan in 1971. No one believed that the worm would turn one day, that Kashmiri teenagers would react to and defy popular stereotypes to pick up guns and give the Indian army a run for its money. They were out to assert their masculinity the hard way.

Yet, remarkably, as in Bangladesh in 1971, while Kashmiri men were trying to erase the feminine within themselves, Kashmiri women showed a resilient capacity to meet head-on the violence let loose in Kashmir, the violence that saw Kashmiri suffering and pain as primarily nothing more than necessary blood sacrifice at the altar of nation building and state formation. Kashmiri women, this book suggests, have mostly been a defiant yet healing presence signaling restitution and reconciliation—in a battle-ravaged, terrorized society mediating between yesterday and tomorrow to keep hope alive today. Lalla-Ded, who can be considered the protagonist of this book's narrative, directly in some ways and indirectly in others, is significant by virtue of being a surviving symbol of what Kashmir was and still could be. Nyla Ali Khan uses her as a possible key to a future that contemporary politics chooses to see as only a red-ribboned fantasy produced by fevered imagination.

The memory and imagination of that singular woman seems to emerge out of the pages of this book to acquire an autonomous existence that mocks the merchants of war. She waits to become the presiding deity and moral pivot of another Kashmir that lives in the hearts of the Kashmiris—and perhaps also in the rest of South Asia—as a political possibility that has not yet been erased by the war dogs of our times.

Nyla Ali Khan's passionate, affectionate portrait of Kashmir looks to the future with hope because her reading of Lalla-Ded and the Kashmiri women's struggle for survival is the story of the possibilities that may not have been crushed by the combined efforts of fanatic militants and the Indian army. Kashmir can still be, under an imaginative visionary arrangement, a culture mediating between South Asia and Central Asia, between India and Pakistan, and perhaps even between Islam, Hinduism, and Buddhism.

A few suspicious of the format of contemporary nation-states speak of Tibet not as a cat's-paw that may help break China, but as a country that might someday help resume a number of vital dialogues, some ancient and some new—such as those between the Sinic and the Indic civilizations; between Confucianism, Buddhism, and Hinduism; between a rigid, copybook version of a nation-state and a loosely territorial, proudly soft state; and perhaps even the secular, the non-secular and the postsecular. Like Tibet, Kashmir can also become a location of our experiments with ourselves, outside the apparently inescapable frame of the European-style, nineteenth-century idea of progress. In any case, most Kashmiris, like most Tibetans, carry three invisible, imaginary passports and, spiting the rules of well-defined citizenship, they may in the future want to be simultaneously citizens of Kashmir, India, and Pakistan. That imagination has nothing to do with the nation-states in the region; it will have something to do with the conversations among cultures and civilizations going on for centuries in this part of the world.

Appendix A

KASHMIR'S ACCESSION TO INDIA: MAHARAJA–MOUNTBATTEN CORRESPONDENCE

(His Highness the Maharaja Bahadur of Jammu and Kashmir State, in a letter to His Excellency the Governor General of India, announcing the accession of Jammu and Kashmir State to the Dominion of India stated:)

My dear Lord Mountbatten,

I have to inform Your Excellency that a grave emergency has arisen in my State and request the immediate assistance of your Government.

As your Excellency is aware, the State of Jammu and Kashmir has not acceded to either the dominion of India or to Pakistan. Geographically my State is contiguous to both the dominions. It has vital economic and cultural links with both of them. Besides my State has a common boundary with Russia and China. In their external relations the dominions of India and Pakistan cannot ignore this fact.

I wanted to take time to decide to which dominion I should accede, or whether it is not in the best interests of both the dominions and of my State to stand independent, of course with friendly and cordial relations with both.

I accordingly approached the dominions of India and Pakistan to enter into a standstill agreement with my State. The Pakistan Government accepted this arrangement. The dominion of India called further discussions with representatives of my Government. I could not arrange this in view of the developments indicated below. In fact the Pakistan Government, under the Standstill Agreement, are operating the Post and Telegraph system with the State.

Though we have got a Standstill Agreement with Pakistan Government, that Government permitted steady and increasing strangulation of supplies like sugar, salt and petrol to my State.

---

* The three appendices are from the archives of the National Conference, with the kind permission of Sheikh Nazir Ahmad, General Secretary of the National Conference.

Afridi soldiers in plain clothes and desperados with modern weapons have been allowed to infiltrate into the State, at first in the Poonch area, then in Sialkot, and finally in mass in the area adjoining Hazara district on the Ramkote side. The result has been that the limited number of troops at the disposal of the State had to be dispersed and thus had to face the enemy at several points simultaneously so that it has become difficult to stop the wanton destruction of life and property and looting.

The Mohora power house, which supplies electric current to the whole of Srinagar, has been burnt. The number of women who have been kidnapped and raped makes my heart bleed. The wild forces thus let loose on the State are marching on with the aim of capturing Srinagar, the summer capital of my Government, as a first step to over-running the whole State.

The mass infiltration of the tribesmen, drawn from distant areas of the N.W.F.P. (North West Frontier Province) coming regularly in motor trucks and using the Mansehre-Muzzaffarabad road and fully armed with up-to-date weapons, cannot possibly be done without the knowledge of the provincial Government of N.W.F.P. and the Government of Pakistan. In spite of the repeated appeals made by my Government, no attempt has been made to check these raiders or stop them from coming to my State. In fact both Pakistan Radio and the Press have reported these occurrences. Pakistan Government even put out a story that a provisional Government had been set up in Kashmir. The people of my State both Muslims and non-Muslims, generally have taken no part at all.

With the conditions obtaining at present in my State and the great emergency of the situation as it exists, I have no option but to ask for help from the Indian Dominion. Naturally they cannot send the help asked for by me without my State acceding to the Dominion of India. I have, accordingly, decided to do so, and I attach the Instrument of Accession for acceptance by your Government. The other alternative is to leave my State and my people to free-booters. On this basis no civilized Government can exist or be maintained. This alternative I will never allow to happen so long as I am the Ruler of the State, and I have life to defend my country.

I may also inform Your Excellency's Government that it is my intention at once to set up an Interim Government and ask Sheikh Abdullah to carry the responsibilities in this emergency with my Prime Minister.

If my State has to be saved, immediate assistance must be available at Srinagar. Mr. Menon is fully aware of the gravity of the situation, and he will explain to you, if further explanation is needed.

In haste and with kindest regards,
Yours Sincerely
Hari Singh, The Palace Jammu
October 26th 1947.

In reply Lord Mountbatten wrote to His Highness The Maharaja Bahadur of Jammu & Kashmir State.

Government House, New Delhi
October 27, 1947.

My dear Maharaja Saheb,
Your Highness' letter dated October 26, has been delivered to me by Mr. V. P. Menon. In the special circumstances mentioned by Your Highness, my Government have decided to accept the accession of Kashmir State to the Dominion of India. Consistently with their policy that, in the case of any state where the issue of accession has been the subject of dispute, the question of accession should be decided in accordance with the wishes of the people, it is my Government's wish that, as soon as law and order have been restored in Kashmir, and her soil cleared of the invader, the question of State's accession should be settled by a reference to the people. Meanwhile, in response to your Highness' appeal for military aid, action has been taken to-day to send troops of the Indian Army to Kashmir to help your own forces to defend your territory and to protect the lives, property, and honour of your people. My Government and I note with satisfaction that your Highness has decided to invite Sheikh Abdulla to form an Interim Government to work with your Prime Minister.

With kind regards,
I remain,

Yours very Sincerely,
Mountbatten of Burma.

[HEADNOTE: 1947, ADDRESSED TO THE INTERNATIONAL COMMUNITY, Abdullah's noncommunal politics were vindicated by the ruthlessness of the Pakistani tribal raiders' miscalculated attack, which drove various political forces in the state to willy-nilly align themselves with India. Although the raiders, or *Qabailis*, were unruly mercenaries, they were led by well-trained and well-equipped military leaders who were familiar with the arduous terrain, and the raiders launched what would have been a dexterous attack if they had not been tempted to pillage and plunder on the way to the capital city, Srinagar (Dasgupta 1968: 95). En route to Srinagar, the tribal raiders committed heinous atrocities: they raped and killed several Catholic nuns at a missionary school, and tortured and impaled an NC worker, Maqbool Sherwani (Copeland 1991: 245). The brutal methods of the raiders received strong disapprobation from the people of the Valley who had disavowed a quintessentially Muslim identity and replaced it with the notion of a Kashmiri identity. This political and cultural ideology underscored the lack of religious homogeneity in the population of Kashmir. The raiders antagonized their coreligionists by perpetrating atrocities against the local populace, including women and children. The undiplomatic strategies of the tribal raiders and Pakistani militia expedited the attempts of the All India National Congress to incorporate Kashmir into the Indian Union.

Appendix B

JUDGE O' Ye HUMAN BEINGS!

"THIS" MEANS PAKISTAN

During the last few years, a war-torn world has been witness to the dark depths to which treachery can sink in pursuit of conquest through Aggression. But what happened to Kashmir, I dare say, adds altogether a new pattern to perfidy. Thousands of tribal Pathans equipped with mechanized weapons of war, swooped down on us not merely as armed bandits but as a centrally directed force with the avowed object of subjugating our land to the vassalage of Pakistan at the point of the gun. Unawares of such danger ahead of us, and without any warning from outside, we found that the invader had almost pierced through the heart of our country. They were perilously threatening Srinagar, the capital itself. Our people were literally stunned, not because they were afraid of losing their lives, but because they realized how serious a challenge it was to their will to be independent to decide their own destiny.

Sincerely,
Sheikh Mohammad Abdullah

[As the first Prime Minister of India-administered J & K from 1948 through 1953 Abdullah, with his socialist politics, many times reiterated his commitment to challenge the safely guarded domain of privilege and power that had disenfranchised the Muslim majority, reinforced the seclusion of Kashmiri women, and made their support irrelevant for the Dogra sovereigns and later for the regimes installed by New Delhi. Interestingly, it was the Kashmiri Muslims led by Sheikh Mohammad Abdullah who rallied around the notion of regional nationalism].

Appendix C

ABDULLAH'S CALL TO HIS PEOPLE TO STAND AGAINST EXPLOITERS OF ISLAM

My fellow people of Jammu and Kashmir,

For a long time you have been prey to poverty and heart breaking sufferings. For ages you have groaned under slavery, tightly shackled, only to die slowly from the tortures of hunger and pitiless want. You bore it in the ultimate hope that the dawn of deliverance will surely dispel darkness and distress from your benighted existence.

With that hope in front of us, I made the freedom of my people the first purpose of my life. It was a holy resolve which found an echo in many patriotic hearts, who are today by my side as most devoted colleagues, all sworn unto death to serve you and bring the happy gift of free and prosperous life. For years now we have faced bullets and bayonets. In that cause you have been with us as determined crusaders. Our martyrs, whom we salute, bear testimony to the purity of our purpose and the grandeur of our ideals as lovers of freedom.

Head of State,
Sheikh Mohammad Abdullah

Glossary

Abdullah, Sheikh Mohammad: Popularly known as the Lion of Kashmir, Abdullah reigned as prime minister of J & K from 1948 to 1953. When the pledge to hold a referendum was not kept by the Indian government, Abdullah's advocacy of Kashmir independence led to his imprisonment. He was shuttled from one jail to another until 1972 and remained out of power until 1975. During the period of Abdullah's incarceration, Congress Party-led governments in New Delhi made covert arrangements with puppet regimes they had installed. Prior to the 1975 accord between the Sheikh Mohammad Abdullah-led National Conference and the Indira Gandhi-led Congress, Abdullah demanded the revocation of all central laws extended to the state that delegitimized the popular demand for plebiscite. The then prime minister, Indira Gandhi, forged an accord with Abdullah in 1975 by promising to partially restore the autonomy of the state by revoking certain central laws that had arbitrarily been imposed on J & K. The same year, Abdullah returned as chief minister of the state. Sheikh Abdullah and his National Conference won an overwhelming victory in the election of 1977, and he remained in office until his death in 1982.

Association of Parents of Disappeared Persons (APDP): The APDP is an apolitical organization comprising mothers of Kashmiri Muslim boys who were victims of custodial disappearances or deaths. It was founded in the early 1990s by Parveena Ahangar, an illiterate and desperate mother whose son was arrested by Indian paramilitary forces on grounds of suspicion and taken to an unknown destination for interrogation. His whereabouts are still unknown. The APDP doesn't receive funding from any regional or national political organization. Parveena organizes demonstrations in Kashmir to protest the use of unwarranted torture and other brutal methods of interrogation by the police or military forces in various parts of the Valley.

Bharatiya Janata Party (BJP): A party that advocates Hindu nationalism and claims to protect the unitary identity of India's Hindu majority.

Border Security Force (BSF): The largest part of the enormous Indian paramilitary apparatus in Indian-administered J & K, deployed in counterinsurgency operations since 1990.

Buddhism: A set of philosophical and religious teachings, Buddhism was founded in the fifth century BC by Siddhartha Gautama, or the Buddha. Buddhism was a corrective to the social and political inequities perpetrated by ritualistic Hinduism.

Central Reserve Police Force (CRPF): A paramilitary force deployed in Indian-controlled J & K.

Congress: The party that spearheaded India's independence struggle against British colonial rule and superseded other organizations in India's political arena for almost four decades. Over the years, the Congress has acquired dynastic overtones and has come to be closely associated with Jawaharlal Nehru, first prime minister of independent India (1947–1964), and his progeny, Indira Gandhi (prime minister 1966–1977 and 1980–1984), Rajiv Gandhi (prime minister 1984–1989), and Sonia Gandhi (president of the Congress 1991–present).

Dogra: A martial Hindu community located in the Jammu region. A Dogra dynasty founded the principality of J & K and was the indisputable ruling house from 1846 to 1947.

Dukhtaran-e-Milat ("Daughters of the Nation"; DM): The only women's reactionary organization in Kashmir claiming that the Arabized version of religious scriptures to which this vigilante group subscribes is the authentic version. A large percentage of the Kashmiri populace looks upon the moral policing undertaken by this group in the Valley rather unfavorably. The DM advocates accession to Pakistan as the only viable option for Indian-controlled J & K.

Gujjar: Gujjars are a pastoral people who trace their lineage to the Rajputs of Rajasthan in India.

Hinduism: The world's oldest religion, Hinduism comprises diverse beliefs and traditions. It is a conglomerate of philosophy, theology, and mythology.

Hizb-ul-Mujahideen (HM): This guerilla outfit was formed in 1989. It has pro-Pakistani leanings and espouses a conservative religious ideology.

Instrument of Accession: The accession of J & K to the Indian Union took place under the provisions of the Constitution of India and was legitimized on 15 August 1947 and accepted by the governor-general, Lord Mountbatten. The subtext of the Instrument of Accession was that the wishes of the Kashmiri people would be taken into consideration once political stability had been established in the newly formed nation-states of India and Pakistan. The United Nations Commission for India and Pakistan (UNCIP) decreed a plebiscite for Kashmir on 13 August 1948 and 5 January 1949. Needless to say, a plebiscite was never held.

Inter-Services Intelligence (ISI): The ISI is the Pakistani military's well-organized and well-funded intelligence and covert operations wing. It has been actively supporting and charting the course of the insurgency in Indian-controlled Kashmir since the late 1980s.

Jammu and Kashmir Liberation Front (JKLF): An organization founded in the 1960s in Pakistani-controlled J & K, it espouses the political ideology of reuniting the entire territory of the former princely state of J & K as an autonomous state. JKLF activists pioneered the insurgency that started in Indian-administered J & K in 1990.

Jehan, Begum Akbar: Sheikh Abdullah's spouse, Jehan's maiden name was Nedou. She was part Austrian and part Gujjar. Akbar Jehan supported Abdullah's struggle and represented Srinagar and Anantnag constituencies in J & K in the Indian parliament from 1977 to 1979 and 1984 to 1989, respectively, and was the first president of the Jammu & Kashmir Red Cross Society from 1947 to 1951.

Kashmiri Saivism (Shaivism): A philosophy founded and propounded by Vasugupta and his contemporary, Somanand, in the eighth century AD. Vasugupta revealed the philosophy in his *Spanda Shâstra*, and it was further expounded by Somanand in his Pratyabhigyâ Shastrâ, Sanskrit works. It is a monistic philosophy that underlines the oneness of the self and the supreme deity. Kashmiri Saivism (Shaivism) is an idealistic philosophy that doesn't completely deny the objective reality of the world and propounds egalitarianism as opposed to an orthodox religious hierarchy.

Kashmiriyat: The doctrine of Kashmiriyat was shrewdly used by Abdullah's National Conference in order to create a secular ethos that would enfold both the Pandits and the Muslims of Kashmir. This secular ideology was intended to keep the intrusive policies of New Delhi at bay and to maintain the autonomous status of J & K. This notion of cultural harmony was, however, predicated on the maintenance of Kashmiri Pandit privileges. The political, economic, and social rights of the Muslim majority were barely incorporated into the larger political necessity of protecting the rights and privileges of the Pandit minority.

Lalla-Ded: A poetess syncretizing the Gnostic traditions of Sufism with Saivism (Shaivism), Lalla-Ded was born in 1334 into a Kashmiri Brahman home in Simpur village, about four miles from Srinagar, the summer capital of Kashmir. She witnessed Kashmir's transition to Islam, a period of tremendous upheaval as a new ruling dynasty was installed and a new religious ideology engendered tremendous zeal. The most significant contribution of Lalla-Ded to the Kashmiri language and literature is that she translated the sophisticated, esoteric concepts of Shaiva philosophy and her mystic experiences into the vernacular and made them accessible to the masses. She incorporated seemingly ordinary and mundane images into the philosophical teachings, enabling laypeople to relate to them.

Line of Control (LOC): This 740-kilometer dividing line between Indian-controlled J & K and Pakistani-controlled northern territories was created as a cease-fire line in January 1949 at the cessation of the first Indo–Pak war. It remained the LOC by amicable agreement between the two governments in July 1972. While the Indian administration refers to its portion of the territory as J & K, the Pakistani administration refers to its part of the territory as Azad (Free) J & K. The cease-fire line between the Republic of India and the People's Republic of China in the Aksai Chin is referred to as the Line of Actual Control.

Maurya Empire: Ruled by the Maurya dynasty from 322 to 185 BC, it wielded extraordinary political dominance and military prowess in ancient India. Founded in 322 BC by Chandragupta Maurya, it was probably the largest empire to control the Indian subcontinent.

Mughal Empire: An imperial power that politically and militarily controlled most of the Indian subcontinent from the early sixteenth to the mid-nineteenth centuries. The classic Mughal period began with the crowning of Jalauddin Akbar in 1556 and ended with the death of Aurangzeb in 1700. Emperor Jalauddin Akbar's army captured Kashmir in 1589. His successor, Jahangir, built the magnificent Shalimar Garden in Srinagar, Kashmir, a testimonial to the captivating charms of the Valley and to the sophisticated aesthetic sense of the Mughals. His empress, Nur Jahan, built the imposing Pathar mosque on the banks of the river Jhelum, which fell into disuse during the Dogra period but was restored to its former glory in 1932 after the upsurge of Kashmiri Muslim nationalism. Jahangir's successor, Shah Jahan, and his heir apparent, Dara Shikoh, further enhanced the aesthetic appeal of the Valley and its beauteous landscape by building mosques and gardens of unparalleled architectural grace. Subsequent political inefficacy, military feebleness, inability to quell local revolts, and growing dominance of British colonialism led to the decline of the Mughal Empire.

Muslim Conference (MC): Sheikh Mohammad Abdullah created a legitimate forum for himself and the state's Muslim population by founding the All Jammu and Kashmir Muslim Conference in 1932. Abdullah's disillusionment with the marginalization of the Muslim majority drove him to forge a movement that would focus on the structural inequities legitimized by the state. A unitary national identity was fashioned by the young leadership of the MC, including Sheikh Mohammad Abdullah, Bakshi Ghulam Mohammad, and Maulana Sayeed Masoodi, in order to expound upon the political expediency of the institution of a constituent assembly, adult suffrage, and protective measures for minorities. Eventually, the MC was replaced by the secular All Jammu and Kashmir National Conference, presided over by Abdullah in June 1939. Its first president was Abdullah's Communist ally, G.M. Sadiq.

Muslim United Front (MUF): An unwieldy coalition of nonmainstream, antiestablishment groups, the MUF remained a structureless organization besieged by multiple and intractable political ideologies. In 1987, the emphasis laid by the MUF on regionalism and cultural pride enabled it to woo a large number of Kashmiri youth.

National Conference (NC): The Muslim Conference (MC) was converted into the All Jammu and Kashmir National Conference in 1939. In 1944, the NC sought a reconstitution of the political, economic, and social systems of J & K. The NC came to be identified with the socially leftist republicanism and personality of Sheikh Mohammad Abdullah. Abdullah's NC was responsible for the eradication of a feudal structure and its insidious ramifications; giving the right of the land he worked on to the tiller; rescinding any political solution that did not take the aspirations and demands of the Kashmiri people into consideration; asserting the right of Kashmiris to high offices in education, bureaucracy, and government; and forming of the Constituent Assembly of J & K to institutionalize the constitution of the state in 1951, which was an enormous leap toward the process of democratization. The unwelcome alliance of the NC with the Congress in 1986 and with the Hindu nationalist BJP in 1997 under the leadership of Sheikh Mohammad Abdullah's older son, Farooq Abdullah, eroded its mass base and diminished its popularity in the Valley. Currently, the NC is the major opposition party within the political spectrum of the state, but it has greatly diminished in popularity and strength. It worked to restore its popular base for the 2008 elections. In a replay of history, the Congress with a total of 17 Assembly seats and the NC with a total of 28 Assembly seats, the same number it had in 2002 when it shunned the possibility of power-sharing and chose to sit in the opposition, have formed a coalition government headed by Farooq Abdullah's son and current NC president, Omar Abdullah. But the NC has greatly diminished in popularity and strength.

Pandits: A small Hindu minority, the Pandit population of the Valley enjoyed privileges and perks in the political, civil, and economic structures of which the Muslim majority was deprived. After the emergence of insurgency in Indian-administered J & K in 1990, most Pandits left the Valley. Some Pandits have either continued to remain in the Valley or have maintained their properties from abroad.

People's Democratic Party (PDP): Formed in Indian-controlled J & K in 1999 under the patronage of Mufti Mohammad Sayeed, the PDP ostensibly has pro-India leanings but prior to the 2002 elections was successful in formulating and foregrounding its populist measures. In the 2002 elections, to elect a new legislature in the state, the PDP won 16 of 46 assembly seats in the Valley and Sayeed formed a tottering coalition government with the Congress. Although the PDP is currently in the opposition in the political spectrum of the state, its authority remained unchallenged in the rural areas of the Valley in the 2008 assembly elections.

Plebiscite Front (PF): In August 1955, a group comprising eight legislators from the Constituent Assembly initiated a political movement called the Jammu and Kashmir Plebiscite Front. The first president of this organization was Abdullah's trusted lieutenant, Mirza Afzal Beg. Beg spearheaded this movement during Abdullah's probationary period. The credo of this organization was the restoration of civil liberties, right of the Kashmiri people to decide their political fate through a plebiscite under UN auspices, withdrawal of the armed forces of both India and Pakistan from Kashmir, and democratic and impartial elections. The oppositional stance of this organization met with state-sponsored violent repression. The PF had a popular mass base in Indian-administered J & K between 1955 and 1975. It particularly enjoyed tremendous support in the Kashmir Valley.

Rashtriya Rifles (RR): Regular Indian army troops involved in counterinsurgency operations in Indian-administered J & K since the inception of insurrection in 1990.

Rishiism: An order that practiced Lalla-Ded's doctrine of religious humanism, founded by the followers of Sheikh Noor-ud-Din Wali, also known as Nand Rishi and Sahazanand, after his death. Lalla-Ded facilitated Sheikh Noor-ud-Din Wali's immersion into the intellectual radicalism generated by her philosophy of religious humanism.

Shah Hamadan: A famous saint, Mir Sayyid Ali Hamadani, also known as Shah Hamadan, Amir Kabir, and Ali Sani, was a leader of the renowned Suhrawardy order of Sufism (Kubrawi sub-order), unorthodox iconoclasts who were rigorous believers in social justice and who protected the marginalized from political oppression. Hamadan is said to have arrived in Kashmir between 1379 and 1380, where he acquired political and religious clout over the monarch, Sultan Kutbuddin. He exercised tremendous influence in the conversion of predominantly Brahmanical Kashmir to Islam.

Sikhism: Founded by Guru Nanak in the fifteenth century, Sikhism's historic homeland is the Punjab region in India. Guru Nanak was a social reformer and a religious leader. The religious and sociopolitical identity of Sikhism was institutionalized by Guru Gobind Singh in the seventeenth century. The Sikhs established a militarily and politically powerful nation under Ranjit Singh in the nineteenth century. Traditionally, Sikhs are known for their military prowess and, more recently, for their demand for secession from India and the formation of a separate nation-state. The Sikhs comprise about 2 percent of the Indian population.

Singh, Hari: The Hindu Maharaja of Kashmir, Hari Singh signed the Instrument of Accession on 26 October 1947, formally acceding J & K to the newly formed nation-state of India.

Special Operations Group (SOG): A paramilitary division of the Indian-controlled J & K police force accused of heinous human rights abuses. The SOG continues to run amok and is a law unto itself.

Special Task Force (STF): A militia group comprising renegade militants that alongside the SOG has been responsible for egregious crimes.

Sufism: A Gnostic movement in Islam. Sufis were eclectic and unorthodox, imbued with Asiatic, European, and Hindu thought. Sufiism generated oppositional and dissident resistance to orthodox Islam.

Wali, Sheikh Noor-ud-Din: The founding father of the predominant Sufi sect in the Kashmir valley, Rishiism, acknowledged Lalla-Ded as his spiritual mentor. He is said to have been an older contemporary of

Shah Hamadan. Wali is also known as Nund Rishi and Sahazanand. Lalla-Ded facilitated Sheikh Noor-ud-Din Wali's immersion into the intellectual radicalism generated by her philosophy of religious humanism. His inimitable poetry significantly enriched Kashmiri literature and is a defining aspect of Kashmiri culture. Noor-ud-Din Wali's paradigmatic sayings have had a considerable impact on Kashmiri cultural discourse.

Bibliography

Interviews

Ahangar, Parveena, founder of the Association of Parents of Disappeared Persons (APDP), Srinagar, July 2006.

Ahmad, Sheikh Nazir, general secretary of the National Conference (NC), April 2008 and January 2009.

Begum, Pathani, Gujjar matriarch, Srinagar, July 2006.

Dar, Farida, activist of outlawed militant organization Ikhwan-ul-Muslimeen, November 2009.

Dhar, Amar Nath, professor of English and scholar of Lalla-Ded's religious philosophy, April 2008.

Duda, P.N., senior advocate of the Supreme Court of India, April 2008.

Firdous, Shamim, former member of the Legislative Council, Assembly of Jammu and Kashmir, and current president of the Women's Wing of the National Conference and member of the J & K Legislative Assembly, Srinagar, July 2006.

Hangloo, R.L., chair of history department at the University of Hyderabad, November 2009 and January 2010.

Khan, Mohammad Ishaq, emeritus professor of history at the University of Kashmir, and author of *Biographical Dictionary of Sufism in South Asia*, December 2009.

Malik, Yaseen, chairman of the breakaway faction of the Jammu and Kashmir Liberation Front (JKLF), April 2008.

Margoob, Mushtaq, director of the Psychiatric Diseases Hospital, Srinagar, June 2009.

Matto, Suraiya Ali, vice chairperson of *Behboodi Khwateen*, an organization for the upliftment of downtrodden women and children, Srinagar, April 2008, and Kearney, NE, November 2009.

Mattoo, Neerja, emeritus professor of English at Maulana Azad Government College for Women, Srinagar, April 2008.

Misri, Krishna, former principal of Government College for Women, Nawakadal, Srinagar, and Maulana Azad Government College for Women, Srinagar, April 2008.

Naeem, Hameeda, professor of English at the University of Kashmir, and human rights activist, Srinagar, July 2006.

Political activists of the National Conference (NC) and the People's Democratic Party (PDP), Srinagar, July 2006 and 2007.

Shah, G.M., former chief minister of Jammu and Kashmir, and president of the Awami National Conference, April 2008.

Singh, Karan, former crown prince of the princely state of Jammu and Kashmir and Sadr-i-Riyasat (governor) of J & K, New Delhi, July 2007.

Taing, Mohammad Yousuf, former secretary of the Cultural Academy and director general of culture, J & K government, July 2007 and December 2009.

Wahid, A., retired chair of the Department of Internal Medicine, Sher-e-Kashmir Institute for Medical Sciences, Srinagar, March 2008.

Zameer, Sajjida, member of the 1947 Women's Militia organized by the National Conference, and former director of the Education Department, J & K, April 2008.

Documents

Amnesty International. "'If They Are Dead Tell Us': 'Disappearances' in Jammu and Kashmir." London: Amnesty International, February 1999.

———. "India." November 2005. http://web.amnesty.org/report2004/indsummary-eng (accessed 15 December 2005).

———. "India Must Prevent Torture." Kashmiri–Canadian Council, November 2005. http://www.kashmiri-cc.ca/quarterly/kq2-4/AMNESTY2.htm (accessed 10 January 2007).

Asia Watch, Reports, June 1993.

Census of India, 1981. Series 1: India. Part II-B (i), New Delhi: Office of the Registrar General, 1983.

Human Rights Commission of Pakistan. *Newsletter.* January 1994.

Human Rights in Kashmir, Report of a Mission. Geneva: International Commission of Jurists, November 1994.

Indiagram. No. 333. Washington DC: Embassy of India, 18 November 1953.

Mahato, Prabal. "The Impact of Terrorism on Women and Children in Jammu and Kashmir." Unpublished report, 1999.

Speeches and Interviews of Sher-e-Kashmir Sheikh Mohammad Abdullah. 2 vols. Srinagar: Jammu and Kashmir Plebiscite Front, 1968.

United Nations Security Council. *Security Council Official Records.* 3rd year, nos. 1–15. United Nations, 1948.

Speeches

Nehru, Jawaharlal. Speech, 17 September 1953. In *Jawaharlal Nehru's Speeches: 1949–1953.* Vol. 2. Delhi: Government of India, 1963.

———. Speech, House of the People, 29 December 1953. In *Jawaharlal Nehru's Speeches: 1949–1953.* Vol. 2. Delhi: Government of India, 1963.

———. Speech on the floor of the Indian Parliament, 11 August 1951. In *Jawaharlal Nehru's Speeches: 1949–1953.* Vol. 2. Delhi: Government of India, 1963.

Opening Address by Honorable Sheikh Mohammad Abdullah, Jammu and Kashmir Constituent Assembly, Srinagar, 1951.

Books

Abdullah, Farooq. *My Dismissal.* Delhi: Vikas, 1985.

Abdullah, Sheikh Mohammad. *Flames of the Chinar: An Autobiography.* Translated by Khushwant Singh. New York: Viking, 1993.

Aitchinson, C.V., ed. *A Collection of Treaties, Engagements and Sanads.* Vol. XII, Part I. Calcutta: Government of India Central Publication Branch, 1931.

Akbar, M.J. *India: The Siege Within: Challenges to a Nation's Unity.* New York: Penguin, 1985.

Ali, Tariq. "The Story of Kashmir." In *The Clash of Fundamentalisms: Crusades, Jihads and Modernity,* 217–52. London: Verso, 2003.

Bamzai, Prem Nath Kaul. *Culture and Political History of Kashmir.* 3 vols. Delhi: M.D. Publications, 1994.

Bazaz, Prem Nath. *Daughters of the Vitasta.* New Delhi: Pamposh Publications, 1959. Reprint, Srinagar: Gulshan Books, 2005. (Page references are to the 2005 edition.)

————. *Inside Kashmir.* Mirpur, Azad Kashmir: Verinag, 1941. Reprint, Srinagar: Gulshan Books, 2002. (Page references are to the 2002 edition.)

————. *Kashmir in Crucible.* New Delhi: Pamposh Publications, 1967. Reprint, Srinagar: Gulshan Books, 2005. (Page references are to the 2005 edition.)

————. *Truth about Kashmir.* Delhi: Kashmir Democratic Union, 1950.

Behera, Navnita Chadha. *Demystifying Kashmir.* Washington, DC: Brookings Institution Press, 2006.

Bhattacharjea, Ajit. *Kashmir: The Wounded Valley.* New Delhi: UBS, 1994.

————. *Sheikh Mohammad Abdullah: The Tragic Hero of Kashmir.* New Delhi: Roli Books, 2008.

Bose, Sumantra. "Hindu Nationalism and the Crisis of the Indian State: A Theoretical Perspective." In *Nationalism, Democracy and Development: State and Politics in India.* Edited by Sugata Bose and Ayesha Jalal, 104–64. Delhi: Oxford University Press, 1997.

————. *Kashmir: Roots of Conflict, Paths to Peace.* Cambridge: Harvard University Press, 2003.

Bose, Tapan, Dinesh Mohan, Gautam Navlakha, and Sumanta Banerjee. "India's Kashmir War." In *Secular Crown on Fire: The Kashmir Problem.* Edited by Ashghar Ali Engineer, 224–53. Delhi: Ajanta, 1991.

Brecher, Michael. *The Struggle for Kashmir.* Toronto: Ryerson Press, 1953.

Chadha, Vivek. *Low Intensity Conflicts in India: An Analysis.* New Delhi: Sage Publications, 2005.

Chengappa, Raj. "End the Wink and Nudge Approach." In *Weapons of Peace: The Secret Story of India's Quest to Be a Nuclear Power*, 352–66. New Delhi: Harper Collins, 2000.

"'Cloth,' saith Custom—Doth that sanctify?" In *The Word of Lalla the Prophetess*. Translated by R.C. Temple. London: Cambridge University Press, 1924. Reprint with introduction by Shafi Shauq, Srinagar: Gulshan Books, 2005. (Page references are to the 2005 edition.)

Cohen, Stephen P. *The Idea of Pakistan*. Washington, DC: Brookings Institution Press, 2004.

Copeland, Ian. "The Abdullah Factor: Kashmiri Muslims and the 1947 Crisis." In *Political Inheritance of Pakistan*, edited by D.A. Low, 218–54. London: Macmillan, 1991.

Dasgupta, Jyoti Bhusan. *Jammu and Kashmir*. The Hague: Martinus Nijhoff, 1968.

Diakov, A.M. *Natsional' nyi Vopros I Angliiskii Imperialism v Indii*. Ogiz, 1948.

Felman, Shoshana, and Dori Laub, M.D. Testimony: Crises of Witnessing in Literature, Psychoanalysis and History. New York: Routledge, 1992.

Gandhi, Leela. Postcolonial Theory: A Critical Introduction. New York: Columbia, 1998.

Ganguly, Sumit. *The Crisis in Kashmir: Portents of War, Hopes of Peace*. New York: Woodrow Wilson Center Press, 1997.

Ganju, M. *Textile Industry in Kashmir*. New Delhi: Premier, 1945.

Gottlieb, Gidon. Nation against State: A New Approach to Ethnic Conflicts and the Decline of Sovereignty. New York: Council on Foreign Relations, 1993. Quoted in Robert Wirsing. India, Pakistan, and the Kashmir Dispute, 233. New York: St. Martin's Press, 1994.

Grierson, G.A. *Standard Manual of the Kashmiri Language*. 2 vols. Calcutta: Asiatic Society, 1911.

Hagerty, Devin T. *South Asia in World Politics*. Lanham, MD: Rowman and Littlefield, 2005.

Hassnain, F.M. *Freedom Struggle in Kashmir*. New Delhi: Rima Publishing House, 1988.

Hewitt, J.P. *Dilemmas of the American Self*. Philadelphia: Temple University Press, 1989.

Hoodbhoy, Pervez Amirali, and Abdul Hameed Nayyar. "Rewriting the History of Pakistan." In *Islam, Politics, and the State: The Pakistan Experience*. Edited by Asghar Khan, 164–77. London: Zed Books, 1985.

Jain, R.K., ed. *Soviet–South Asian Relations: 1947–1978*. Vol. 1. Atlantic Highlands, NJ: Humanities Press, 1979.

Jayawardena, Kumari. *Feminism and Nationalism in the Third World*. London: Zed Books, 1986.

Jha, Prem Shankar. *Kashmir, 1947: Rival Versions of History*. Bombay: Oxford University Press, 1996.

Kampani, Gaurav. "Kashmir and India–Pakistan Nuclear Issues." In *South Asia in World Politics*. Edited by Devin T. Hagerty, 161–86. New York: Rowman and Littlefield, 2005.

Kaul, R.N. Kashmir's Mystic: Poetess Lalla Ded, Alias Lalla Arifa. New Delhi: S. Chand, 1999.

Kaura, Uma. Muslims and Indian Nationalism: The Emergence of the Demand for India's Partition 1928–40. Columbia: South Asia Books, 1977.

Kaw, M.K., ed. Kashmir and Its People: Studies in the Evolution of Kashmiri Society. New Delhi: A.P.H., 2004.

Khan, Amanullah. *Free Kashmir*. Karachi: Central Printing Press, 1970.

Khan, Mohammad Ishaq. *Biographical Dictionary of Sufism in South Asia*. New Delhi: Manohar, 2009.

——— History of Srinagar, 1846–1947: A Study in Socio-Cultural Change. Ann Arbor: University of Michigan Press, 1978.

———. Kashmir's Transition to Islam: The Role of Muslim Rishis. New Delhi: Manohar, 1994.

Khan, M. Zafarullah. *The Kashmir Dispute*. Karachi: Institute of International Affairs, 1958.

Kodikara, Sheldon U. "South Asian Security Dilemmas in the Post-Cold War World." In *South Asia after the Cold War: International Perspectives*. Edited by Kanti P. Bajpai and Stephen P. Cohen, 47–65. Boulder, CO: Westview Press, 1993.

Korbel, Josef. *Danger in Kashmir*. Princeton: Princeton University Press, 1954. Reprint, New York: Oxford University Press, 2002. (Page references are to the 2002 edition.)

Krishen, Rajbans. *Kashmir and the Conspiracy against Peace*. Bombay: People's Publishing House, 1951.

Kumari, Abhilasha, and Sabina Kidwai. *Crossing the Sacred Line: Women's Search for Political Power*. New Delhi: Orient Longman, 1998.

"Lal Ded's Vakhs." In *Kashmiri Saints and Sages: Ancient and Modern Ascetics in Kashmir*. Kashmir Overseas Association. http://www.koausa.org/Saints/LalDed/Vakhs1.html (accessed March 2005).

Lamb, Alastair. *Kashmir: A Disputed Legacy, 1846–1990*. Hertingfordbury: Roxford Books, 1991.

Lawrence, Walter R. *The Valley of Kashmir*. London: H. Frowde, 1895. Reprint, Srinagar: Gulshan Books, 2005. (Page references are to the 2005 edition.)

Mahjoor, Ghulam Ahmad. "Vwolo Haa Baagvaano" ("Come, Gardener!"). Translated and edited by Trilokinath Raina. In *An Anthology of Modern Kashmiri Verse (1930–1960)*. Poona: Sangam Press, 1972.

Malik, Iffat. *Kashmir: Ethnic Conflict International Dispute*. Karachi: Oxford University Press, 2002.

Manchanda, Rita. "Guns and Burqaa: Women in the Kashmir Conflict." In *Women, War and Peace in South Asia*. Edited by Rita Manchanda, 42–101. New Delhi: Sage Publications, 2001.

Margolio, Eric S. War at the Top of the World: The Struggle for Afghanistan, Kashmir, and Tibet. Toronto: Key Porter Books, 1999.

McClintock, Ann. *Dangerous Liaisons: Gender, Nation and Postcolonial Perspective.* Minneapolis: University of Minnesota Press, 1997.

Mehta, Jagat S. "Resolving Kashmir in the International Context of the 1990s." In *Perspectives on Kashmir: The Roots of Conflict in South Asia.* Edited by Raju G.C. Thomas, 388–409. Boulder: Westview Press, 1992.

Minh-ha, Trin T. *Woman, Native, Other.* Bloomington: Indiana University Press, 1989.

Mir, Imraan. A New Kashmir: Religion, Education and the Roots of Social Disintegration. Napa Valley: Valley House Books, 2003.

Mohanty, Chandra. *Third World Women and the Politics of Feminism.* Bloomington, IN: Indiana University Press, 1991.

Murphy, Paul E. *Triadic Mysticism: The Mystical Theology of the Saivism of Kashmir.* Columbia: South Asia Books, 1999.

Nandy, Ashis. The Intimate Enemy: Loss and Recovery of Self under Colonialism. Oxford: Oxford University Press, 1983.

Noorani, A.G. *The Kashmir Question.* Bombay: Manaktalas, 1964.

Parimoo, B.N. The Ascent of Self: A Reinterpretation of the Mystical Poetry of Lalla-Ded. Delhi: Motilal Banarsidass, 1978.

Perkovich, George. *India's Nuclear Bomb: The Impact on Global Proliferation.* Berkeley: University of California Press, 1999.

Puri, Balraj. Jammu and Kashmir: Triumph and Tragedy of Indian Federalism. Delhi: Sterling, 1981.

———. *Kashmir: Towards Insurgency.* New Delhi: Orient Longman, 1995.

Qasim, Syed Mir. *My Life and Times.* New Delhi: Allied, 1992.

Rahman, Mushtaqur. Divided Kashmir: Old Problems, New Opportunities for India, Pakistan, and the Kashmiri People. Boulder, CO: Lynne Rienner, 1996.

Rai, Mridu. Hindu Rulers, Muslim Subjects: Islam, Rights, and the History of Kashmir. Princeton: Princeton University Press, 2004.

Ray, Sangeet. En-Gendering India: Woman and Nation in Colonial and Postcolonial Narratives. Durham: Duke University Press, 2000.

Ray, Sunil Chandra. *Early History and Culture of Kashmir.* New Delhi: Munshiram Manoharlal, 1970.

Razdan, P.N. Gems of Kashmiri Literature and Kashmiriyat: The Trio of Saint Poets. New Delhi: Samkaleen, 1999.

Rogers, A., trans. *The Tuzuk-i-Jahangir* or *Memoirs of Jahangir.* Edited by H. Beveridge. Vol. 2. London: Royal Asiatic Society, 1914.

Rushdie, Salman. "The Assassination of Indira Gandhi." In *Imaginary Homelands: Essays and Criticism 1981–91*, 41–46. London: Granta Books, 1991.

———. *Shalimar the Clown.* New York: Random House, 2005.

Said, Edward. *Culture and Imperialism.* New York: Knopf, distributed by Random House, 1991.

Saxena, Hari Lal. *The Tragedy of Kashmir.* New Delhi: Nationalist, 1975.

Schofield, Victoria. *Kashmir in Conflict: India, Pakistan and the Unending War.* Second revised edition. London: I.B. Tauris, 2002.

Shibutani, T. *Society and Personality.* Englewood Cliffs, NJ: Prentice Hall, 1961.

Sibtain, Tahira. "The Genesis of the Kashmir Dispute." In *Kashmir: Now or Never.* Edited by Abdul Hafeez Touquir. Islamabad: National Book Foundation, 1992.

Singh, Karan. *Karan Singh: Autobiography.* New Delhi: Oxford University Press, 1994.

Smith, Vincent H. *The Oxford History of India.* Oxford: Clarendon Press, 1928.

Soz, Saifuddin. *Why Autonomy to Kashmir?* New Delhi: India Centre of Asian Studies, 1995.

Spivak, Gayatri Chakravorty. Critique of Postcolonial Reason: Toward a History of the Vanishing Present. Cambridge: Harvard University Press, 1999.

Stromquist, Nelly P. "The Theoretical and Practical Bases for Empowerment." In *Women, Education and Empowerment: Pathways Towards Autonomy.* Edited by Carolyn Medel-Anonuevo, 12–22. Hamburg: UNESCO Institute for Education, 1995.

Sufi, Ghulam Muhyi'd Din. *Islamic Culture in Kashmir.* New Delhi: Capital Publishing House, 1979.

Talbot, Ian. *Pakistan: A Modern History.* London: C. Hurst, 1988.

Taseer, Bilquis C. *The Kashmir of Sheikh Mohammad Abdullah.* Lahore: Feroze Sons, 1986.

Tellis, Ashley. Stability in South Asia: Prospect of Indo–Pak Nuclear Conflict. Dehradun: Natraj, 2001.

———. "Toward a Force-in-Being: Understanding India's Nuclear Doctrine and Future Force Posture." In *India's Emerging Nuclear Posture: Between Recessed Deterrent and Ready Arsenal,* 251–475. Santa Monica: Rand, 2001.

Temple, Richard Carnac. *The Word of Lalla the Prophetess.* London: Cambridge University Press, 1924. Reprinted with introduction by Shafi Shauq, Srinagar: Gulshan Books, 2005. (Page references are to the 2005 edition.)

Verghese, B.G. "Kashmir: The Fourth Option." *Defence Today* 1, no. 1 (1993). Quoted in Robert Wirsing. *India, Pakistan, and the Kashmir Dispute,* 229. New York: St. Martin's Press, 1994.

Verma, P.S. *Jammu and Kashmir at the Crossroads.* New Delhi: Viking, 1994.

Warner, Susan, and Kathryn M. Feltey. "From Victim to Survivor: Recovered Memories and Identity Transformation." In *Trauma and Memory.* Edited by Linda M. Williams and Victoria L. Banyard, 161–174. London: Sage Publications, 1999.

Widmalm, Sten. Kashmir in Comparative Perspective: Democracy and Violent Separatism in Kashmir. New York: Routledge, 2002.

Wirsing, Robert. *India, Pakistan, and the Kashmir Dispute*. New York: St. Martin's Press, 1994.

———. *Kashmir in the Shadow of War: Regional Rivalries in a Nuclear Age*. New York: M. E. Sharpe, 2003.

Younghusband, Sir Francis. *Kashmir*. New Delhi: Sagar, 1970.

Zutshi, Chitralekha. *Languages of Belonging: Islam, Regional Identity, and the Making of Kashmir*. New York: Oxford University Press, 2004.

Articles

Akhtar, Shaheen. "Elections in Indian-held Kashmir, 1951–1999." *Regional Studies* 18, no. 3 (2000): 12–29.

Armitage, Richard. Interview. PBS transcript, 30 August 2002. http://www.outlookindia.com (accessed 4 July 2006).

Barve, Sushobha. "Bridging Divides." *Dawn*, 5 February 2008. http://www.dawn.com/2008/02/05/op.htm (accessed 12 March 2008).

Battye, Michael. "Angry India Accuses U.S. Tilt to Pakistan." Reuters, 30 October 1993.

Bhagat, Pamela. "Women in Kashmir: Citizens at Last." *Boloji Media*, November 2005. http://www.boloji.com/wfs/wfs110.htm (accessed November 2005).

Bhatnagar, Rashmi Dube, Renu Dube, and Reena Dube. "Meera's Medieval Lyric Poetry in Postcolonial India: The Rhetorics of Women's Writing in Dialect as a Secular Practice of Subaltern Coauthorship and Dissent." *Boundary 2* 31, no. 3 (2004): 1–46.

Bisnath, S., and D. Elson. "Women's Empowerment Revisited." UNIFEM, November 2002. http://www.undp.org/unifem/progressww/empower.html (accessed 10 August 2006).

Chaudhuri, Pramit Pal. "Why a War against Terrorism Has Pakistan Terrified." *Hindustan Times* (http://www.hindustantimes.com), 16 September 2001. http://www.ofbjp.org.news/0901/10html (accessed August 2006).

Cohen, Stephen P. and S. Dasgupta. "U.S.–South Asia: Relations under Bush." *Oxford Analytica*. 2001. http://www.brookings.edu (accessed March 2008).

Daily Etalaat. "Another Pugwash on Kashmir." 3 April 2008. http://etalaat.net/english/?p=10 (accessed 8 April 2008).

Das, Taraknath. "The Kashmir Issue and the United Nations." *Political Science Quarterly* 65, no. 2 (1950).

Dawn. "Delhi Positions Missiles on Border." 27 December 2001. http://www.dawn.com/2001/12/27/top4.htm (accessed December 2007).

Delhi Express. 1 January 1952.

Delhi Radio. Indian Information Service. Delhi, 31 March 1952.

Desmond, Edward W. "The Insurgency in Kashmir 1989–1991." *Contemporary South Asia* 4, no. 1 (1995): 5–16.

Emirbayer, Mustafa, and Ann Mische. "What Is Agency?" *American Journal of Sociology* 103 (1998): 962–1023.

Fazili, Ehsan. "Sentimental Return for Pandits." 2000. *Tribune News Service.* http://www.tribuneindia.com/2000/20000610/j&k.htm#3 (accessed January 2008).

Friese, Kai. "Hijacking India's History." *New York Times*, 30 December 2002, sec. A: 17.

Fuchs, Stephan. "Beyond Agency." *Sociological Theory* 19, no. 1 (2001): 24–40.

Greater Kashmir. "Eleven Policemen Indicted for Custodial Murder of Two Civilians." 20 March 2008. http://www.greaterkashmir.net/full_story. asp?Date21_4_2008&ItemID=22&cat=1 (accessed 20 March 2008).

———. "Family Seeks Whereabouts of Youth." 25 March 2008. http://www. greaterkashmir.com/full_story.asp?Date=26_3_2008&ItemID=54&cat= 14 (accessed 20 March 2008).

———. "Five Lecturers Among 30 Injured: Protests Continue in Sopur." 13 September 2007. http://www.greaterkashmir.com/full_story.asp?Date =14_9_2007&ItemID=52&cat=1 (accessed December 2007).

———. "GOI Responsible for Exodus of Kashmiri Pandits." 12 November 2007. http://www.greaterkashmir.com/full_story.asp?Date=13_11_2007 &ItemID=23&cat=1 (accessed 12 November 2007).

———. "Grave Concern." 31 March 2008. http://www.greaterkashmir.com/ full_story.asp? Date=10_4_2008&ItemID=15&cat=10 (accessed 31 March 2008).

———. "Soldiers Go Berserk in Pulwama." 13 September 2007. http://www. greaterkashmir.com/NewsItem.asp?Date=14_9_2007&Show=1(accessed January 2008).

———. "Statement Unrealistic." 22 March 2008. http://www.greaterkashmir. net/NewsItem.asp?Date=3_3_2008&Show=10 (accessed March 2008).

Guha, Ramachandra. "Opening a Window in Kashmir." *World Policy Journal, Reconsiderations* 21, no. 3 (2004): 1–17.

Hayward, C.R. "De-facing Power." *Polity* 31 (1998): 22–34.

The Hindu (Madras). 26 March 1952.

The Hindu. "Text of PM, Musharraf Statement." 6 January 2004. http:// www.hindu.com/2004/01/07/stories/2004010706041100.htm, (accessed July 2007).

The Hindustan Times (Delhi). 26 October 1953.

The Hindu Weekly Review. 1953

India Today. 31 March 1987: 26; 15 April 1987: 40–43; 30 April 1990: 10; 31 March 1993: 27.

Iqbal, Anwar. "Outgoing Prime Minister Says Kashmir at Root of Nuclear Arms Race." United Press International, 18 October 1993. http://web. lexis-nexis.com. (accessed 26 August 2006).

Johnson, Robert. "Russians at the Gates of India? Planning the Defense of India, 1885–1900." *The Journal of Military History* 67, no. 7 (2003): 697–743.

Kabeer, N. "Resources, Agency, Achievements: Reflections on the Measurement of Women's Empowerment." *Development and Change* 30 (1999): 435–64.

Kampani, Guarav. "India's Compellence Strategy." *CNN Research Story of the Week*, 10 June 2002. http://cns.miis.edu/pubs/week/020610.htm (accessed November 2007).

Kashmir Human Rights Site. "Impact of Conflict Situation on Children and Women in Kashmir." http://kashmir.ahrchk.net/mainfile.php/articles/45/ (accessed November 2005).

The Kashmir Times (Jammu). 28 August 1998.

Kashmir Times. "Militancy in Kashmir Valley Completes Fourteen Years." 1 August 2002. http://www.kashmirtimes.com/archive/0208/020801/index.htm (accessed March 2004).

Kashmiri Women's Initiative for Peace and Disarmament. "Probe Gimmick." 2004. *Voices Unheard: A Magazine.* http://www.geocities.com/kwipd2002 (accessed November 2005).

Kelly, John H. "Prepared statement by John H. Kelly, assistant secretary for Near Eastern and South Asian Affairs before Subcommittee on Asian and Pacific Affairs, House Foreign Affairs Committee." U.S. Department of State, 2 November 1990. http://web.lexis-nexis.com (accessed 2 April 2008).

Kohli, Atul. "Can Democracies Accommodate Ethnic Nationalism? Rise and Decline of Self-Determination Movements in India." *Journal of Asian Studies* 56 (1997): 325–44.

Lok Sabha. "Obituary References." 2000. http://parliamentofindia.nic.in/lsdeb/ls13/ses4/24072.htm (accessed August 2005).

The London Times. 6 September 1950.

Mattoo, Neerja. "Lalla-Ded as the Voice of the Marginalized." Paper presented at the Series on Mystic Masters, India International Centre, New Delhi, March 2007.

Misri, Krishna. "Kashmiri Women Down the Ages: A Gender Perspective." *Himalayan and Central Asian Studies* 6, no. 3–4 (2002): 3–27.

Nair, A.R. "Two Unforgettable Days: Tour with Sheikh a Happy Revelation." *Minorities' View* (1968): 24–33, 44.

Pickering, Sharon. "Undermining the Sanitized Accounts: Violence and Emotionality in the Field in Northern Ireland." *The British Journal of Criminology* 41 (2001): 485–501.

Prasad, Shally. "Medicolegal Response to Violence Against Women in India." *Violence Against Women* 5 (1999): 478–507.

Puri, Balraj. "Analysis of the J & K Permanent Resident Bill." *PUCL Bulletin*, April 2004. http://www.pucl.org/Topics/Law/2004/jk-pr-bill.htm (accessed November 2005).

Ramachandran, Sudha. "Suicide, Just Another Way to Fight in Kashmir." *Asia Times Online*, 24 July 2002. http://www.atimes.com/atimes/South_Asia/DG24Df02.html (accessed March 2008).

Reuters. "Pakistan Court Expected to Rule on Gang-Rape Case." *Khaleej Times*, 27 August 2002. http://www.khaleejtimes.com.ae/ktarchive/270802/subcont.htm (accessed 24 August 2007).

Rushbrook-Williams, L.F. "Inside Kashmir." *International Affairs* 33, no. 1 (1957): 26–35.

Schofield, Victoria. "Pakistan's Northern Areas Dilemma." BBC News, 15 August 2001. *BBC News Online*. http://news.bbc.co.uk/1/hi/world/south_asia/1491179.stm (accessed 15 March 2008).

The Statesman (Calcutta). 15 September 1950, 16.

Talbott, Strobe. Interview. *The Hindu*, 14 January 2000. http://www.hinduonnet.com.

The Times (London), 26 April 1952.

Whitehead, Andrew. "Kashmir's Conflicting Identities." *History Workshop Journal* 58 (2004): 335–40.

Wirsing, Robert. "Kashmir in the Terrorist Shadow." *Asian Affairs* 33, no. 1 (2002): 91–97.

Index